# Enterprise Networking for Information Systems Professionals

## Other VNR Business Technology/Communications Books...

Designing TCP/IP Internetworks
*by Geoff Bennett*

Information Proficiency: The Key To The Information Age
*by Thomas J. Buckholtz*

Doing More Business on the Internet
*by Mary J. Cronin*

Networking Device Drivers
*by Sanjay Dhawan*

Routing in Today's Internetworks
*by Mark Dickie*

Spinning the Web: How To Provide Information On The Internet
*by Andrew Ford*

Digital Signal Processing in Communications
*by Marvin E. Frerking*

The Complete Cyberspace Reference and Directory
*by Gilbert Held*

Working With NetWare: For Network Supervisors and Users
*by Gilbert Held*

Global Expansion In The Information Age: Big Planet, Small World
*by Thomas J. Howard*

Online Marketing Handbook: How To Sell, Advertise, Publicize, and Promote Your Products and Services On the Information Superhighway
*by Daniel S. Janal*

Digital Telephony and Network Integration, 2nd Edition
*by Bernhard E. Keiser and Eugene Strange*

Low-Cost E-Mail With UUCP: Integrating UNIX, DOS, Windows and MAC
*by Thomas Wm. Madron*

The Illustrated Network Book: A Graphic Guide to Understanding Computer Networks
*by Matthew G. Naugle*

Making Telecommuting Happen: A Guide for Telemanagers and Telecommuters
*by Jack M. Nilles*

JPEG Still Image Data Compression Standard
*by William B. Pennebaker and Joan L. Mitchell*

Successful Reengineering: An Implementation Guide To Using Information Technology
*by Daniel Petrozzo and John C. Stepper*

Using Wireless Communications in Business
*by Andrew M. Seybold*

Fax Power: High Leverage Business Communications
*by Philip C. W. Sih*

Applications for Distributed Systems and Network Management
*by Kornel Terplan and Jill Huntington-Lee*

SNMP Application Developer's Guide
*by Robert L. Townsend*

A Network of Objects: How To Lower Your Computing Cost and Improve Your Applications Delivery
*by Thomas C. Tsai*

Communications Standard Dictionary, 2nd Edition
*by Martin H. Weik, DSc.*

Enterprise Networking for Information Systems Professionals
*by Norman Witkin*

# Enterprise Networking for Information Systems Professionals

Norman Witkin

VAN NOSTRAND REINHOLD
I(T)P™ A Division of International Thomson Publishing Inc.

New York • Albany • Bonn • Boston • Detroit • London • Madrid • Melbourne
Mexico City • Paris • San Francisco • Singapore • Tokyo • Toronto

Copyright © 1995 by  Van Nostrand Reinhold.

 Published by Van Nostrand Reinhold, a division of
International Thomson Publishing Inc.
The ITP logo is a trademark under license.

Printed in the United States of America.
For more information, contact:

Van Nostrand Reinhold
115 Fifth Avenue
New York, NY 10003

International Thomson Publishing GmbH
Königswinterer Strasse 418
53227 Bonn
Germany

International Thomson Publishing Europe
Berkshire House 168-173
High Holborn
London WCIV 7AA
England

International Thomson Publishing Asia
221 Henderson Road #05-10
Henderson Building
Singapore 0315

Thomas Nelson Australia
102 Dodds Street
South Melbourne, 3205
Victoria, Australia

International Thomson Publishing Japan
Hirakawacho Kyowa Building, 3F
2-2-1 Hirakawacho
Chiyoda-ku, 102 Tokyo
Japan

Nelson Canada
1120 Birchmount Road
Scarborough, Ontario
Canada M1K 5G4

International Thomson Editores
Campos Eliseos 385, Piso 7
Col. Polanco
11560 Mexico D.F. Mexico

1 2 3 4 5 6 7 8 9 10 QEBFF 01 00 99 98 97 96 95

**Library of Congress Cataloging-in-Publication Data**

Witkin, Norman
    Enterprise networking for information systems professionals / Norman Witkin.
        p.     cm.
    Includes index.
    ISBN 0-442-01875-4
    1. Local area networks (Computer networks) 2. Business enterprises—Communication systems.
  3. Information technology.
  I. Title.
  TK5105.W58     1995
    004.6—dc20                                                95-11498
                                                                CIP

Project Management: Raymond Campbell • Art Direction: Jo-Ann Campbell • Production: mle design • 562 Milford Point Rd. Milford, CT 06460 • 203•878•3793

To my wife Adrienne,
without whose encouragement and loving support
this book would not have been possible.

# Contents

# Preface

I wrote this book hoping to eliminate for others the sorts of difficulties I myself encountered in exploring and understanding the key issues and concepts in the fast-changing world of data communications. On many occasions, as a computer professional working on applications and systems for mainframes, minicomputers and personal computers, I found myself confronted with new data communications tasks. Each time the issues seemed tougher, while the job of getting clear and concise information about the subject was even more challenging.

Data communications are, of course, an increasingly important, if not the most critical, component in today's Information Systems. In the past, communication capabilities and functions were "peripheral" to the computer. Today the computer is itself viewed as a workstation or server peripheral to the network. The network has become the lifeblood of the organization. It is one thing to accept this opinion as a valid maxim, but a wholly different matter to know what to do about it.

An Information Systems professional needs a thorough grasp of the organization's requirements in order to design and implement the new enterprise network applications. This is challenging enough, but in many cases the applications are themselves suggested by the available technology. The professional must, therefore, be aware of all current and potential data communication capabilities. To deliver top-quality, economically sound services to users, he or she must know all the concepts (and acronyms!). In a field that changes so fast, this is a formidable undertaking and can be daunting.

My hope is to provide help in this respect. The book is intended to be a general tutorial and a single-point compendium of information on data communication technologies and choices. For more detail, the bibliographical Appendix lists a number of books that I found helpful in clarifying topics once puzzling.

Today's enterprise networks link heterogeneous computer systems that communicate across global boundaries, connecting organizations to customers, vendors and business partners. Substantial rewards are to be claimed by those enterprises that choose the right protocols, standards and technologies.

## ORGANIZATION OF THE BOOK

Chapter 1 traces the development of three generations of Information Systems. The goals of each generation are examined in the light of prevailing communication and computer technologies. As technological capabilities changed in each generation, the scope of organizations' attainable goals changed. We observe how organizations restructured their communications functions in response, evolving over time to today's enterprise-wide networks.

Chapter 2 describes issues and options affecting the communication of information. Beginning with a brief data communications history from the early days of telegraphy, it deals with the technical choices. These include code systems (ASCII, EBCDIC, Morse, and Baudot), mode (parallel or serial, synchronous or asynchronous, character or block), resource usage (circuit, message or packet switched), connectionless, or connection-oriented services (datagrams, circuits and virtual circuits), channel type (simplex, half- or full-duplex), integrity validation (echoplex, parity, CRC, block check), overrun protection and flow control (XON/XOFF, or sequence number acknowledgement), and access (balanced or unbalanced, ACK/NAK usage, polling or selection, poll/final alternation).

Chapter 3 discusses the rationale for modular architectures for systems in general, and the layered approaches suggested by ITU-TS and ISO for designing communication systems. It examines the layering approach in standards such as the IEEE 802 and ISO 8802 for the data link and physical layers of LANs. It explains the layering software process of message encapsulation at a sending station and, reciprocally, of decapsulation at the receiver.

The abstract geography or mapping of the connections making up a network is its topology. When a network contains multiple stations, different cabling layouts are possible. These feature different costs, access and data transport capabilities. Chapter 4 looks at the different configurations of network topologies and the various medium access methods. Star, bus, ring and mesh topologies are described, as are the considerations for gaining access within them. These include reserving facilities, allotting time to each user for the different resources, and applying different policies to dedicating or sharing facilities among users so as to avoid message collision. The chapter explores managing resources from a central point or from a distributed- or peer-management perspective.

Chapter 5 examines the characteristics of the communications media themselves in more detail. Studying media, such as copper wire and fiber optics, equips us to compare the benefits and limitations accorded by different media for transporting data, voice, image or video.

No data communications would be meaningful without quality signaling, reliably converting 1s and 0s at the source to some form of energy (electricity or light), and then doing the converse at the destination. Different signaling technologies yield different reliabilities. Chapter 6 discusses these different signaling methods.

Local area networks are high-speed communication networks characterized by limited geographical coverage. Chapter 7 discusses the major LANs, namely Ethernet, Token Ring and Token Bus. StarLAN, MAP and TOP are also described.

We describe Metropolitan Area Networks in Chapter 8. These networks evolved primarily to permit LANs to interconnect across a metropolis or a county. The two MAN technologies examined are DQDB and FDDI. The Bellcore-defined Switched Multi-megabit Data Services are predicated on using one of these technologies, DQDB.

Geographically remote LANs or MANs interconnect via wide area capabilities. Chapter 9 covers wide area network facilities, technologies and services that figure prominently in today's enterprise networks. Examined and included are voice and data (analog and digital), modems, Frame Relay, T1, T3, SONET, ISDN, and ATM.

The direction taken by commercial communications networks in the 1980s and 1990s was shaped perhaps more by IBM than by any other single company. IBM's influence has been felt through the extension of its communications practices to standards now accepted worldwide. These are implemented not only by IBM in its own products but by the communications industry as a whole. Chapter 10 describes SNA, IBM's premier communications network architecture and its protocols.

The growth in the use, size and number of LANs has stimulated a demand for devices that can interconnect them. Chapter 11 discusses bridges, routers and gateways, the interconnecting devices used to build networks of computers and LANs communicating across wide geographies and diverse functional areas. Source Routing and Transparent Routing are examined. The chapter concludes with a close look at TCP/IP and IBM's APPN, two major technologies of influence in enterprise-wide networking.

---

Special thanks are due my editor, Mr. Neil Levine and his fine team of colleagues at Van Nostrand Reinhold. Also, I want to acknowledge and thank BCR Enterprises, Inc., for permission to use their glossary. Any errors that may exist in the text are, of course, mine.

# 1

# Communications in Information Systems

## EVOLUTION IN INFORMATION SYSTEMS

The role of information systems and communications in organizations is clear: provide the intelligence to enable the organization to perform at its optimum. In business organizations this generally means performing most profitably over a planning period.

The history of computers and computer communications is relatively short. The first computers for commercial use were introduced in the late 1950s, and capabilities to link peripherals to computers over distances exceeding several meters only appeared in the late 1960s.

Three generations of information systems characterize developments since then. The first generation dates from the 1960s to the mid-1970s; the second from the 1970s through most of the 1980s; and the third, current era started in the late 1980s and progresses through the 1990s.

This chapter traces the development of the three generations. We examine the goals of each generation in the light of the prevailing communication and computer technologies. As technological capabilities changed in each generation, the scope of an organization's attainable goals changed. The changes sometimes radically altered and affected the environment. We observe how organizations restructured their communications functions in response, evolving over time to today's enterprise-wide networks.

## ORGANIZATIONS AND INFORMATION

An organization's structure determines how well it acts on opportunities and how well it responds to threats, challenges, or changes to its environment. A plausible theory is that the ideal structure for an organization is one that enables it to handle or "manage" information most efficiently and effectively. For it is information that provides intelligence on the organization's status quo—its functioning and environment—and changes to the status quo.

Actions taken by an organization follow decisions based upon this intelligence. The organization gathers raw data from events and transactions it is involved in or which affect it. It responds to the acquired data by taking immediate action then and there, or it simply records the data for later. At any stage, the data may be consolidated with data derived from other sources. When the data are used and analyzed and meaning or significance is attributed, "information" is created. From this information, the decisions and actions result.

How have businesses structured themselves to best manage information? When we examine corporate structures in the decades of the sixties, seventies, and eighties, we find most were hierarchical. A hierarchy enabled a corporation to be efficient in managing large and geographically dispersed entities. From the top, a board of directors set policy, and charged a president with the responsibility of implementing it. He or she delegated some of the responsibility to vice-presidents. The vice-presidents, in turn, organized their departments into sub-departments, each with a manager. Each manager divided the sub-departmental responsibilities among a number of sections, with their own section leaders. We find this repeating on to the bottom of the hierarchy, regardless of the geographical concentration or dispersion of the components of the corporation.

Time and distance are the key efficiency factors when communicating information between these hierarchical elements. Whatever type of information (text or numerical data, voice, graphics, image or video) is being sent from one location to another, the further apart two locations are, or the greater the volume of material conveyed between them, the longer is the time needed.

Information detail is as voluminous as the transactions with the outside world. Data must be edited, analyzed, and filtered in a timely fashion by the appropriate responsibilities within an organization—else the cost of managing the information could be prohibitive.

As mentioned, the hierarchy is a suitable framework for the handling of data, regardless of the geographical width or size of an organization. It lets an organization balance the need, on one hand, to respond to the smallest detail and the need, on the other, to plan and manage resources with the *essence* of the detail. The organization's higher-level managers depend on summaries, that is, wider perspectives of the essentials. In the efficient organization, each responsibility level processes its own detail. Subordinate hierarchical levels extract and convey only salient data to superior levels (where there is little or no need for the constituent detail). The benefit of this is conciseness and, therefore, shorter communication times and lower costs.

The hierarchical structure is convenient when a large or dispersed organization needs to select one organization member from a set of peers, e.g., the "candidate" best able to serve some defined need of the organization. This candidate could be a person, department, or functional unit. The superior level has information about the status and environment of all subordinates. Historically, it was costly to make this information universally available, so it was frequently viewed as privileged. Without access to the privileged information, or knowledge of the decision-making policy, peer entities could not select a candidate from among themselves "democratically" and efficiently.

## Impact of Today's Computers

But technology, specifically today's computers and communications, undermines the premise of the above scenario. The lowest ranked worker in an organization now can access the organization's information data base via a personal computer (PC) and local area network (LAN). Software within the computers can provide the necessary editing, filtration and analysis on the raw data.

Furthermore, the status, performance, and activities in peer-ranked departments, divisions, and companies can be examined by all others. It is not necessary to structure an organization hierarchically when a less costly, leaner (in terms of overhead), indeed flat organization could do equally well, if not better. Decisions formerly only made by middle-level managers can be made without them; the prerequisite is that information and policy be available to all authorized concerned parties.

One side benefit of implementing a flat structure is that outsiders immediately see a more responsive and flexible organization. Employees engaging in transactions with customers, vendors or business partners, have "one-stop" access to most (if not all) of the organization's products and services. This makes the organization more competitive. Another benefit derives from internal human relations; employees feel empowered and more trusted. This translates into greater competitiveness. Employee loyalty reduces staff turnover and their longer tenures result in lower aggregate hiring costs.

## INFORMATION TECHNOLOGY IN THE '60s

What technology did business exploit in the past three generations of information systems? In the sixties, the standard information processors of business were large mainframes. These were typified by IBM System/360 computers (e.g., 360/40, 360/50, and 360/65) and by competing products from the BUNCH group of companies (Burroughs, Univac, NCR, Control Data, and Honeywell. As an aside, since RCA was a player, too, perhaps the group was BRUNCH!) As decision-making was centralized and hierarchical, so, too, was much of the data processing.

The goal of information systems of this era was to improve the efficiency of clerical procedures (see Figure 1.1). A remedy was sought for the time lost, for example, when operators had to search for ledgers and files in manual procedures. Sometimes, also, operators vied with each other for access to the same records. The time taken to locate the applicable records within these files, to retrieve and update them and then to return the ledgers or files, was too long. The goal was to eliminate delays in the various steps of clerical processing of transactions, making the process more efficient.

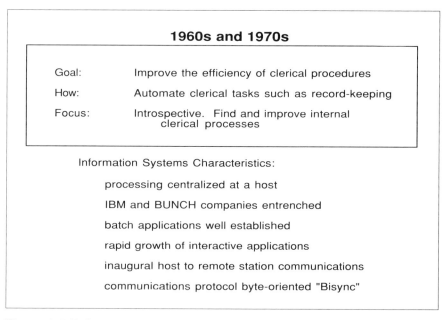

Figure 1.1. Information systems of the '60s and '70s.

Another area needing remedy was the quality of clerical work. In inventory applications, for example, setting appropriate reorder quantities can have significant impact on profitability. A corporation's policy for calculating quantities based upon records of sales or usage of the stock items was usually expressed in an algorithm or mathematical procedure. Errors, either in the data or in executing the algorithm, were costly; numbers too high caused the corporation to order and hold too much inventory, tie up working capital, and incur unnecessary interest expense; numbers too low resulted in out-of-stock situations and lost sales.

Automation was seen as the key to providing the needed improvements. It allowed the speed-up of clerical processing of transactions by eliminating the delays in manual procedures. Automating clerical tasks such as record-keeping led to better data and to swifter decisions. Secondly, automation reduced clerical errors since the computations and algorithms could be performed without human intervention. Automation took shape in magnetic tape or disk "copies" of the ledgers and files, plus computer programs. The computer programs processed the algorithms and processed transactions or changes to the magnetically stored records. The transactions were presented to the programs on some machine-readable medium.

The machine-readable medium of the era was the punched card. The 80-column punched card was a data processing heritage from an earlier "electronic accounting machine" (EAM) era. (In passing, let us note that an alternative medium, punched paper tape, was used successfully by European companies and also by the British—e.g., International Computers Limited (ICL), and English Electric LEO Marconi). Documents reflecting transactions such as customer purchase orders were mailed to a central location. Here they were consolidated into batches prior to the card-punching (key-punch) operation. After a batch of cards was punched, a repeat keystroke process (verification) verified the punching accuracy. The verified batch was then submitted to the computer.

An undesirable aspect of this new process was the time that elapsed between transactions occurring and the computer's records (i.e., the magnetic tapes or disks) actually incorporating them. To improve efficiency, an initial step aimed to ease host site clerical workloads by distributing the card punching operations, moving them away to remote sites where the transactions were themselves generated. Deploying and operating card punch equipment remotely was easy. The next logical step was perhaps more difficult. Connecting card readers remotely to the mainframe introduced the need for communications circuits. These had to be obtained from a non-computer vendor, the telephone company.

Let us examine the equipment that addressed this application. One typical remote card reader (and printer) was the IBM 2780. This communicated with the host through the latter's Transmission Control Unit (TCU). Equipped with a modem, the remote 2780 connected via a private line (leased circuit) to the

TCU at the host site. Reciprocally, the TCU supported the links to multiple remote sites by means of multiple communications circuits and modems. It handled many of the compute-intensive tasks of the communications lines, relieving the host system. IBM's TCUs at that time included the 2701, 2702, and 2703. (Competing products were available from companies such as Memorex).

Having this type of configuration at the remote site meant that as soon as a batch of verified punched cards was ready, it could be submitted to the host. This saved the time of mailing cards or sending them by courier. But there were still periods of time that elapsed before the magnetic tapes or disks actually incorporated the changes brought about by the transactions, and in those periods the computer records did not reflect reality.

The remedy for this was quick in coming. Keyboard/display stations which were components of IBM's 5250 and 3270 Information Display Systems appeared in the early seventies. These devices allowed transaction data to be entered into a mainframe immediately the transaction occurred. No longer was it necessary to group transactions with other transactions in a batch. The architecture of the 3270 Information Display System allowed either local or remote operation. With remote operation, transactions were submitted to a host from a remote site. Transactions needed no prior batching, nor was it necessary that the documents or cards be at the host site.

The equipment used for interactive applications included multiple Model 3278 keyboard/display stations connected by coaxial cables to a cluster controller, the IBM 3271. The 3271, in turn, was connected to the host (via its adjacent 270x TCU) either directly, or remotely. If remotely located, the 3271 cluster controller was equipped with a modem. A private line (leased circuit), provided by the telephone company, connected the modem to the matching modem at the host site.

In the sixties and seventies, many corporations did both remote interactive data entry and remote batch. They installed cluster controllers and keyboard/display stations at the remote sites for applications like order entry and customer inquiry, and batch card-readers/printers for jobs that were less time critical. Products, such as the IBM 3270, processed transactions against the host data base in real time. By contrast, 2780 type products communicated transactions that had been batched over a period of time, usually the previous shift, or day. Each of these applications needed its own communication line to the host site. Each line incurred recurrent monthly lease charges. As we shall see later, this fact was not lost on system managers; they sought ways to consolidate or "multiplex" the batch and interactive communications on one line.

Figure 1.2 shows the information systems paradigm of the 1960s and 1970s. In the era, most application programs were run on the mainframe. Most were written in COBOL, FORTRAN IV or PL/I. But the communications software was typically written in (the lower level, more complex) Assembler language.

To ease the programmer tasks, which were formidable in dealing with the minutiae of the communications functions, IBM and the BUNCH computer companies provided pre-written Assembler program subroutines and "macro instructions." These were communications-oriented system programs that could be tailored to the specifics of the user's configuration by means of parameters. In the case of IBM, the subroutines together formed BTAM, the Basic Telecommunications Access Method. (Perhaps a better title would have been Basic Telecommunications Services, reflecting a broader scope of function than is implied by "access method.") Multiple communications lines demanded multiple co-resident copies of BTAM in the mainframe computer memory. Each line's software was tailored individually. With BTAM, lines that had the same function could not share software. Later, newer developments such as Telecommunications Access Method (TCAM), and Virtual Telecommunications Access Method (VTAM), allowed for some sharing of common software by multiple lines. VTAM is discussed in further detail below.

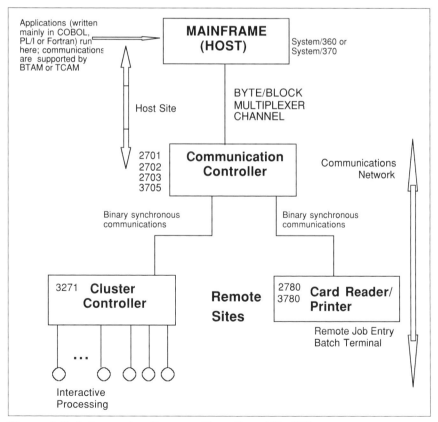

*Figure 1.2. Information Systems Paradigm '60s/'70s.*

## RISE OF MINICOMPUTERS, PCs

Despite the dominance of mainframes in the 1960s and 1970s, there was a growing new trend on the sidelines of the computer field—minicomputers. Digital Equipment Corporation's (DEC's) PDP/8 and PDP/11 were successful in finding application in thousands of niches too small for mainframe consideration. Many new minicomputer companies flourished with successful products including Data General (with the Nova), Basic Four, and Hewlett-Packard. The latter introduced a number of HP2000 products leading to the HP3000. IBM itself introduced a family of Report Program Generator-based minicomputers that included the standalone System/3, /32, and /34. Over time, the System/36 and System/38 appeared. Most recent in this IBM progression is the AS/400. IBM's Series/1 and System/7 should also be added to the list of minicomputers, although these products were less business-office and more scientific/industrial oriented.

Figure 1.3 suggests that in the decade of the 1970s the dominance and (largely) exclusiveness of centralized host processing was vulnerable. In particular, because the large, centralized mainframe was unsuited to certain distributed processing applications, minicomputers and, later, personal computers and local area networks, were attractive for these tasks. The computing landscape had changed.

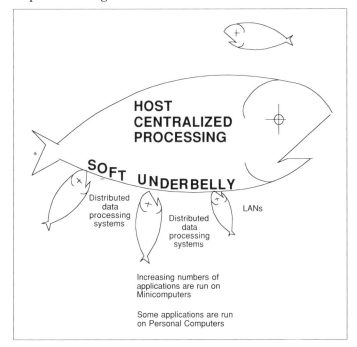

*Figure 1.3. Vulnerability of the centralized host role in period from mid-1970s to early 1980s.*

Furthermore, it was the minicomputer that presented the opportunity to eliminate one of the two communications lines linking a remote site to the host. In the 1970s and 1980s, while an increasing number of new applications were being introduced with minicomputers, many of them functioned additionally as intelligent controllers linked to and remote from the mainframe. Using a single line, they emulated the 3270 or 2780 (later 3780) products, taking care that host software need not be altered. Minicomputers, like the IBM 3790 and 8100, went one step further; they processed both batch and interactive applications, but required just one line to the host. Products from Computer Automation (SyFA), Four Phase, Datapoint, and Microdata had similar capabilities.

The minicomputer ushered in an era of distributed data processing and interactive data entry. The 80-column punched card became obsolete. Minicomputers emulating 3270s and 2780/3780s replaced the remote cluster controllers and card-readers/printers. Later, PCs equipped with communications adapters followed the role of the minicomputer, doing the same thing, emulation.

The communications functions in the 2780/3780 and the 3270 conformed with a protocol called Binary Synchronous Communications. Had this protocol been the only one on the market at the time, the users' programming and operating tasks may have been simpler. But IBM (and other vendors) had many other products that also communicated with the host, most with different protocols! This led to confusion on the part of users and of the non-IBM vendors whose products emulated IBM's protocols.

## SNA ARRIVES ON THE SCENE

IBM introduced the Systems Network Architecture (SNA) in the early 1970s, seeking to rationalize the communications functions of its own product offerings. Among SNA's earliest features was Synchronous Data Link Control (SDLC). SDLC was a superior protocol to its predecessor (Binary Synchronous Communications), overcoming deficiencies that the latter had, for example, in dealing with transparent data.

Figure 1.4 illustrates the (still) host-centric nature of the typical information system in the 1970s and 1980s. The host CPU had itself matured to an IBM System 370 (e.g., the 4300, 308x, 3090 or 9370). But, as in the 1960s and 1970s, most of the corporation's applications were still running on it. On closer examination, the key change seen in the communications arena is the hardware and systems software introduced to conform with IBM's Systems Network Architecture. New software called "Virtual Telecommunications Access Method" (VTAM) replaced BTAM or TCAM on the mainframe. Also, new "Front-end Processor" (FEP) equipment (e.g., IBM 3705, 3720 and 3725) succeeded the earlier IBM 270x TCUs. These FEP devices were programmable. Software in the FEP known as Network Control Program (NCP) was subordinate to VTAM at the host, complemented VTAM's functionality and helped serve multiple lines. At the host itself, regardless of the number of lines supported, a single copy of VTAM software was resident in memory. In an era when memory was expensive, this provided a memory-saving benefit, particularly when compared to BTAM installations.

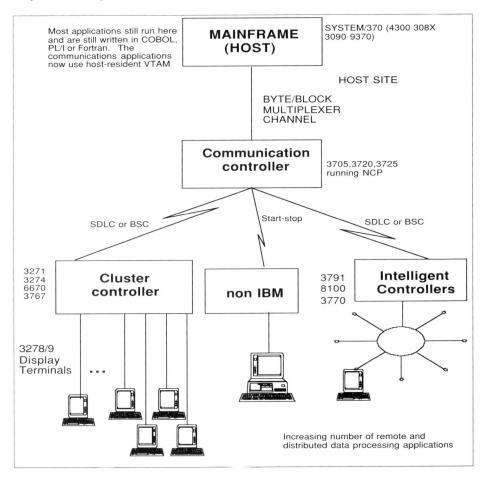

*Figure 1.4. Information Systems paradigm 1970s / 1980s.*

## PCs—GROWTH, ISSUES AND IMPACT

Whereas the goal of information systems in the 1960s and 1970s was to improve the centralized clerical processes, the newer goal of the 1970s and 1980s was to improve the decision-making processes in operations as well. Figure 1.5 highlights the characteristics of information systems in that era that focused on company procedures. An important characteristic of the era was the shift from centralized to distributed processing. Initially, this was made possible by the low-cost minicomputers. They made it economical for computing power or "intelligence" to be at remote locations, and for the integration of interactive and batch applications.

---

### 1970s and 1980s

| | |
|---|---|
| Goal: | Improve the decisions on operations |
| How: | Automate decision support systems |
| Focus: | Largely with Company procedures, but now involving vendor and business relationships (e.g., "just-in-time") |

Information Systems Characteristics:

  processing not totally host centered

  rapid growth of distributed data processing

  ascendance of  minicomputers

  integration of batch and interactive communications

  rapid growth of interactive applications

  initial shipments of personal computers

  communications protocol bit-oriented "SDLC"

---

*Figure 1.5. Information Systems of the '70s and '80s.*

But the most significant factor affecting information systems in the 1970s and 1980s was the personal computer (PC). The early 1980s witnessed rapid growth of personal computer shipments. Fueled by low cost and increasing power of the PC components, notably its CPU and memory chips, the population of installed PCs soared. The market acceptance of Intel's 8088 and Motorola's 6502 chips as *de facto* standards helped propel the industry growth. Intel and Motorola enhanced their products with releases of greater capability every year. The ensuing 80x86 and 68000 families of the standards attracted new manufacturers and vendors of PC "clones" to the industry. The industry produced huge quantities, contributing to a price decline that made the product more attractive to the consumer. This stimulated demand, prompted even greater production quantities and helped accelerate a mutually-reinforcing spiral of lower prices and increased supply.

PCs were used for personal productivity, initially spreadsheet and word-processing applications for individual users. PCs gained foothold in business, in the otherwise monolithic domain of mainframes, because their low cost allowed them to be purchased on department budgets. Procurement of PCs did not need MIS management approval, were not subject to MIS project implementation schedules, and were generally installed and deployed in a matter of hours. This contrasted markedly with MIS's cumbersome performance for mainframe projects.

## LANs Arrive

The wider use of the PC gave rise to a number of new resource-related issues. PC users increasingly needed to share printers and also demanded access to local data storage devices. In the early 1980s the costs of PC peripherals, notably printers and disk drives, were relatively high. The LAN made printer and data storage resources economically available to more than one adjacent PC user. It linked PCs, designating some as sharable print "servers" and file "servers." The concept of client (workstation) and server (more powerful PC or a minicomputer) crystallized. This concept, accepted by most businesses, introduced strains on the hegemony of the mainframe. Users wanted the mainframe to assume a role of server in what would become essentially a peer-to-peer network.

The technology of LAN connectivity was introduced primarily by Xerox, DEC, Intel, Datapoint, and IBM. The ease of installation was a contributor to the growth of LANs in corporate America. The new technology linked PCs (including those designated as servers) on locally-strung cables. Ethernet, invented by Xerox, DEC, and Intel, featured a "bus" cable with drop-cables tapped from it providing access to the PCs. Datapoint's ARCNET was another technology with the same aim. IBM introduced—at a later date—the Token Ring technology. (At the outset, IBM also offered Ethernet connectivity in its PC Network, using an adapter developed by Sycor.)

Again, in the 1970s and 1980s, the approach taken to achieve improvement in information processing was to focus on automation that had already demonstrated its usefulness in improving clerical procedures. Automating *communications* was seen as a way to eliminate or minimize the delays in responding to customers, and in notifying vendors or business partners of the organization's own requirements. The closer one got to the deadline time for a task or process, the more exactly could one specify requirements for its services or products. This better accuracy, or precision, could lead to reduced work or production-line stoppage, less wastage, minimal over- or under-stocking of inventory and consequently, more efficiency. So the scope of automation widened to embrace personal and operational productivity, using communications to improve clerical and operations processes. Providing data links for operational processes that were located internally within the organization, was the first priority. However, pressures mounted to link to an increasing number of parties external to the organization, creating the *enterprise* network.

## COMMUNICATIONS AS STRATEGIC WEAPONS

By the end of the 1980s, technology itself was seen not only as a vehicle for automation, but as the means for corporations to achieve strategic competitive advantage. A number of major organizations had established significant competitive advantage by employing better ways of dealing with customers. They used technology to develop new ways of doing business, overturning prior methodologies.

One example is airline reservation systems, where airlines granted travel agents direct access to the airlines' data bases from the terminals on their desks. No longer did the travel agent need to make phone calls to airlines where an airline employee would perform the same task. In banking, as another example, Automatic Teller Machines revolutionized the decades-old practice of making checking and savings account deposits and withdrawing cash; no longer was a human teller required for this function.

Companies that availed themselves of these technologies flourished. Those that did not, foundered, or failed.

In the 1990s, the focus of information systems became more extroverted in contrast with the more inward-looking (prior two) generations.

The concept of an enterprise network evolved, challenging corporations to design and implement information systems that extended beyond their doors to customers, vendors, and business partners. The concept involves applications of all types, featuring voice (both conversational mode and message), E-mail, on-line data entry, inquiry response, bulk file transfer, facsimile, image, graphics, and video transmission. The question is how to design such networks. To start with, at the more general level, what communications medium should be selected, over what geographical span and with what topology of connectivity? We examine some of these issues now.

## BANDWIDTH DEMAND ON MEDIUM BY APPLICATION

Figure 1.6 associates different applications with selected media. Different media accommodate specific ranges of performance, with some media more suitable for certain applications than others. The figure lists *voice* as the first application. Through the medium of air, voice tones as high as twenty thousand cycles per second [20 kilohertz (20 kHz)] are accommodated. In the "plain old telephone service" (POTS), "twisted pair" copper wire is the medium for carrying an electrical signal that is the analog of the voice energy in air. (The characteristics of twisted pair are described in Chapter 5.) We shall see later that, in POTS circuits, tones higher than 3 kHz are filtered out, but, despite that, enough of the characteristic inflections and tonalities of the speech are retained for a listener to satisfactorily identify or recognize the speaker.

| Application | Medium | Mode | Performance/Bandwidth |
|---|---|---|---|
| Voice, speech high fidelity | air | Analog | tones to 20 kHz |
| POTS (plain old telephone service) | Twisted Pair | Analog | tones 300 Hz to 3300 Hz 3 kHz BW |
|  | Twisted Pair | Digital PCM compressed | 64 kbit/s, 8-16 kbit/s with codec |
| Data Transaction | Twisted Pair | Analog with modems (tones modulated/ demodulated) conditioned line for higher rates | tones 300 Hz to 3300 Hz (3 kHz BW) speeds to 9600 bit/s typical; 14.4-19.2 kbit/s less typical but exist |
| Data File | Twisted Pair | Conditioned analog line ISDN (Basic Rate) fractional T1 Switched 56 Accunet DS1 (T1) digital DS3 (T3) digital | 14.4-19.2 kbit/s 64 kbit/s incr. of 64 kbit/s 56/112 kbit/s 1.544 Mbit/s 44.736 Mbit/s |
|  | Coaxial and and Fiber Optic |  |  |

*Figure 1.6  Bandwidth demand on medium by application. (Continued on next page)*

| Application | Medium | Mode | Performance/Bandwidth |
|---|---|---|---|
| Data<br><br>(Files and Transactions) | Coaxial<br>and<br>Shielded T/P<br>and<br>Unshielded Twisted Pair (EIA/TIA Category 3, 4, 5) | LAN<br>baseband<br>LAN<br>baseband<br>RF LAN<br>broadband<br>RF LAN<br>broadband | 10 Mbit/s<br>20 MHz BW<br>16 Mbit/s<br>16 MHz BW<br>2 Mbit/s<br>12 MHz BW<br>10 Mbit/s<br>20 MHz BW |
| Image and Graphics | Twisted Pair, Coaxial and Fiber Optic | Digital FDDI and DQDB MANs and LANs | 10-100 Mbit/s |
| Video | Coaxial Cable and radio Twisted Pair | Broadband (analog) CATV, VHF, UHF RF Codec (digital, compressed) | 5 MHz/channel<br><br>128 kbit/s to 1.5 Mbit/s |

*Figure 1.6 Bandwidth demand on medium by application. (Continued)*

The next application listed in Figure 1.6 is the transport of *data* in its myriad forms. Although the public telephone network was designed for voice, it proved amenable for the transport of data. Transaction data representing at most a few hundred bytes, may be transferred in reasonable time using modems at speeds to 9600 bits per second (bit/s). With "conditioned" lines, and the appropriate modems, higher transfer rates are possible.

Different applications demand different bit rates and different media support different bit rates. Figure 1.7 illustrates the time taken to transmit *exemplars* of different applications at say 1200 or 9600 bits per second. Certain applications are misfits; an extreme example is the digital transmission of a 30-second movie or video. What is needed for these applications is transmission capabilities in the range of tens or hundreds of megabits per second. Returning to Figure 1.6, the transfer of large, multi-megabyte files of data over long distances is better served by some type of *digital* service. Among the services offered by the industry are DS 1 (colloquially, "T1," the name of the hardware facilities of the DS 1 service), "Fractional T1," "DS 3," "Digital Data Services," "ISDN Basic and Primary Rate Services," "Switched 56," and "Accunet." These services are discussed in *Chapter 9—Wide Area Networks*. Over short distances, by contrast, files are routinely transferred at multi-megabit per second speeds by most LANs.

---

## TRANSMITTING AT 1200-9600 BITS/S

APPLICATION:

| | |
|---|---|
| ASCII file 1MB | ~ from $1/4$ hr to 2 hrs |
| black & white graphic<br>      8 $1/2$ x 11  300 dpi<br>      (no compression) | ~ from $1/4$ hr to 2 hrs |
| compressed graphic (100x): | ~ 9 secs to 70 secs |
| color graphic<br>      (24 bits Cyan Magenta Yellow): | ~ 3 $1/2$ mins to $1/2$ hr |
| video:  30 sec."commercial":<br>      full color, compressed<br>      full color studio quality | ~ 1 $1/3$ hrs to 10 $3/4$ hrs<br>~ 1 $2/3$ days to 13 days |
| audio: 10 sec. "spot": | ~  67 secs to 9 mins |

---

*Figure 1.7. The need for bandwidth illustrated by some typical applications. Column on the right is time taken to transmit at 9,600 and 1,200 bits/s, respectively.*

To transmit images and color-graphics efficiently also requires at least LAN speeds, ideally to 100 megabits per second (Mbit/s).

The resources for transmitting video are the most demanding. Video is communicated either on an analog circuit (a la cable or CATV) or digitally. The latter requires a "codec" to convert the analog signal of moving images to a digital format.

## GEOGRAPHIC SPAN

The second issue raised by the question of how one designs the enterprise network is that of geographic span. Figure 1.8 illustrates the geographic span of the different types of network. Three types of networks together span the globe. First among these are Wide Area Networks (WANs), traditionally the province of telephone companies or the Post, Telephone and Telegraph (PTT) entities of governments, with a range in hundreds to thousands of kilometers. The second type is the Metropolitan Area Network (MAN). It extends across a city, or perhaps several adjoining cities or counties, covering distances of several hundred kilometers. The third type in this classification is the LAN. LANs are local in scope, and cover areas such as a campus or several buildings. LAN cabling is typically tens of kilometers in length, or less.

| GEOGRAPHY | NETWORK TYPE | SPAN (kM) | COMMENTS |
|---|---|---|---|
| World | WAN | 1 to 10,000 + | Realm of PTTs and Telcos; ITU-TS standards; analog lines with modems; digital X.25, ISDN, Frame Relay, T1 |
| Nation | | 100s - 1000s | DMS100, #5ESS switches; proprietary SNA, DNA and other networks; routers |
| County/ Metropolis/ City | MAN | 10s - 100 | DQDB, FDDI, 802.6 SMDS service |
| Campus | LAN | 1s - 10 | Privately owned higher speed client/ server networks; largely Ethernet, Token Ring (also ARCNET, StarLAN); IEEE 802 standards; router connectivity to WAN, MAN, and other LANs |
| Highrise | | <5 | |
| Building | | <5 | |
| Room | BUS | .001 - .01 | ISA, EISA, SCSI, µchannel |
| Cabinet | | .000001 - 0.001 | Parallel processing |

*Figure 1.8. Geographic span of communication networks.*

## Communications Taxonomy

Although not handled in this book as a communications network, the internal "Bus" wiring within a computer is indeed a fourth type of network. Here the communicating partners are, at most, a few meters apart. In the 1970s, Metcalfe and Boggs proposed the following taxonomy for communications:

|  | Distance kM | Bit Rate Mbit/s |
|---|---|---|
| Remote Networks | > 10 | < 0.1 |
| LANs | 0.1 to 10 | 0.1 to 10 |
| Multiprocessors | < 0.1 | > 10 |

*Table 1.1.*

Today, using this taxonomy, we may substitute the words "WANs and MANs" for "Remote Networks." Today, also, we find that the trend for bit rate is much higher. Technology, particularly fiber optics, is driving toward, and enabling, multi-megabit per second speeds even in "Remote Networks" WANs and MANs.

## MODERN INFORMATION SYSTEMS

Figure 1.9 provides a picture of how the modern information system may take shape, and be interconnected. The entire network is characterized as client/server. LANs provide access for client workstations to servers. Bridges, routers, and gateways interconnect the various LANs with others. The host system assumes a role of data base server. Its communication controller becomes a router. Client workstations that are all on a par cooperate regardless of platform or operating system. In addition to the IBM PC running the PC DOS operating system (and clones of it running MS-DOS or Windows) there are specialized workstations such as Apple's Macintosh, DEC's MicroVax, Sun workstations and HP/Apollo workstations. Higher performance workstations than the PC that are on the network may also include IBM's own PS/2 with the OS/2 operating system. The specialized workstations address niche markets. Servers include mainframes, minicomputers or specialized PCs. Finally, we note that while "dumb" terminals like the 3270 display stations or VT100s have been superseded by PCs emulating them, the original mainframe applications are still available to them.

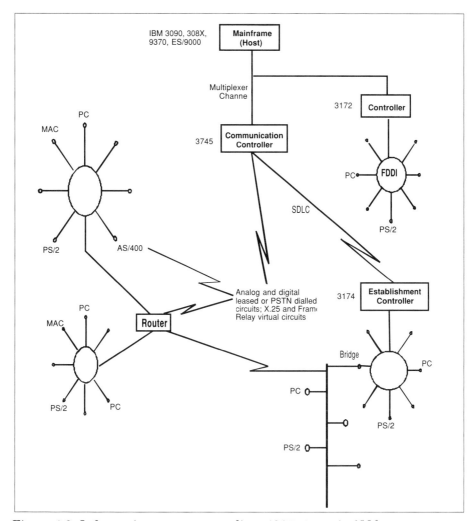

*Figure 1.9. Information systems paradigm 1980s to early 1990s.*

The aim is to provide a wide spectrum of network resources to any client regardless of location. At one end of the spectrum may be a post-office-like mail system, satisfying the needs of applications where delay from the time of submission to the receipt of the communications could be considerable. Examples include sending information from paper documents, plus magnetic and optically encoded floppy disks, cartridge tape, compact disks and videotape. For these applications, where the delay is acceptable to the communicating partners, it makes sense to include the mail system as part of the network. At the other end of the spectrum, the applications may demand real-time, fraction-of-a-second delay. This type of application is usually interactive, with the end-points alternating in their roles as transmitter and receiver of information with each transmission.

Figure 1.10 lists media options available for communicating with partners in close proximity, or at a distance. In practice, the media for communications are mainly chosen from electrical conductors (twisted pair and coaxial cables) and fiber-optics. Wireless media such as radio, microwave, infrared and satellite are, however, not only viable alternatives, they make new applications possible.

Whether the medium is wireless or not, whether the application is real-time or not, and no matter how the network is characterized (be it LAN, MAN or WAN) or inter-operates with other networks, today's communication environments share a common attribute. As Information Systems managers are aware, the inexorable trend is toward the transfer of rapidly increasing volumes of information at ever higher performance rates. Coupled with this are expectations of reliability (which must be superb), network management (which must be easy) and cost-effectiveness. Fortunately, technology, and product and service trends, are afoot to meet the challenges.

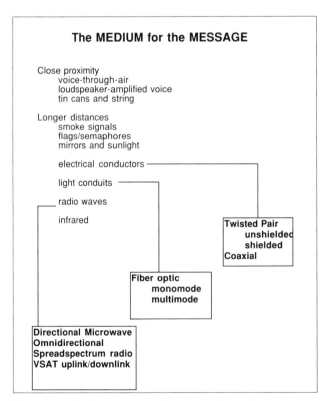

*Figure 1.10. Communications media options.*

# 2

# Choices in Transmission

## INTRODUCTION

Chapter 1 reviewed the objectives and use of technology over three generations of Information Systems. In this chapter, we take a closer look at information and the different options for communicating it.

Information is useful or usable representations of reality. Representations are needed when it is impossible or impractical to transfer abstract or concrete objects in order to communicate meaningfully about them with others.

Perhaps the easiest representation of a physical object is a picture. Someone communicating with a remote partner about an object may send a picture as simple as a drawing of it. A color photograph would improve the quality of the communication. Better yet would be multiple views of the object in a number of photographs. A moving picture (video) would be more successful, and a 3-dimensional or holographic video representation may possibly be the best. The closer the "analog" approximates the object so that it seems real, the greater is the likelihood that the concept transmitted will be interpreted as intended. Generally, the more real and true the representation appears, the more complex is the technology required.

A visual picture avails only the sense of sight. Invoking the senses of touch, hearing, taste and smell could add to the quality of the communication if media for these were involved as well.

The less "real" the analogs or models, the simpler the technology needed, and the more we need to resort to written words and symbols.

Human language enables us to communicate not only about objects, but concepts too. We use words and symbols that common experience associates with them. These words and symbols conjure up the concepts and objects in the recipient's mind. If you have an object at hand, say an orange, you know its nature from the aggregate of sensory stimuli (look, smell, taste, sound, feel) and analytical perceptions. Later, a label such as the word "orange" may create an image of the original in your mind. The success of a word or symbol in representing the real thing varies with the association the observer makes with his or her experience of the object. To gain a concept of unfamiliar objects, on the other hand, the observer needs descriptions using other familiar words or symbols. Someone never exposed to an orange can only perceive it with adequate descriptions of its weight, smell, color, size, taste, structure, succulence, feel, temperature, appearance, etc.

To convey words and symbols to persons in close proximity, we speak through the air (see Figure 1.10). Under noisy conditions, we may amplify the speech with loudspeakers. Loudspeakers can also be used to extend the range of speech, but at most their span is a few hundred meters.

Extending the range of speech brings to mind children's experiments with tin cups and string. The issue and challenge of doing this is not child's play, however.

## A Brief Communications History

From earliest times, man has grappled with the challenge of communications over distance. Perhaps primitive man's first communications were designed to alert the community of danger or the presence of enemies. Successes in this area were achieved by beating a drum or lighting one or more fires. These signals had the advantage of message timeliness over the alternative: dispatching a messenger.

Tracing the history of rapid communications leading to the modern era, we find a number of key applications. In Britain, during the early 1800s, the railroads needed a method to signal between stations, primarily for safety reasons. In 1837, Wheatstone and Cooke demonstrated a "telegraph" to the London and Birmingham Railway. This was based on the Danish physicist Oersted's discovery that a compass needle was deflected when current changed in an electrical circuit near it.

Wheatstone and Cooke's telegraph exploited this phenomenon in a configuration of several circuits using wires strewn between two stations. At the receiving station, each circuit had a compass needle near it. Each letter of the English alphabet was uniquely represented by a combination of circuits. To communicate, the transmitting operator changed the current in one or more circuits. The receiving operator deduced which circuits were changed by observing which compass needles deflected.

In 1835, the American engineer, Morse, proposed an alternative telegraph. His system featured a single circuit in contrast with multiple circuits. At the receiving end, Morse shaped a length of the circuit's wire into a coil and positioned a movable iron plunger within the coil, creating a solenoid. At the plunger's tip was an inked pen. A moving roll of paper was placed nearby.

Electro-magnetism, responding to the absence or presence of current in the wire, moved the pen onto and off the paper.

In Morse code (see Figure 2.1), letters of the alphabet are assigned unique combinations of at most four "dots" or "dashes." Numeric digits are combinations of exactly five dots or dashes. Dots or dashes were sent and received serially, i.e., one behind the other in time on the same single circuit. To transmit a dot, the sender broke the circuit for a short duration; a dash was three times longer. These breaks caused short or longer marks to be inked at the remote receiver respectively.

| | | | | |
|---|---|---|---|---|
| E • | I •• | S ••• | H •••• | |
| | | | V •••— | |
| | | U ••— | F ••—• | 1 •———— |
| | | | •• —— | 2 •• ——— |
| A •— | R •—• | L •—•• | 3 •••—— | |
| | | | •—•— | 4 ••••— |
| | | W •—— | P •——• | 5 ••••• |
| | | | J •——— | 6 —•••• |
| T — | N —• | D —•• | B —••• | 7 ——••• |
| | | | X —•—• | 8 ———•• |
| | | K —•— | C —•—• | 9 ————• |
| | | | Y —•—— | 0 ————— |
| M —— | G ——• | Z ——•• | | |
| | | | Q ——•— | |
| | | O ——— | ———• | , ——••—— |
| | | | ———— | . •—•—•— |

letters occurring less frequently —>>

<<— letters occurring more frequently

Fundamental unit of transmission is the DOT; In telegraphy, the DOT is a "space"; DASH is a "mark" condition three times the duration of a dot; intersymbol spacing is 3 dots duration; interword spacing is 7 dots duration.

*Figure 2.1. Morse Code.*

In Morse code, frequently used letters are assigned combinations of fewer dots and dashes than less frequently used letters. Morse was already seeking ways to cut the transmission time! Note from Figure 2.1 that the letters E and T have a single symbol only to represent them: a dot and a dash respectively. Research led to Morse's discovery that these letters appeared most frequently in English text. After E and T, the next four most frequently appearing letters, I, A, M and N are assigned two symbols each. Each of the next eight most frequent, S, U, R, W, D, K, G, and O is assigned three symbols. The least frequently appearing letters of the alphabet take four symbols each.

The advantages that Morse code enjoyed over its predecessors were its innovative use of printing, plus its economy in terms of number of circuits needed. Interestingly, as operators became familiar with the telegraph, they learned to recognize the letters by sound. The clicks associated with the mechanical creation of the dots and dashes uniquely identified the letters.

However, a disadvantage of Morse code is that specialized operator skills were needed to transmit and receive messages. Also, Morse code has a limited number of punctuation characters. (These use six dot-dash symbols).

## Baudot

Baudot code (see Figure 2.2) redressed the shortcomings. Unlike Morse code which has up to six positions, Baudot is solely a five position code. Thirty two different permutations are possible with five positions, each position adopting a binary value, i.e., either numeral "0" or "1." The 32 codes are shown in the left-most column of the figure. A letter of the English alphabet is associated with a permutation. In addition to the 26 letters, Baudot code can represent the numerals from 1 through 9 and 0, punctuation characters and some special equipment control characters. Baudot represents a total of 64 characters by operating in one of two states at a time: letters mode or figures mode. By convention, at the time messages start, letters mode is assumed to be in effect; the 32 codes in the left-hand column of Figure 2.2 are interpreted as letters per the middle column, until the (FIGS shift) key is struck. Thereafter, the 32 codes are interpreted per the right-hand column as figures until the (LTRS shift) key is struck.

| BINARY | LETTERS | FIGURES |
|--------|---------|---------|
| 00000 | blank | blank |
| 00001 | E | 3 |
| 00010 | line feed | line feed |
| 00011 | A | - |
| 00100 | sp (space) | sp (space) |
| 00101 | S | , |
| 00110 | I | 8 |
| 00111 | U | 7 |
| 01000 | Carriage Return | Carriage Return |
| 01001 | D | $ Who are you? |
| 01010 | R | 4 |
| 01011 | J | bell |
| 01100 | N | , (comma) |
| 01101 | F | ! |
| 01110 | C | : |
| 01111 | K | ( |
| 10000 | T | 5 |
| 10001 | Z | ” (quote) |
| 10010 | L | ) |
| 10011 | W | 2 |
| 10100 | H | # |
| 10101 | Y | 6 |
| 10110 | P | 0 |
| 10111 | Q | 1 |
| 11000 | O | 9 |
| 11001 | B | ? |
| 11010 | G | & |
| 11011 | FIGS shift | FIGS shift |
| 11100 | M | . (period) |
| 11101 | X | / |
| 11110 | V | ; |
| 11111 | LTRS shift | LTRS shift |

*Figure 2.2. Baudot Code. International Alphabet Number 2, North America Teletypewriter (TTY) keyboard.*

The success of Baudot as a code is evidenced by its longevity as the code used in Telex. Telex was a worldwide international public telegraph service introduced by Germany in the 1930s. Successful for many years until superseded by the service called TWX, Telex employed Baudot code. Baudot is also known by the name "International Telegraph Alphabet Number 2—ITA2" given it by the International Consultative Committee for Telephony and Telegraphy, CCITT, which recently changed its title to "International Telecommunications Union—Telecommunications Standardization Sector," or "ITU-TS." This international body sets standards for communications.

## DIGITAL COMPUTER CODES

Use of binary "0" and "1" is of course the coding of the digital computer. IBM and other computer companies introduced their own coding systems to represent the alphabet and numerals.

In the 1960s, IBM introduced Binary Coded Decimal Interchange Code, (BCDIC) for example. This is a 6-position code in contrast with Baudot's 5. In BCDIC, there are no equivalents of "letters shift" and "figures shift." Each position in BCDIC assumes a binary value. The binary digits are called "bits."

### *EBCDIC*

With its introduction of the System/360 line of mainframe computers, IBM replaced BCDIC with Extended BCDIC, EBCDIC, an eight-position code (Figure 2.3). Here too, each position was binary. The 8-bit code spans a wider range of symbols, namely 256. IBM's name for the octet of bits is "byte." The bit numbering convention that IBM adopted differs from international standards, as we shall see below. IBM numbered the byte's bits from left to right. Bit 1 is the highest order or "most significant bit" (MSB) of the byte. The "least significant bit," LSB, the bit of lowest order is at the right-hand end of the byte and is numbered 8.

| b1 | 1 | 1 | 1 | 1 | 1 | 1 | 1 | 1 | 0 | 0 | 0 | 0 | 0 | 0 | 0 | 0 |  |  |  |  |  |
|---|---|---|---|---|---|---|---|---|---|---|---|---|---|---|---|---|---|---|---|---|---|
| b2 | 1 | 1 | 1 | 1 | 0 | 0 | 0 | 0 | 1 | 1 | 1 | 1 | 0 | 0 | 0 | 0 |  |  |  |  |  |
| b3 | 1 | 1 | 0 | 0 | 1 | 1 | 0 | 0 | 1 | 1 | 0 | 0 | 1 | 1 | 0 | 0 |  |  |  |  |  |
| b4 | 1 | 0 | 1 | 0 | 1 | 0 | 1 | 0 | 1 | 0 | 1 | 0 | 1 | 0 | 1 | 0 |  |  |  |  |  |
| hex | F | E | D | C | B | A | 9 | 8 | 7 | 6 | 5 | 4 | 3 | 2 | 1 | 0 |  | b5 | b6 | b7 | b8 |
| 0 | 0 |  |  |  |  |  |  |  |  | . | & | SP |  | DS | DLE | NUL | 0 | 0 | 0 | 0 | 0 |
| 1 | 1 |  | J | A |  |  | j | a |  | / |  |  |  | SOS | DC1 | SOH | 1 | 0 | 0 | 0 | 1 |
| 2 | 2 | S | K | B |  | s | k | b |  |  |  |  | SYN | FS | DC2 | STX | 2 | 0 | 0 | 1 | 0 |
| 3 | 3 | T | L | C |  | t | l | c |  |  |  |  |  |  | DC3 | ETX | 3 | 0 | 0 | 1 | 1 |
| 4 | 4 | U | M | D |  | u | m | d |  |  |  |  | PN | BYP | RES | PF | 4 | 0 | 1 | 0 | 0 |
| 5 | 5 | V | N | E |  | v | n | e |  |  |  |  | RS | LF | NL | HT | 5 | 0 | 1 | 0 | 1 |
| 6 | 6 | W | O | F |  | w | o | f |  |  |  |  | UC | EOB | BS | LC | 6 | 0 | 1 | 1 | 0 |
| 7 | 7 | X | P | G |  | x | p | g |  |  |  |  | EOT | PRE | IL | DEL | 7 | 0 | 1 | 1 | 1 |
| 8 | 8 | Y | Q | H |  | y | q | h |  |  |  |  |  |  | CAN |  | 8 | 1 | 0 | 0 | 0 |
| 9 | 9 | Z | R | I |  | z | r | i |  |  |  |  |  |  | EM |  | 9 | 1 | 0 | 0 | 1 |
| A |  |  |  |  |  |  |  |  | : |  | ! | ¢ |  | SM | CC | SMM | A | 1 | 0 | 1 | 0 |
| B |  |  |  |  |  |  |  |  | # | , | $ | . |  |  |  | VT | B | 1 | 0 | 1 | 1 |
| C |  |  |  |  |  |  |  |  | @ | % | * | < | DC4 |  | IFS | FF | C | 1 | 1 | 0 | 0 |
| D |  |  |  |  |  |  |  |  | ' | - | ) | ( | NAK | ENQ | IGS | CR | D | 1 | 1 | 0 | 1 |
| E |  |  |  |  |  |  |  |  | = | > | ; | + |  | ACK | IRS | SO | E | 1 | 1 | 1 | 0 |
| F |  |  |  |  |  |  |  |  | " | ? |  | \| | SUB | BEL | IUS | SI | F | 1 | 1 | 1 | 1 |

*Figure 2.3. EBCDIC—Extended Binary Coded Decimal Interchange Code 8-bit (byte) code; Bits are numbered left-to-right; b1 is most significant.*

## ASCII

EBCDIC, however, did not become the dominant code for communications and interchange between computers. Another code, shown in Figure 2.4, is today more popular for communications. This is the American Standard Code for Information Interchange, ASCII. ASCII is a 7-position code. The USA Standards Institute, (which later was re-named the American National Standards Institute, ANSI), introduced ASCII as a U.S. Federal standard. It is the standard adopted by the ITU-TS and the International Organization for Standardization, ISO. ITU-TS's designation for ASCII per its Recommendation V.4 is International Alphabet Number 5, IA5. (IA5 and ASCII are almost identical with only minor differences: in IA5, the "$" sign is a country's currency symbol, for example.)

| | 1 | 1 | 1 | 1 | 0 | 0 | 0 | 0 | b7 | | | | |
|---|---|---|---|---|---|---|---|---|---|---|---|---|---|
| | 1 | 1 | 0 | 0 | 1 | 1 | 0 | 0 | b6 | | | | |
| | 1 | 0 | 1 | 0 | 1 | 0 | 1 | 0 | b5 | | | | |
| hex | 7 | 6 | 5 | 4 | 3 | 2 | 1 | 0 | | b4 | b3 | b2 | b1 |
| 0 | p | | P | @ | 0 | sp | DLE | NUL | | 0 | 0 | 0 | 0 |
| 1 | q | a | Q | A | 1 | ! | DC1 | SOH | | 0 | 0 | 0 | 1 |
| 2 | r | b | R | B | 2 | " | DC2 | STX | | 0 | 0 | 1 | 0 |
| 3 | s | c | S | C | 3 | # | DC3 | ETX | | 0 | 0 | 1 | 1 |
| 4 | t | d | T | D | 4 | $ | DC4 | EOT | | 0 | 1 | 0 | 0 |
| 5 | u | e | U | E | 5 | % | NAK | ENQ | | 0 | 1 | 0 | 1 |
| 6 | v | f | V | F | 6 | & | SYN | ACK | | 0 | 1 | 1 | 0 |
| 7 | w | g | W | G | 7 | ' | ETB | BEL | | 0 | 1 | 1 | 1 |
| 8 | x | h | X | H | 8 | ( | CAN | BS | | 1 | 0 | 0 | 0 |
| 9 | y | i | Y | I | 9 | ) | EM | HT | | 1 | 0 | 0 | 1 |
| A | z | j | Z | J | : | * | SUB | LF | | 1 | 0 | 1 | 0 |
| B | { | k | [ | K | ; | + | ESC | VT | | 1 | 0 | 1 | 1 |
| C | \| | l | | L | < | , | FS | FF | | 1 | 1 | 0 | 0 |
| D | } | m | ] | M | = | - | GS | CR | | 1 | 1 | 0 | 1 |
| E | ~ | n | | N | > | . | RS | SO | | 1 | 1 | 1 | 0 |
| F | DEL | o | — | O | ? | / | US | SI | | 1 | 1 | 1 | 1 |

*Bits are numbered right-to-left; b1 is least significant bit of 7-bit code.*

*Figure 2.4. American Standard Code for Information Interchange ASCII.*

Unlike EBCDIC, ASCII bits are numbered from right to left. However, like EBCDIC, symbols are grouped together conveniently in columns. For example, characters designed to control the receiving terminal are in the two right-hand columns of Figure 2.4. These are generally non-printing characters.

In transmission, the 7-position ASCII code is usually accompanied by an eighth bit. This is used as a parity bit. We discuss the concepts of parity and asynchronous and synchronous transmission later. For now, let us mention that ITU-TS recommends even parity for asynchronous communications, odd parity for synchronous.

By convention, the least significant bit (a 0 in Figure 2.6 for the ASCII "V") is transmitted first; the most significant bit, followed by parity bit, last.

Morse, Baudot, BCDIC, EBCDIC and ASCII all represent "characters" by codes. Except for Morse, each character code has a fixed number of positions: Baudot has five, BCDIC six, ASCII seven and EBCDIC has eight. A common feature of all the codes is that each position is binary. Even the dot or dash of Morse code could be interpreted as a binary representation.

## PARALLEL OR SERIAL?

Is it preferable to transmit the character on parallel paths, with one path per position of code, or to transfer the bits of the character serially one after the other on the same path, as pioneered in Morse code?

Figure 2.5 shows an example of transmitting the letter "V" (expressed in ASCII) in parallel. Physically, eight paths or circuits are used, one for each bit of the character, plus parity. All eight bits move simultaneously (hence "in parallel") from sender to receiver. Parallel transfer transmission lines are characteristically short, normally less than a meter. Parallel transfer is usually reserved for moving bits within the chassis of computers on internal buses or channels such as the ISA, SCSI, EISA and Microchannel. The SCSI bus is also external to the computer chassis, though its length is not more than a few meters.

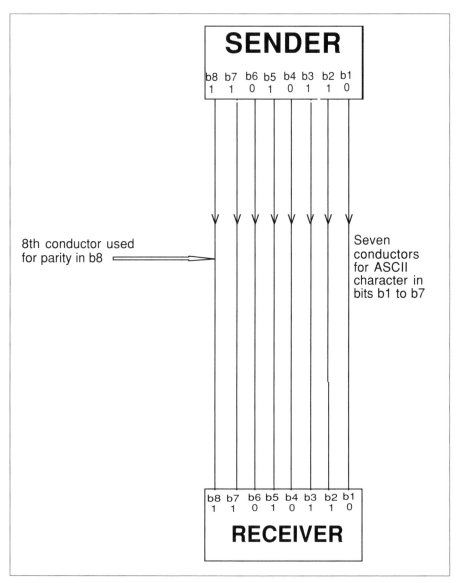

*Figure 2.5. Parallel transmission of ASCII "V" (hexadecimal 56).*

Parallel transfer is expensive. Part of the expense is the electronics to synchronize the transfer of all parallel bits, ensuring the simultaneous transmission of all the bits in each character and the simultaneous reception, later, of all the bits in the character.

Figure 2.6 illustrates the alternative to parallel transmission: bit serial transmission. There are two types of bit serial: asynchronous and synchronous transmission. In both types, the bits that make up the character are sent and received one after the other. An advantage of bit serial—synchronous or asynchronous—is lower equipment cost than for parallel. However, *n path* parallel transmission is *n* times as fast as serial.

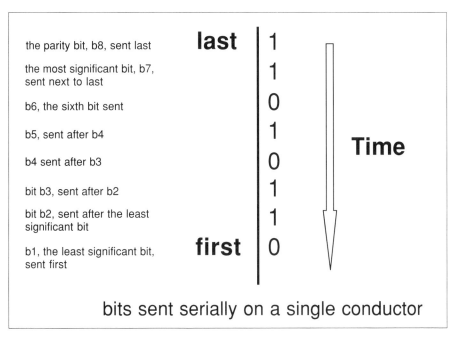

*Figure 2.6. Serial transmission of ASCII "V" (hexadecimal 56 with odd parity).*

### Reliability and Distance

The quality of received signals deteriorates with increasing distances. This applies equally to serial and parallel transmission. It is serial, not parallel transmission that is usually used for communicating over distances exceeding a few meters. Lines may need some mechanism to restore the signal's quality. Regenerating amplifiers or repeaters are placed between the sender's and receiver's equipment. With voice-grade telephone service, the inter-repeater distances are typically the manhole to manhole distances in streets, i.e., approximately 6,000 feet.

## IDLE, SPACE AND MARK; VOLTAGES

Given that the strength of the signal itself is successfully restored, how does the receiver know *when* the communication starts? One approach is to follow telegraphy practices. In ITU-TS Recommendation V.1, a communication line is said to have two states, defined as condition A and condition Z. Initially, an idle line with no signals being sent is in condition Z, the IDLE/MARK state. Condition Z means "line idle" only until a start bit is transmitted. A start bit is transmitted when the line switches to condition A for one bit time. After that, each bit time for which the line is in condition A signals binary 0 ("space"), and each bit time in condition Z signals a 1 ("mark"). Condition A is also called the SPACE state. The terms "space" and "mark" signifying binary 0 and 1 respectively, are inherited from telegraphy.

As an example, to define the two conditions of a line, two voltage levels may be used. Let us illustrate the asynchronous transmission of a character, say the letter "V" (in ASCII, hexadecimal 56). In Figure 2.7, the two discrete voltage levels are represented on the vertical axis. The horizontal axis is time. To alter the state, the voltage is varied by a discrete amount. Binary 0 or 1 is transmitted by placing one of two voltages on the line for a bit time. Initially, the line is in an IDLE/MARK state, shown at the left of the illustration by the flat horizontal line voltage. No information is communicated until the voltage changes. The change is a step increase in voltage level (a convention chosen arbitrarily for this illustration). This higher voltage is the SPACE state: its first occurrence is the start bit. After start, each interval of time for which the line is at the higher or lower voltage state signals binary 0 or 1 respectively. After the last bit of the character and its parity bit, if any, have been transmitted, the line is reinstated to the IDLE/MARK voltage.

In the previous discussion, discrete voltages described states. The state could equally have been represented by the presence or absence of current. In a later chapter, we discuss other ways in which networks represent 1s and 0s.

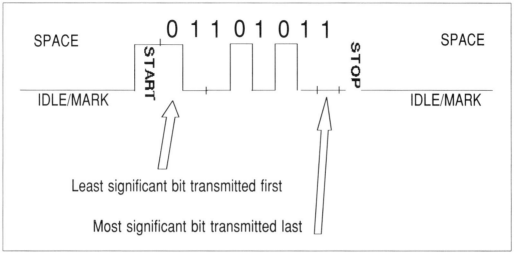

*Figure 2.7. Asynchronous transmission features variable intercharacter (idle) times plus start/stop bits.*

## Asynchronous, Start-Stop

The majority of *asynchronous* applications involve operators entering keyboard data. Inter-character keystroke delay is orders of magnitude longer than the time between successive bits within a character. Also, the delay between keystrokes is unpredictable. Keyboard data entry characterizes asynchronous, alias "start-stop," or "teletype (TTY)" bit serial applications.

With bit serial, two timing mechanisms are in play. One of these is used to signal to the receiver the imminent arrival of the character; the other arranges for constant intervals of time between successive bits. In asynchronous applications, the first mechanism has the sender and receiver use a "start bit" immediately prior to transmitting the first bit of a character on a communication line. The receiver is alerted to the impending arrival of the first information bit by this start bit.

Regardless of the technique used to mark the time the first bit is "on the line," a second timing mechanism arranges for constant bit times between subsequent bits of the character. For asynchronous communications (and, as we shall see presently, for synchronous communications as well), all bits transmitted after the start has been signaled appear on the line at a fixed bit rate. This is achieved by an electronic timer such as a crystal that oscillates at a fixed rate.

After the last bit of an asynchronous character is transmitted, the sender reinstates the line to idle. By convention, sender and receiver agree on a minimum period of idle time between characters, expressed in bit times. Usually, 1, or 2 bit times are specified; however, some equipment stipulates 1.5 bit times.

These are the 1, 2, or 1.5 *Stop* bits. In practice, applications are not slowed by the stop-bit requirements since human typing speed is usually a limiting factor.

## SYNCHRONOUS

While asynchronous transmission uses start and stop bits, the alternative type of bit serial transmission, *synchronous*, does not. In synchronous transmission, the intervals between characters are constant. Typically, synchronous messages are sent as blocks of multiple characters. Exactly one bit time after the transmission of the last bit of a character is the first bit of its successor. After the first character is transmitted, the subsequent characters follow at predictable intervals of time.

The advantage that synchronous enjoys over asynchronous is that the stream of bits is all payload; there are no start and stop bits. A separate mechanism, described below, is needed to determine when each block of characters starts. But first we describe isochronous transmission.

## ISOCHRONOUS

*Isochronous* (from the Greek *iso*=same, *kronos*=time) transmission on digital circuits is characterized by the transmission times for all equal-length sequences of consecutive bits being identical. (For analog circuits, read *events* e.g., wave-forms, for "bits.") Thus, in an isochronous transmission, if one chooses any bit sequence length, say $n$ bits, the interval of time between the transmission of the bit at position number $b$ and of that at $b+n$ is always constant. This holds true for every bit position $b$ in the message provided, of course, that there is a bit at position $b+n$. If there isn't, then the constancy must apply, symmetrically, to the interval of time between the transmission of the bit at position number $b-n$ and of that at $b$.

So, the individual bits within any individual start-stop (**asynchronous**) character are transmitted isochronously. However, a sequence of start-stop characters, transmitted as it is being keyed, cannot be called isochronous. The likelihood of every set of two bits, say, taking exactly the same amount of time is infinitesimal. It would require that the intervals be identical between the time of the last bit transmitted in any character and the first bit of the next. But sequences of these characters are intrinsically subject to variability in the inter-character times.

Likewise, "synchronous" transmission is isochronous *within any one block of characters* (all the individual bits within each block being transmitted at a constant rate). But "synchronous" transmission in general (i.e., covering two or more blocks) is not isochronous because the inter-block times vary.

Note that network equipment such as repeaters, nodes or routers must be careful not to introduce any delay to isochronous traffic that could change its nature.

## EFFICIENCY SYNC VS. ASYNC

Synchronous is the preferred method for communicating messages already present in the memory of the sending equipment. It is a more efficient method than asynchronous when efficiency is measured as the percentage of transmitted bits that is payload. While in practice one may find legitimate reasons to use asynchronous communications to send blocks of data that are already in the memory of the sending equipment, the efficiency of so doing is never higher than 80% and may be as low as 70%. The following table shows that the efficiency of asynchronous mode varies, depending on the number of STOP bits chosen:

| Overhead Bits | Overhead Ratio | | Efficiency |
|---|---|---|---|
| 1 start+ 1 stop | 2/9 | 22.2% | 77.8% |
| 1 start+ 2 stops | 3/10 | 30% | 70% |
| 1 start+ 1.5 stops | 2.5/9.5 | 26.3% | 73.7% |

*Table 2.1.*

Because asynchronous is simpler than synchronous as a type of transmission to implement in hardware, it is cheaper. The more complex mechanisms needed to signal the start of a block of characters for synchronous communications are more costly.

As we said, synchronous mode requires that the block be available in the memory of the sending equipment; strictly speaking, it only requires that the next bit be available in time for transmission. Usually (but not necessarily) this means that the bit to be transmitted is taken from a character in the block already in memory. If this is not the case, then, at a minimum, the next single bit must be available in time for its transmission.

## THREE WAYS TO START SYNC BLOCKS

At least three mechanisms are available to signal the start for a synchronous block of characters. In the three that we describe below, the block of characters is prefaced by overhead bits.

Firstly, in products using IBM's Binary Synchronous Communications protocol and DEC's Digital Data Communications Message Protocol (DDCMP), the block is prefaced by two or more SYN characters. These are the EBCDIC and ASCII unique synchronizing characters respectively.

A second mechanism does not rely on characters being recognized. Instead, the preface is a "Start Frame Delimiter" which may appear as a sequence at any bit time. Two possibilities apply, the first for communications protocols called High Level Data Link Control (HDLC) and Synchronous Data Link Control (SDLC). The pattern 01111110 on an HDLC or SDLC link (for example, on the wire between two communications partners) signals the start of a frame. HDLC/SDLC transmitters and receivers are programmed to preface and recognize the start of each frame by this pattern. The pattern is called a flag.

To ensure that no data within a frame is mistaken for a flag, every time the transmitter sends a bit, it examines the pattern of the last six bits it sent. The transmitter is sensitive to the pattern 011111 i.e., a 0 followed by five 1s. It does nothing special unless it recognizes that it has transmitted this pattern. Then, it inserts a superfluous 0 after the transmission of the fifth 1. Reciprocally, a receiver receiving bits one at a time looks for the same pattern 011111. When it recognizes the 0 followed by five 1s pattern, if the next bit is a zero, the receiver discards it, being the superfluous 0 inserted by the sender. Otherwise, five 1s followed by a 1 could be part of a flag. Figure 2.8 shows an algorithm whereby the SDLC/HDLC Receiver "strips off" (unstuffs) superfluous 0 bits, recognizes flags, and recognizes abort conditions.

So far, we have described the use of SYN characters and 01111110 flags as mechanisms for "Start Frame Delimiter" to indicate the start of a block of characters. Another approach is found in Token Passing Ring and Token Passing Bus LANs. The Start Frame Delimiter is signalled by using electrical patterns that are "violations" of rules for physically forming binary 1s and 0s. We describe these violations later in Chapter 6 under the discussion of Manchester encoding.

Yet another—the third—example of prefacing a block of characters is found in the implementation of Ethernet. Ethernet receivers recognize a "preamble" sequence of 56 alternating 1s and 0s, followed by eight 1s. The IEEE specification for essentially the same technology, viz. CSMA/CD 802.3, uses a sequence of 62 alternating 1s and 0s followed by 11.

As an aside, Ethernet's 64-bit preamble and, as we shall see later, its minimum block size, make its use for asynchronous keyboard data entry unattractive.

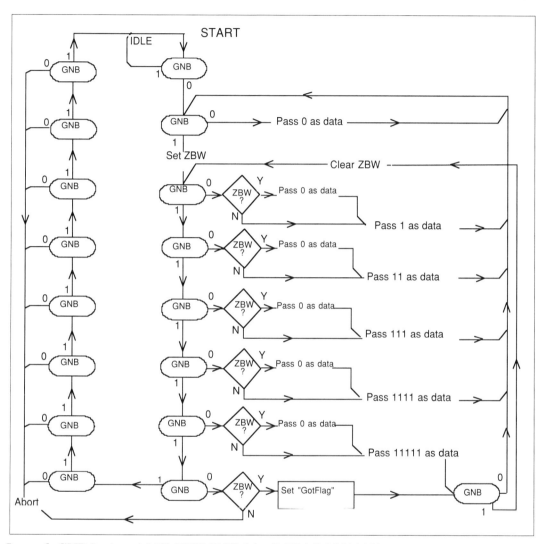

Legend: GNB "get next bit"; ZBW "0 Waiting"; FLAG 01111110
Rule: 15 successive 1s: line idle; else 7 or more successive 1s: abort

*Figure 2.8. SDLC/HDLC Receiver's Bit Unstuffing Algorithm.*

## RESOURCE SHARING FOR ECONOMICAL REASONS

We indicated earlier that, because it is more efficient, synchronous mode is nearly always preferred over asynchronous mode for the transmission of blocks of characters. But, efficiency is also measured by how well resources are used. Were it practical, every possible pair of communicating partners would have a dedicated point-to-point link. Since this is not practical, resources have to be shared among many users. Users need to gain access to or reserve these resources as needed. Prior to communications taking place, the partners must arrange for their exclusive use of certain facilities either for the duration of the upcoming conversation, or permanently.

Figure 2.9 shows a topology of switching nodes called a *mesh*. While every end-point in a mesh may not be directly connected to every other end-point, any pair of end-points may be connected indirectly via one or more intermediate nodes. Except for situations where every pair of end-points must always be connected, mesh networks are an economical choice. When pairs of end-points are connected in a mesh, they use the intermediate nodes either on a temporary or permanent basis. The links are set up as needed and, thereafter, if they were temporary, are made available for other connections. The economy of the mesh network derives from the fact that not every end-point needs always to be continuously linked to every other one.

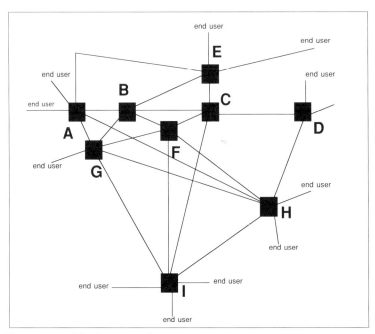

*Figure 2.9. Mesh network.*

## Circuit Switching

A mesh is used in *circuit switched* or *packet switched* fashion. In the *circuit switched* environment, the resources that connect a pair of communicating end-points include one or more electrical circuits. Circuit switched networks provide either temporary or permanent (private line) services. Dialing a telephone number in a circuit switched network, (and getting through!) establishes a temporary connection. For the duration of the dialed telephone call, each link in the connection is dedicated to the communicating pair of end-points alone. Until the parties disconnect i.e., "hang up," the circuits and equipment used for the communication are unavailable for use by other parties even if there are periods of complete inactivity when no communications are taking place. This problem is exacerbated when a private line is provisioned. With a private line, no dialing is necessary (to start a conversation) since a permanent connection exists. But when the parties terminate their conversation, the circuits and equipment used for the communication are never available for use by other parties.

Choosing a private line or dialed connection in a circuit switched network is usually decided by issues of economics, efficiency and by security needs.

The key feature of circuit switched networks is that there is no delay or variability in the delay at nodes in the connection. Circuit switching can, therefore, provide the *isochronous* communications demanded by voice and video applications. It is ideal for voice, for example, because there are no delays that would otherwise cause the listener to hear broken speech.

Many applications, however, do not need isochronous transmission. For these cases, (particularly data), transmission may be accomplished by means of other, more economical methods such as message or packet switching.

## Message Switching

The nature of data communications is "bursty;" transactions or files are transmitted in bursts. Furthermore, unlike voice, data applications do not require isochronous communications. This is because the integrity of data is not compromised by any (small) delays that may occur at nodes in a connecting path. As long as all the bits sent are received, the data application is satisfied. A private line is frequently suggested for data when call-establishment and tear-down times for each transaction could be too lengthy and cumbersome. But private lines are less economical than dialed. Network managers prefer to be able to share the resources among other users when idle time occurs between data bursts.

One alternative that finds successful configuration and use of resources for certain data applications is the *message switching* network. Rather than have the communicating partners control what facilities to use, and when, this type of network allows the nodes to allocate resources as and when they see fit. The user composes a message, and submits it to the network (the first node). In each node, the network's software seeks a path for the message to the destination. It uses its own criteria as to what resources to use and when. The path is constructed dynamically, each node selecting the next interim destination. As the message works its way through the network, it is stored at each node in its path. The node decides on the next destination, retrieves the message and forwards it. The final node delivers the message to the intended destination.

Note the *store-and-forward* nature of the message switching network. The entire block of characters representing the message is in the memory of the sending node prior to its first character being transmitted. The store-and-forward nature allows the network the flexibility of sharing or "multiplexing" circuits and facilities among concurrent pairs of communicators. The message may take a variable time in its transit, compared with a predictable time using a circuit switched network.

## E-mail

Many electronic mail applications are implemented using the store-and-forward approach. IBM's SNA Distribution Services (SNADS) provides a store-and-forward distribution capability analogous to a mail service. Its advantage is that the end-points of the communication do not need to be in active session with each other. The open, non-proprietary X.400 series of Recommendations from the ITU-TS defines a standard for similar message handling services. Many vendors comply with X.400 for inter-operability.

## *Packet Switching*

Even greater efficiencies in the sharing of resources could be realized when communicating partners agree on a single, common format for the messages. The *packet switched* network is a special case of the store-and-forward message switch network. Here the sender, in conformity with others, breaks the outgoing message into convenient size blocks, or "packets," usually 128 or 256 bytes long. All the communicating partners, including the interim nodes, agree to the common format. The standard size of the packet enables the efficient use of memory in the network, since the nodes do not have to cater for different size blocks from different users.

## Virtual Circuits Allow Sharing

Packets need identities or addresses to enable nodes in the network to forward them. One of two identification approaches is taken, usually dependent on the number of packets that will constitute the message.

The first approach generally applies to multiple packet messages such as files. This approach uses a *virtual circuit*. To set up a virtual circuit in the first place, an originator must take some administrative steps. This entails a business contract with the network service provider. The customer defines the endpoints of the path, i.e., the source and the destination. In a sense, the originator seeks to establish the equivalent of a private line, or permanent circuit-switched connection. Unlike their circuit-switched counterparts, however, the resources assigned to a virtual circuit are not dedicated. They will be shared among different requesters at different times. The service provider identifies the virtual circuit with a unique number. Packets provided at the source are tagged by the customer with this virtual circuit number. The service provider's proprietary network practices determine the route packets will take through the network. Regardless of how the route is chosen, prior to the transmission of the message proper, the software in each node has already been primed with the preferred "next node" numbers for each virtual circuit. This information is in tables. When a node is about to forward a packet, it uses the packet's tagged virtual circuit number as an index to the "next node" number in the table. Should a problem such as congestion arise with the selected node, the storing-and-forwarding node selects another node.

## Connectionless Datagrams

The second approach applies to single-packet and few-packet messages, or *datagrams*. Here, when a packet is submitted to the network for delivery, it does not have a virtual circuit number; instead, the message header contains the address of its final destination. As interim nodes receive and store the datagram, they examine the header and decide to what node the packet should be forwarded, in order to get it closer to the destination.

Datagrams are *connectionless* communications: no pre-arranged allocation of communications resources has been established: neither a circuit-switched call nor packet-switched virtual circuit has been set up. (Dialed circuit-switched calls and packet-switched virtual circuits are examples of *connection-oriented* communications, discussed below). The advantage that connectionless messages have is speed. No time is needed and no delay is incurred for call establishment prior to the transmission of the datagram. The disadvantage is that the sender initiates a transmission unmindful of any problems that the network may incur in transporting the message.

Many popular protocols use connectionless communications, among them the "IP" or Internet Protocol of TCP/IP, the technology of the global *Internet*. Tens of thousands of networks are linked in this publicly-accessible global network. The actual transfer and delivery of individual packets are handled by the IP portion of TCP/IP. Application programs using TCP/IP's User Datagram Protocol (UDP), transmit datagrams on a "mail-it-and-pray-it-gets-there" basis. No assumption is made about the availability or reliability of the connection.

### Paths are Pre-set for Connection-oriented

A dialled circuit-switched conversation is an example of *connection-oriented* communications because the dialing pre-sets a path for the ensuing communications traffic to follow. In packet switching with virtual circuits, the paths are also pre-set although the actual use of the links occurs only when the packets are at hand. So, virtual circuit packet switching is also an example of connection-oriented communications. Prior to accepting the first transmission, the connection-oriented network has assigned either a dedicated path (circuit-switching scenario) or a sharable path (packet-switching, virtual circuit scenario) to the destination. Only if the various necessary intermediate links are available will the network allow the transmission to proceed.

Although IP is connectionless, the applications using *Transmission Control Protocol* in TCP/IP (as opposed to UDP) can derive the advantages of connection-oriented services. TCP uses the connectionless IP for the transport of individual datagrams. Embedded in each datagram is a protocol number that alerts the receiving node to pass the datagram to the TCP software in the node. Called and calling parties, or programs, can check for errors in the packets, confirm that packets are received in the right sequence and control the flow of the messages exchanged.

Among the more popular connection-oriented networks used for data transmission are those described as X.25 packet networks. X.25 is a "Recommendation" of the ITU-TS. Commercial products that offer public packet switching services compliant with the X.25 standard include British Telecom's Tymnet, GTE's Telenet, Canada's Datapac, and France's Transpac. The successor to X.25, *Frame Relay*, is also connection-oriented. Both X.25 and Frame Relay virtual circuits provide customers with the services almost equivalent to private lines.

## SIMPLEX, HALF- AND FULL-DUPLEX

As indicated above, the connection-oriented network assigns either a dedicated path (circuit switching scenario) or a sharable path (packet-switching scenario) to the destination. The path permits messages to flow between the two end-points in any of three ways:

1. always from point A to point B or

2. always from point B to point A or

3. sometimes from point A to point B; the rest of the time from point B to point A.

In #1 or #2 above, the direction of messages in a path is exclusively one-way. The path is *simplex.*

#3 describes either a bi-directional half-duplex or full-duplex path. The *half-duplex* path acts as a simplex path for some of the time, alternating also as a simplex path in the other direction at other times.

The *full-duplex* path is more strongly bi-directional. Here, both end-points of a path may receive or send simultaneously, or at any time.

Note that the definitions of simplex, and half- and full-duplex say nothing about the wiring or cabling that may be necessary for the bi-direction. Figure 2.10 illustrates the bi-direction (simplex, half- and full-duplex) concepts by arrows representing direction of transmission pointing either one or both ways. Simultaneous bi-direction does not mean that the use of two distinct electrical circuits is necessary. Shown in the lower half of Figure 2.10 is the scheme used by the original full-duplex Bell 103 modem to provide two-way simultaneous communication on one circuit.

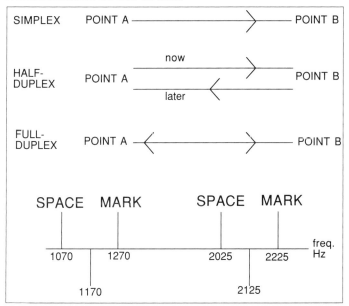

*Figure 2.10. (Top): Simplex, half- and full-duplex, (Bottom): Full-duplex frequency assignments in a single circuit using Bell 103 frequency shift keying modem.*

## ERRORS, ACKNOWLEDGMENTS AND ORDER

With communications flowing between two points A and B, three issues bear on quality. The first relates to data integrity—how does the receiving party know that the data received is what was sent? If an error occurs, how can it be detected? Must it be corrected? The second relates to acknowledgment—does the sending party need verification from the receiving party for messages already sent prior to it sending more messages? The third relates to order— which party communicates first and how and when does it know its turn to transmit?

### *Error Handling by Humans*

How do communicating parties know that the data received is what was sent? In the standard asynchronous mode of transmission, for example, one validates that keystrokes entered at a "dumb" terminal are transmitted without error to a remote computer. A popular approach has the computer echo the character it receives for the keystroke back to the terminal's display. The human keyboard operator gets visual feedback from the CRT or printer. The operator backspaces and corrects erroneous characters.

Note that the process of echoing characters works efficiently for terminals operating in the asynchronous mode. Connecting a keyboard/display terminal to a computer using Ethernet would not work efficiently: the overhead associated with each keystroke would be prohibitive. Consider keyboard entry and 'echoplex' confirmation in Ethernet, where the minimum packet size is 512 bits (64 bytes):

| **TERMINAL** | **ETHERNET** | **HOST** |
|---|---|---|
| operator presses "V" key | handles 64 bytes | receives 63 overhead bytes with the V |

**then**

| **HOST** | **ETHERNET** | **TERMINAL** |
|---|---|---|
| transmits a "V" for the CRT to display | handles 64 bytes | V to screen is one of 64 bytes |

*Table 2.2.*

The efficiency (really inefficiency!) is 1.56% since 98.44% of what is transmitted is overhead.

## Parity, by Machine

Echoplexing allows the human operator to confirm character-by-character transmission visually. By contrast, *parity* is a mechanism whereby equipment, not humans, validates character-by-character transmission. The parity mechanism requires the attachment of a redundant or "parity" bit to each character. ASCII 7-bit codes become 8 bits of parity-protected transmitted data, for example. When this is done, the parity is called *vertical parity*.

Parity detects the loss or corruption of an **odd** number of same-valued bits within a character. It detects the error where a single 1 bit within an octet is damaged and is interpreted as a 0 or when a single 0 is interpreted as 1. It also detects when three, five or seven 1s within a character are all received as 0s; or where three, five or seven 0s are all received as 1s. Parity does not catch all errors. Examples include an even number of 1s being received as 0s, an even number of 0s received as 1s or the loss of an entire character.

The user selects one of two conventions for the entire transmission. In the **odd parity** convention, the sending equipment transmits (and the receiving equipment checks for) a 0 or 1 value in the parity bit so that the count of 1s in the octet is odd. If **even parity** is selected instead of odd, the value of the parity bit is chosen so that the count of 1s in the octet is even.

## Longitudinal Parity

Longitudinal parity is a technique that extends the scope of parity protection to an entire block of characters. It requires the transmission of a redundant character at the end of the block. Each bit in this special character protects the *same* bit number $n$ position for all characters in the block, $n$ being 8, 7, 6,..,1. Using a similar approach to vertical parity, this bit is chosen to be 0 or 1 so that the count of all the 1 bits in this position of every character in the block (including the redundant character), yields an odd number. (This is the **odd parity** convention; for **even parity**, the bit is chosen to be 0 or 1 to make the count of 1s even.) As it receives each bit of each character, receiving equipment counts and recomputes an expected longitudinal parity character. The transmission is deemed successful if this computed parity character agrees with the transmitted longitudinal parity character. Otherwise, the receiver signals an error to the sender and the entire block must be retransmitted.

Unfortunately, longitudinal parity cannot catch all errors. It cannot detect when an even number of 1s, in the same bit position in two or more characters, are received as 0s or when an even number of 0s are received as 1s. Also, should entire characters be dropped from the block during transmission, only if the count of dropped 1s is odd can the mechanism detect the loss. Conversely, should erroneous "characters" be inserted into the block during transmission, only then if the count of inserted 1s is odd for any bit position can the mechanism detect the erroneous insertions.

## Block Length Counts, Too

One way of ensuring that the same number of characters is received as was sent is to count the number of characters in the block. This is done, for example, in "XMODEM" and "Kermit," two software packages used for communicating files. Both these software packages arrange to preface each block of characters for transmission with a special *block length character*. The block length is expressed as a (binary) number, e.g., to 128 in the case of XMODEM. The receiver counts how many characters it receives in the block. If the count differs from the number specified in the prefix, the receiver signals an error to the sender and the block must be re-transmitted.

## Checksums, for Parity, Block Length

Despite the improvement derived by a combined use of longitudinal parity with block length checks, stronger error detection schemes are sought. One approach replaces the longitudinal parity character with *checksum* characters. The checksum may be simply a binary sum of all the characters in the block. As the sender transmits each character, it adds it to the checksum. Carry bits overflowing the checksum field are ignored. The receiver recomputes the checksum and compares it with the sender's. Unless bits in the checksum field itself were damaged, yielding a faulty "error received," if the checksums do not match, the transmission was bad. The probability of a good transmission is (only) high when the two checksums match.

The checksum transmitted may also be the *twos complement* of the binary sum of all the characters in the block. This approach has the feature that when added to the receiver's cumulative checksum it generates an answer of zero. The advantage is practical: when the end of block is detected, successful addition of the checksum (that results in zero) prepares the field for its use in checking the next block.

## CRC to the Rescue

The strongest methodology for validating transmissions is through the use of *cyclical redundancy checks* or *CRC*. (Depending on context, the acronym CRC could read as *Cyclical Redundancy Characters*.) The idea behind the CRC is to view the entire block of characters as one long binary number that will be protected by a mathematical process. The sender affixes redundant bytes to the end of the block, in much the same way that a checksum character is appended. But the value placed by the sender in the CRC is actually a remainder after division of the long binary number by a divisor. Readers interested in the use, theory and implementation of CRC will find this topic covered in *Appendix C— Cyclical Redundancy Checks (CRC)*.

The topic of CRC (and, earlier, block check characters and parity) addressed one of three issues bearing on the attainment of quality communications between two points A and B. For the communicating parties to know that the data sent was received correctly, mechanisms to detect errors were needed.

## ACKNOWLEDGMENT

A second issue relates to acknowledgment. Prior to sending more messages, does the sending party need a "green light" from the receiving party? Regarding messages already sent, if there were errors, is the sender to be notified of them? If so, are they to be corrected? How? Even if the block was received error-free, the receiver may be unable to accept the next transmission because of congestion, saturation of processing capability, or another reason. Is there a mechanism whereby the receiver can forestall the sender when it is not ready for the next blocks? We discuss these issues now. (The third issue relates to order—whose turn it is next to communicate and how each party knows when it is its turn to transmit).

We have been focusing above on synchronous transmissions but the problem of errors in transmission and *overruns* can equally occur in *asynchronous* applications. With keyboard data entry, the possibility of overrun is rare since the operator's typing speed is slower than the acceptance rate of the receiver. An operator is alerted to something being wrong when the confirmations of entered keystrokes (echoes) are not seen on the screen or printer. This prompts the operator to re-key, and the problem is resolved.

### XON and XOFF

Additionally, in some asynchronous applications not involving operators, receiving equipment may request the sending equipment to halt transmission. An example is a printer application. With paper problems such as jams or paper-outs, the printer needs to alert the computer to stop sending it records. Operating on a full-duplex link, *XON* and *XOFF* controls could be used. The printer transmits XOFF to the computer to get transmission suspended; it subsequently transmits XON to the computer when the transmission may resume. Although not mandatory, the symbols typically selected for this purpose are ASCII Device Control 1 and 3 (DC1 and DC3), hexadecimal 11 and 13 for XON and XOFF respectively.

## Async for Files?

While synchronous transmission is preferred for efficiency in transmitting blocks of data, file transfer is sometimes accomplished asynchronously. A number of software packages support the asynchronous capability. For example, XMODEM (which we introduced earlier), allows two linked computers to transmit files between themselves. For transmission, XMODEM segments a file into 128-byte blocks and numbers them sequentially. At the end of each block, a 2-byte checksum is transmitted. If the XMODEM software at the receiver agrees with the sequence number of the block received, and also with its checksum, it transmits an ACK character. Otherwise, a NAK is sent, requesting XMODEM at the sender to re-transmit. (As an aside, the ASCII ACK is hexadecimal 06 and NAK is hexadecimal 15.)

## Binary Synchronous's ACK and NAK

ACK/NAK is used in the Binary Synchronous (BSC) protocol. Receipt of a block is confirmed by the receiver to the sender. The sender may not send a block unless the previously sent block has been acknowledged as received correctly.

BSC receivers send (short) acknowledgment blocks containing the ACK character. Successive acknowledgment blocks contain, alternately, a 0 or a 1 character appended behind the ACK. This guards against the undetected loss of a block *and* its acknowledgment.

In the event an error is detected by the receiver, a NAK is sent instead of an ACK. This Negative Acknowledgment signals the original sender to re-transmit.

(For synchronous communications, acknowledgment is not always accomplished by means of ACKs and NAKs . In protocols like HDLC/SDLC and IEEE 802 Logical Link Control, sequence numbers are used. Token Ring and Token Bus frames in Local Area Networks also use an *Address Recognized/Frame copied bit* in the frame status byte. We examine these approaches in detail later).

## BSC and Satellites

One problem with BSC is that time could be lost waiting for acknowledgments to arrive at the sender. This applies particularly when the transit time for a signal between source and destination is long. Delay is exaggerated, for example, with satellite communications. The distance from earth to satellite is about 22,300 miles. The signal travels from source earth station to the satellite, and then to the destination, a total of 44,600 miles. The speed of light is 186,000 miles per second, so travel time is one-quarter second. The return acknowledgment takes another one-quarter second.

To see what impact this physical constraint has on performance, consider 256-byte packets transmitted at 2,400 bits per second. Recognize that each packet can only be transmitted after its predecessor has been acknowledged. A transmitter will be busy sending a packet for

$$\frac{8 \times 256}{2400} = 0.85 \text{ seconds.}$$

The sender waits one half of a second once the last bit has been transmitted before receiving the first bit of the acknowledgment. In other words, its transmitter is active at most

$$\frac{0.85}{0.5 + 0.85} = 63\% \text{ of the time.}$$

Ironically, this ratio worsens the faster the transmitter operates! For the same 256-byte packet, a 4800-bit/s transmitter would be busy for

$$\frac{8 \times 256}{4800} = 0.43 \text{ seconds.}$$

Once again, after the last bit has been transmitted, the sender waits one half of a second before receiving the first bit of the acknowledgment. In this case, its transmitter is active at most

$$\frac{0.43}{0.5 + 0.43} = 46\% \text{ of the elapsed time.}$$

Similarly, at 9600 bit/s, the transmitter can be active no more than

$$\frac{0.21}{0.5 + 0.21} = 30\% \text{ of the time.}$$

One suggestion for improving the performance is to increase packet size. Nevertheless, regardless of the packet size chosen, the maximum equipment utilization efficiency will drop the faster the transmitter operates.

## Acknowledging in HDLC

The protocol *HDLC*, and variations of it like *SDLC*, overcome the performance deficiency by permitting more than one packet at a time to be in the process of being communicated. With HDLC/SDLC, lack of receipt of an acknowledgment of one or more packets will not delay the transmission of their followers. A maximum number of unacknowledged packets does, however, apply. The maximum number of unacknowledged packets is known as a *window*. We see the implementation of windows in the HDLC/SDLC frame. The frame structure is detailed later. Suffice to say here that its fields are: "Flag, Address, Control,

Information, Frame Check Sequence, Flag." Table 2.3 details the third, i.e., the *control* field within the HDLC frame. ITU-TS notation is used, with the low-order (least significant) bit on the left. The N(R) and N(S) fields apply windows as described below.

| 1 | 2 | 3 | 4 | 5 | 6 | 7 | 8 | Format |
|---|---|---|---|---|---|---|---|---|
| 0 | N(S) | | | P/F | | N(R) | | Information |

O R

| 1 | 0 | * | * | P/F | | N(R) | | Supervisory |
|---|---|---|---|---|---|---|---|---|

O R

| 1 | 1 | # | # | P/F | # | # | # | Unnumbered |
|---|---|---|---|---|---|---|---|---|

**Legend:**
P/F = Poll/Final bit
** = supervisory code
## = unnumbered code
N(R) = Receive Sequence Number
N(S) = Send Sequence Number

*Table 2.3. HDLC control field.*

The fields marked N(R) and N(S) are each 3 bits long. The field N(S) is used to advise the recipient of the sender's sequence number for the current frame. N(R) is used to advise the recipient what number the sender of the current frame *will expect* to find in the N(S) field of the next packet it gets from the recipient. It also implies that packets with earlier N(R) numbers i.e., numbers N(R) *minus* 1, N(R) *minus* 2, etc. were received successfully from the other party.

The N(R) and N(S) numbers are expressed *modulo 8*. (A number expressed Modulo 8 is its remainder after division by 8. Modulo 128, which uses a 2-octet control field, is optionally available. For simplicity, we discuss just the one case here.)

HDLC and its derivatives, including SDLC, allow full-duplex transmission between two end-points. No ACK/NAK transmission is done. However, information packets transmitted include fields for both "frame check sequence" (equivalent to a CRC) and sequence number. Each end-point confirms not only the frame check sequence of a received packet, but that the packet's send sequence number N(S) corresponds to an expected number. Every time an end-point sends a packet, it sends updated N(R) and N(S) fields, enabling its partner to do the same thing reciprocally.

## Pacing/Flow Control in HDLC

An end-point may not transmit a packet if the maximum *window* size (here seven) of packets remains unacknowledged. Otherwise, were the end-point to send a packet without waiting, its N(S) number would duplicate that of an as yet unacknowledged frame. With duplicates, the parties would not know which frame has been acknowledged. The end-point calculates the modulo 8 sum of its planned send sequence number *plus* 1. It checks that this sum does not equal the N(R) field seen in the last inbound packet. If they are the same, the transmitter waits until an inbound packet arrives with a different N(R).

---

In the discussions that led to this point, the goals and techniques that have been examined focused on how to get quality transmission by various mechanisms: echoing, parity, block check sums, cyclical redundancy checks, and sequence numbering. We also saw how overruns at the receiver could be guarded against, by allowing the flow of transmission to be controlled by the receiver with mechanisms such as XON/XOFF and sequence numbers.

Acknowledgments alert the sender that the transmission of a block was good or bad. Bad reception usually results in re-transmission. Different schemes are used for acknowledgment, including echoing, ACK/NAK in protocols such as XMODEM and BSC, and monitored N(R) and N(S) numbers in HDLC and its variants. Automatic Request for Repeat or Automatic Request for Re-transmission (*ARQ*) are error control procedures that rely on detection and re-transmission. Alternatively, there are error control procedures that enable the receiver to perform *error correction* without requiring re-transmission. We call these *Forward Error Correction* techniques.

### Forward Error Correction

Forward error correction techniques require the transmission of redundant bits. These are appended to or inserted in the message. In the event that an error is detected by the receiver, the receiver uses the redundant bits to help reconstruct and correct the data rather than require the sender to retransmit the message. In using the *Hamming Code*, for example, the transmitter and receiver are aware of the sequence number of each bit transmitted. This sequence number is used in an algorithm that creates the redundant bits. The transmitter examines each message bit as sent. If a 1, the bit's position within the message, expressed as a binary number, modifies (by Boolean logic Exclusive Or, *XOR*) a counter that was reset to zero prior to the transmission.

(The XOR function is defined in Step 3 of Appendix C). For example, if bit 19 of the message is a 1, the binary number 10011 is XORd with the contents of the counter. Results of each XOR replace the counter's previous contents. The final XOR result is transmitted as the redundant bit Hamming code.

The counter is $r$ bits wide. (Mathematically, $r$ is chosen to be the smallest number of times that the integer 2 must be multiplied by itself to reach a number just as large or larger than the bit length of the message, plus $r$ plus 1. More formally: $r$ is the smallest integer satisfying $2^r \geq m + r + 1$). The $r$ individual bits of the counter are themselves inserted in arbitrary positions within the message. Whilst arbitrary, this pattern for placement of the bits within the message is, of course, known to both sender and receiver. These bits are counted for position, but their contents do not participate in the XOR process.

The benefit of the Hamming code is that any single bit error occurring within the message is not only detectable by the receiver, but correctable by it as well. The error, if any, is detected when the receiver compares the calculated counter value with that submitted. With no errors, the Hamming codes of both sender and receiver are the same. An error is assumed to have occurred if they differ, and an XOR of the submitted counter with the receiver's counter, yields (if non zero) the position number of the erroneous bit. The receiver simply inverts the bit value at that position.

Hamming code's disadvantage is that it assumes that any errors will occur only once per message, i.e., it is good for handling a single bit failure within the entire message. If more than one bit in the message is in error, a valid bit elsewhere within the message will be erroneously "corrected," the error bits themselves remaining uncorrected. Also, an error, or errors, in any of the redundant bits themselves will cause a valid data bit within the message to be erroneously "corrected."

## Order of Transmission—Who's Next?

Apart from the above issues that bear on quality of transmission, the communicating parties may need to agree on communication order. Who communicates next? This applies particularly when the path between the parties is half-duplex. It also applies when the parties operate in half-duplex mode using a communication path capable of full-duplex operation.

To see the different ways in which access is controlled, we examine two configurations. These are illustrated in Figure 2.11 as "unbalanced" and "balanced" configurations.

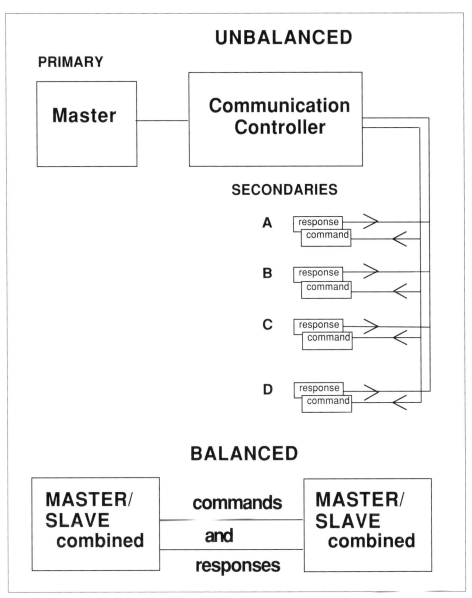

*Figure 2.11. Unbalanced and balanced station relationships.*

In the *unbalanced* configuration, one of the communicating parties is designated as *primary* and the others (one or more) are *secondary*. This designation is established beforehand by the network manager and does not vary from day to day. In the upper half of Figure 2.11 is an example of a network containing, perhaps, a host computer with remotely located equipment. In this figure, the primary, or Master station, could be an IBM System/370 or System/390 coupled together with its 3745 communication controller. At any one point in time, the secondary could be one of the four slave devices labelled A, B, C, and D in the figure.

## Poll and Select

*Commands* flow from the host side via its communication controller to a secondary. *Response* communications flow from the secondary A, B, C or D back to the communications controller and host. A command may be a solicitation for the secondary to transmit. In this case, the solicitation is called a *poll*. Or, the host could *select* the secondary to receive from it one or more blocks of transmission. All communications are under control of the host. No secondary may transmit unless it has been polled by the host. And, at any time, the secondary must be prepared to accept a transmission from the host and its communications controller.

From a connectivity viewpoint, (not explicitly shown in Figure 2.11), a modem is connected to the communication controller. Its tones for 1s and 0s go over the network to multiple pieces of remote equipment that may, for example, be emulating 3780s. Each of these pieces of equipment has a matching modem, connected in a multi-dropped fashion on a half-duplex line. Since all are tied to the same line, they simultaneously receive the communication controller's commands: whenever the latter sends a command, all four secondaries hear it. The 3780 poll-and-select protocol addresses a specific unit; only the addressed secondary responds. (As an aside, prior to sending the response message, the secondary's modem generates a *carrier* signal for its half-duplex path back to the communications controller. Only the communication controller hears and receives this transmission, though.)

In HDLC, a station may transmit a special packet (*not* an information packet, but rather a network management type of message) to alert the network of the mode that the station is communicating in. For example, to operate multidrop lines in standard IBM SNA fashion (as just described above), the command "Set Normal Response Mode" would be sent.

## Poll/Final

In HDLC, a station transmits one packet after another until its final packet. At that time, it flags the receiving party that it is complete by setting the Poll/Final bit in the Control Field of the frame. This technique also applies to the derivatives of HDLC such as SDLC, as well as the IEEE 802.2 Logical Link Control, shown in Figure 2.12.

When the Poll/Final bit is set in polling by the primary, it effectively says to the recipient: "Your turn, now. Please respond."

In the unbalanced mode, there is never doubt as to whose turn it is to communicate. Right from the outset, the primary station controls the communication sequence. On the other hand, in balanced mode configurations each station combines primary and secondary functions, so doubt could arise as to whose turn it is to communicate. Balanced mode, shown on the lower part of Figure 2.11, is often used when PCs or minicomputers connect with one another, e.g., on an Ethernet LAN. Problems could arise if two stations want to transmit simultaneously. The communications protocol, or the network itself, must resolve the conflict. When we examine Ethernet operation in detail later, we will see that it uses a technique called "exponential back off" for this purpose. The technique resolves the colliders' conflict by staggering the time that a station will attempt to regain access to the medium.

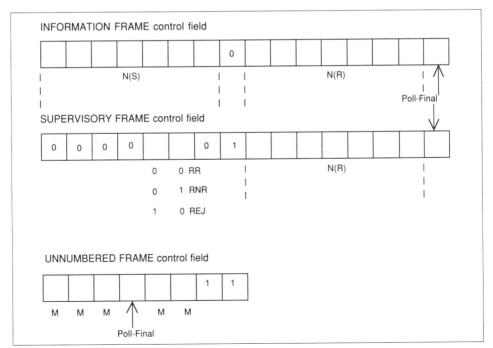

*Figure 2.12. Formats of the three LLC Control fields.*

## X.25 is Balanced—LAP-B

The public packet switching service X.25 also offers the use of its facilities in balanced mode. To interface to an X.25 network, equipment known as a Packet Assembler and Disassembler (PAD) may be used. All PADs are equal in status. The data link protocol in X.25 is derived from HDLC. In networks capable of supporting multiple modes, an unnumbered (non-information) packet containing the command *Set Asynchronous Balanced Mode (SABM)*, may alert the network that a station plans to communicate in the X.25 balanced mode. For this reason, the X.25 data link control standard is known as link access protocol, balanced (LAP-B). (The use of the word "asynchronous" in the command *Set Asynchronous Balanced Mode* is unfortunate. Its usual communications sense does not apply. Rather, it denotes that the submission of packets by a station may occur at any time.)

---

The fact that a link access protocol is balanced does not necessarily mean that all stations using it gain fair or predictable access to the medium. In some instances, an unbalanced mode may provide greater equitability for the participating secondaries than they would enjoy as individual composite primary/secondary stations. At least in the unbalanced mode, the primary station always determines when a secondary gets control of the medium. This is one example of *deterministic* access. Balanced mode may make the access to the medium for LAN connected PCs or minicomputers more random. If the problem of two stations "colliding", i.e., simultaneously transmitting, is resolved by techniques such as Ethernet's (staggering the time at which a collider will attempt to regain access to the medium) then access to the medium for the participating PCs and minicomputers is *probabilistic*.

Yet, this is the era for peer-to-peer communications. *Balanced* mode is the preference of current and future networks. PCs or minicomputers (and even mainframes) connected via a LAN are equal in status on the network. No single machine is designated primary; all are. If the drawback of the probabilistic access cannot be tolerated, the user employs another access method. For most office applications, the unpredictable delay in Ethernet access is tolerable. Otherwise, the user employs deterministic access methods such as Token Passing. These are examined in detail later.

# 3

# Layered Communications Architectures

## RATIONALE FOR MODULES

Chapter 2 described issues and options affecting the communication of information. It dealt with some of the technical choices that a designer of a data communications system faces. These include mode (parallel or serial; synchronous or asynchronous; character or block); resource usage (circuit, message, or packet switched); connectionless or connection-oriented services (datagrams, or virtual circuits); bi-direction (simplex, half- or full-duplex); integrity validation (echoplex, parity, CRC, block check); overrun protection and flow control (XON/XOFF or sequence number acknowledgment); and access (balanced or unbalanced, ACK/NAK usage, polling or selection, poll/final alternation).

Each decision is ultimately realized by means of a hardware choice of physical equipment, or by software function.

In choosing the features for a communication system or network, the designer recognizes that, as time progresses, conditions change, and some decisions may have to be reversed. For example, an application today may call for coaxial cable as the transmission medium. At a future date, however, fiber optic cable may be the medium preferred to meet new demands, say for image transfers. Another example is the choice of a format for electronic mail messages. The proprietary format of a software package may be acceptable for a network limited in the number of stations using it. But if the scope of the E-mail application must be expanded to extend services to other networks, a more widely accepted format such as ITU-TS Recommendation X.400 for Message Handling Services may be needed.

The perfectly maintainable system permits elements to be substituted *without* necessitating changes in the aggregate of choices elsewhere. Most communications networks cannot aspire to this perfection because of the interdependence among their elements. Changing one element in these systems requires changing other elements simultaneously.

A well-engineered system, on the other hand, is an acceptable compromise between freedom to interchange a single element and the chore of having to change many or all other elements with it. It groups interdependent elements and functions together in a single *module*. In the well-engineered system, changing a single module or replacing it by another, does not require changing the other modules. Modules conform in a standard way in how they interface. The modules that are together in a system handle mutually exclusive functions.

## OPEN SYSTEMS INTERCONNECTION

Presumably mindful of the benefits of modular design, the ITU-TS in conjunction with ISO developed and specified an archetypal or reference *communications model*. This is known as the *Open Systems Interconnection (OSI) Reference Model*. OSI organizes any and all the functions and attributes of a communications station into seven distinct modules or *layers*. It numbered the layers 1 to 7 and established the rule: layer $n$ interfaces with layers $n+1$ and $n-1$ only. Layer $n$ requests services of layer $n-1$ only and provides services to layer $n+1$ only, never dealing directly with other layers.

The layering of communication tasks may be viewed as onion-like, with different functions residing in the different shells. One shell corresponds to the interface to the application. Another shell is the interface to the communication medium itself, linking the station with its communicating partner. (This partner in turn has a compatible, if not identical, functionality.) Other shells correspond to functionality handling more general or more detailed tasks as required.

The OSI model's advantage is that *protocol suites* can be easily defined. A suite contains explicit choices and functionality. For two stations to communicate, both must use the same or *compatible* suites. Given an architecture like OSI, it is easy to implement new suites: onc replaces a layer or module of functions by another. Obviously, this must be replicated in all communicating stations. Table 3.1 summarizes the ISO OSI Reference Model, described in ISO specification 7498 and ITU-TS Recommendation X.200:

| Layer 7 | Application | Inter-networking |
|---------|-------------|------------------|
| Layer 6 | Presentation | i.e., interpretation and handling |
| Layer 5 | Session | |
| Layer 4 | Transport | Interconnection |
| Layer 3 | Network | i.e., delivery |
| Layer 2 | Data Link | |
| Layer 1 | Physical | |

*Table 3.1.*

Layer 1, the *Physical Layer* concerns itself with the mechanical, electrical, electronic and, in general, physical issues of interfacing to a communications medium. It converts bits to and from electrical or optical pulses or entities that are transmitted. Interestingly, OSI does not define the characteristics of the medium itself—only the interface to it.

Layer 2, the *Data Link Layer* concerns itself with the integrity of link-to-link transmission e.g., error checking, retransmission, frame flag generation and recognition.

Layer 3, the *Network Layer* is associated with routing: it concerns itself with the issues of addressing and node selection in moving packets through the network.

Layer 4, the *Transport Layer* deals with the issues of end-to-end transport, including end-to-end data integrity, sequence numbering, and multiplexing.

Layer 5, the *Session Layer* concerns itself with the establishment, maintenance and tear-down of sessions; also provides for checkpoint and restart.

Layer 6, the *Presentation Layer* allows for the communications to be presented in different codes, formats, and syntaxes e.g., EBCDIC or ASCII or Graphical User Interfaces (GUI).

Layer 7, the *Application Layer* provides services to the applications that are communicating. Message Handling Services, File Transfer, and Terminal Emulation are some examples of the services.

## LANs AND NOSs

In a discussion on Local Area Networks, it is important to bear in mind the scope of the functions: what OSI layers apply? LAN operating systems, also called *network operating systems (NOSs)*, are provided by vendors like IBM (LAN Server), Novell (NetWare), Banyan (VINES) and Microsoft (LAN Manager). The NOSs cover not only the full range of communications functionalities, that is all seven OSI layers, but they also embrace computational and data base functions. Some NOSs handle network management and operational functions that apply to all layers as well.

## MESSAGE PASSAGE THROUGH THE LAYERS

We now describe the format and processing of a message as it passes between the software elements that form the OSI (and, as we shall see later, IEEE) layers.

A computer application hands a message over to the highest OSI layer of communications software, layer 7. To do this, it places the message in a memory buffer and calls a subroutine, pointing to the address of the message with a hardware or software register.

The subroutine is a layer of communications software. It performs its functions within the local station. The software also must alert corresponding software at the receiving end as to the communications needs at the destination. To do this, the subroutine uses additional bits of 1s and 0s as flags, indicators and parameters. The bits accompany the message, either in front of it in the form of a header, or behind it, as a trailer.

In the OSI Reference Model, after layer 7 has processed a message and created header and trailer appendages for it, layer 7 calls layer 6 for further services.

Layer 6 views the elongated data unit passed to it by layer 7 as simply a data unit. It too performs whatever local functions are decreed. When it passes the message to layer 5 it has prefaced it with its own header and trailer.

This continues iteratively with all the layers of the OSI model. The final message handled by the physical layer is the original message encapsulated by the successive headers and trailers of higher layers. Then the message is placed on the medium.

When the message arrives at the destination station, it is first processed by software (and hardware) in physical layer 1. The layer strips off the flags, indicators, and parameters that were appended in the header and trailer by the same layer number in the sending station. It interprets these according to agreed rules for the chosen medium and access method. Then the software calls layer 2 which responds to the information nested in the next header and trailer. This process repeats for successive higher numbered layers. Each layer interprets its header and trailer information according to agreed conventions.

## LAN STANDARDS AND IEEE

Local Area Networks (LANs) of communicating stations use standards for compatibility reasons. The most widely quoted LAN standards are described in the Institute of Electronic and Electrical Engineers (IEEE) 802 specifications. ISO recognize these in ISO 8802 specifications. They focus on physical and data link layers number 1 and 2, the two lowest layers of the OSI model. Network operating systems adopt the IEEE 802 (ISO 8802) standards in connecting any two network end-points. A measure of the versatility of a NOS is its number of concurrently offered different IEEE protocols for linking pairs of end-points.

IEEE 802 standardizes the interchange of modules. When a NOS changes any choice of network functions at a low OSI level without changing any of its higher layer functions, it is complying with and taking advantage of the IEEE 802 specifications.

The IEEE 802 specifications describe standard interfaces to specific media: twisted pair copper wire, coaxial cable and fiber optic strands. Furthermore, they define different Medium Access Control (MAC) procedures. In general, these procedures need to be executed by a participating station to gain permission to transmit an individual message.

### Three Key IEEE Protocols

In what follows, we describe the three different IEEE 802 LAN protocols or procedures. The approach the IEEE uses complies with the ISO model layering: IEEE 802 encapsulates the user's message with layers of headers and trailers. The merit of the approach is ease of change and maintenance. For example, if at some future date a link such as coaxial cable and Ethernet needs replacement by another medium or access method, the software task is to substitute new headers and trailers. No changes need be done at layers above or below this layer. Figure 3.1 defines the IEEE 802 encapsulation steps; LLC is described next.

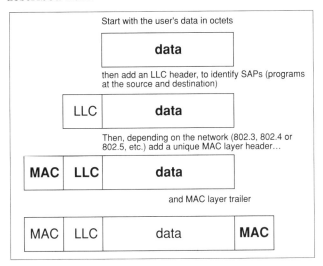

*Figure 3.1. IEEE 802 message encapsulation.*

## Logical Link Control

In LANs conforming to IEEE 802, regardless of what physical medium is used and what MAC is chosen, the processing of messages is handled by the same, single *Logical Link Control*. This software function is encountered by the message after it departs from the source application and has passed down through OSI layers 7, 6, 5, 4, and 3. In other words, when a unit of data is passed from the Network layer to the Data Link layer, it encounters the Logical Link Control (LLC) sub-layer residing at the upper reaches of the Data Link Layer, layer 2. Conversely, at the destination station, the arriving message encounters the LLC function after it passes up through layer 1 and (nearly all of) layer 2.

Among its tasks, LLC associates messages with the applications at the source and destination. This is critical because multiple applications within the same station may avail themselves of communications services. While this is more likely the case if the station is a minicomputer, it may also pertain to any LAN workstation capable of handling multiple tasks. LLC software supports these applications as *Service Access Points* or SAPs (not to be confused with **service advertising protocol** in some networks).

(As an aside, the concept of service access point closely approximates the concept of a port or socket in TCP/IP networks or of *logical unit* used in IBM SNA networks. Also, SAPs are used in ISDN wide area networks, enabling the station to process multiple types of messages: signaling; operations, administration and maintenance; and packet-mode user data).

### LLC Structure and Operation

There are three different LLC formats. All three are headers defining the destination and source service access point fields (DSAP, SSAP), plus a control field. For a detailed description of the three formats and how LLC handles flow control through the use of "windows," readers should consult *Appendix D— LLC Structure and Protocol* of this book. Of primary interest to us at this stage, however, is how the services are provided. The technique is called *encapsulation*.

## ENCAPSULATION

As the original user message moves down the OSI layers from layer 7 through layer 1, it accumulates successive layers of headers and trailers. In LANs, after layer 3 has handled the message, the Logical Link Control sub-layer adds its header. The contents in the LLC header will be the same regardless of what transmission medium, or medium access control (MAC) method is chosen to control the shared use of the medium. As can be seen in Figure 3.2, the MAC header and trailer wrap around the concatenation of the LLC and (layer 3) data.

| | | data | |
|---|---|---|---|
| | LLC header | data | |
| MAC header | LLC header | data | |
| MAC header | LLC header | data | MAC trailer |

*Figure 3.2. IEEE MAC Header and Trailer Fields*

Three unique sets of MAC header and trailer apply to IEEE 802.3, 802.4 or 802.5, respectively. These three major categories of LANs are discussed in detail in Chapter 7. It suffices at this stage to see how the different headers and trailers encapsulate the concatenation of "LLC and Data."

### CSMA/CD Encapsulation

Let us examine the packet format used in the first of the three standards mentioned. Figure 3.3 is the format of a packet when it is encapsulated by the header and trailer of the IEEE 802.3 standard. 802.3 refers to Carrier Sense, Multiple Access/Collision Detect CSMA/CD networks, essentially Ethernet.

| preamble | SFD | D addr | S Addr | length | LLC + data | pad | FCS |
|---|---|---|---|---|---|---|---|

*Figure 3.3.*

### 802.3 MAC Header

The 802.3 *MAC header* comprises the five fields Preamble, Start Frame Delimiter (SFD), Destination Address (D Addr), Source Address (S Addr), and length. The 56 bits of preamble consist of repeating 1s and 0s yielding a 1010... pattern. In conjunction with the SFD bit pattern 10101011, the bits may be regarded as a Physical header enabling the receiver to synchronize the start of the packet.

The station's source address, S Addr, and the destination address, D Addr, are either 2 or 6 byte long fields, at the discretion of the network designer. When 6-byte addresses are used in a network, 22 of the 48 bits have been set aside by the IEEE as unique *organization* identifiers. The remaining 26 bits are defined by the organization itself. 22 bits can identify four million organizations. Vendors hard code the 48 bit numbers into LAN adapter firmware.

Since the 802.3 packet length may be variable, the length of the LLC control field plus the data field it accompanies is contained in a 2-byte length field.

## 802.3 MAC Trailer

The *802.3 MAC trailer* comprises two fields. The Pad field ensures a minimum frame size of 64 bytes. We shall see later that this guarantees that collisions can be detected even when short length blocks are transmitted. A 4-byte Frame Check Sequence FCS field ensures the integrity of the packet. CRC-32 (explained in *Appendix C—Cyclical Redundancy Checks, CRC*) is used for the FCS.

### Similar Encapsulation: Token Passing Bus

Secondly, let us examine the format of a packet when it is encapsulated by the headers and trailers for the IEEE 802.4 standard. 802.4 refers to Token Passing Bus networks, typified by ARCNET and MAP. Figure 7.6 describes the format of the 802.4 frame.

The *802.4 MAC header* consists of Preamble, Start Delimiter (SD), Frame Control (FC), Destination Address (DA), and Source Address (SA). Once again, Preamble and Start Delimiter are physical header fields enabling the receiver to synchronize the start of the packet.

The preamble is two or more microseconds of PAD or IDLE symbols. SD is the pattern JK0JK000, where J and K are special non-data "bits" in so-called Manchester coding that we examine in Chapter 6. As an aside, we note that the left-most bit of SD (the non-data J) is transmitted first.

## Four Frame Types

There are four different types of frame identified by the Frame Control field. (In Figure 7.6, the right-most bit of the Frame Control field is also the first to be transmitted). If Frame Control's right-most two bits are 00, the field is a MAC token control. Otherwise, the field signifies data.

If the Frame Control field signals a MAC token control frame, its contents are:

00000000    Claim token

00010000    Token

10000000  Solicit successor - 1

01000000  Solicit successor - 2

11000000  Who follows?

00100000  Resolve contention

00110000  Set successor

If Frame Control's right-most two bits are not 00, the field is being used to signal the transmission of data, and the two bits signify whether data in the frame is "normal" LLC data, station management data or special-purpose data (reserved for future use). "Normal" LLC data have a Frame Control

xxx00010  Datagram

xxx10010  Please respond

xxx01010  This is a response

where the xxxs indicate priority of service.

The *802.4 MAC trailer* comprises two fields, Frame Check Sequence (FCS) and End Delimiter (ED). The 4-byte Frame Check Sequence FCS field ensures the integrity of the packet with CRC–32. The End Delimiter ED is the physical trailer consisting of the eight "bits" JK1JK1IE.

As with SD above, J and K are special non-data "bits" in Manchester coding. The I bit performs like a Poll/Final bit: 1 indicates that this is the last frame in a sequence; 0 means more follows. An E bit of 1 indicates that an error occurred.

As a matter of interest, the maximum frame size (including SD and ED) is 8191 octets.

### Encapsulating Token Ring 802.5

Finally, we examine the format of a packet encapsulated by the headers and trailers of the IEEE 802.5 Token Passing Ring layers. There are two types of frame in these networks, the *token* frame and the *information* frame. Formats of these frames are illustrated in Figures 7.4 and 7.5. The token frame is a special null case of an information frame and consists of only three fields. It encapsulates nothing, and is used in managing the network access.

Token Frame: | SD | AC | ED |

Information Frame: | SD | AC | FC | DA | SA | LLC + data | FCS | ED | FS |

## 802.5 MAC Header and Trailer

The *802.5 MAC header* comprises five fields that prefix the combination of user data and its LLC header:

- SD is the physical header Start Delimiter octet JK0JK000. As in 802.4, J and K are symbols, not bits, using the Differential Manchester code violations to enable the receiver to lock on to the start of the packet or frame. J is transmitted first.

- Access Control AC is an octet. If we label its bits RRRMTPPP, the Ps are transmitted first and define the priority of the frame. The priority takes one of eight values. The T bit if 0, indicates that the frame is a Token; if 1 an information frame. If M is 1, it signals that Monitoring (described in Chapter 7) is in process. RRR defines the highest priority level of any station waiting for the token.

- The Frame Control FC octet indicates the frame type. For example, if an LLC frame (with user data) is being transmitted, the frame control is xxx00010. 0 is transmitted first. A MAC frame has frame control xxxxxx00. Once again, the 0 bit is transmitted first. Its six x bits are used for token ring management and signify:

    | | |
    |---|---|
    | 110000 | Claim Token |
    | 000000 | Duplicate Address Test |
    | 101000 | Active Monitor Present |
    | 011000 | Standby Monitor Present |
    | 010000 | Beacon |
    | 001000 | Purge |

- The Destination Address (DA) and Source Address (SA) fields are each six bytes in length. Within DA, if the most significant bit of the address is 0, the destination is a single station, otherwise it is a group. If the first transmitted bit of source address is 1 this indicates that *Source Routing* is present. (As discussed in detail later, a *ROUTING INFORMATION* field follows the SA field in this case.)

The *802.5 Trailer* consists of three fields: Frame Check Sequence (FCS), Ending Delimiter (ED) and Frame Status (FS). FCS is the standard 4-byte CRC field. The Ending Delimiter (ED), which follows it, consists of eight bits labeled JK1JK1IE. As described previously for the starting delimiter SD, J and K are symbols, not bits, using Differential Manchester code violations. In this case, they are present to enable the receiver to discern the frame's end. J is transmitted first. The I bit, if 1, indicates that this is the last frame of a sequence; if 0 that more frames follow. The E bit if 1 flags any error; 0 no error. The third field of the trailer is Frame Status, FS. Its bit format is xxCAxxCA where C bits, if 1, signify *Frame copied* and A bits, if 1, *Address recognized* successfully.

# 4

# Topologies and Medium Access

Chapter 3 discussed the rationale for modular architectures for systems in general. It then described the layered approaches taken by ITU-TS and ISO for communication systems. It examined how the IEEE 802 and ISO 8802 standards are used at the data link and physical layers by important instances of communications systems, LANs. It explained how layering is implemented by a software process, i.e., message encapsulation at the sending station and its reciprocal process at the receiver.

When a network contains multiple stations, different connectivity layouts are possible. These feature different costs, access and data transport capabilities. In this Chapter, we look at the different configurations of network *topologies* and the various *medium access methods*.

The abstract geography or mapping of the connections making up a network is called its *topology*.

## TOPOLOGIES

Four major topologies will be discerned. These are *star, bus (or tree), ring,* and *mesh*. All networks contain stations at which a user (person or computer program) is present. In drawings of the topologies, a station is shown either as a *node* or an *end-point*. If the station is connected to two or more other stations and traffic between those two stations depends on its active cooperation, it is a node. Stations with a single direct connection to the network, or to only one other station are called end-points. The simplest network configuration is that of two end-point stations connected by a cable, but some networks may require the end-points to have node-like capabilities. On the other hand, we frequently find that nodes are implemented as dedicated routers or switches, with no capability for connecting directly to users.

## STAR FOR POINT-TO-POINT

The star topology features at least one node from which more than two connecting links radiate to other nodes or stations. Figure 4.1 illustrates a many-to-many star configuration or the point-to-point connections of a *Private Branch Exchange (PBX)*. The PBX is a switchboard or electronic switching device that connects (usually only temporarily) any pair of users. In other words, the PBX provides the (electrical) connection between the cable of one station and that of another. It may concurrently connect a number of pairs of stations point-to-point. Additionally, a PBX may establish point-to-multipoint connections. These enable "conference calls" between multiple stations.

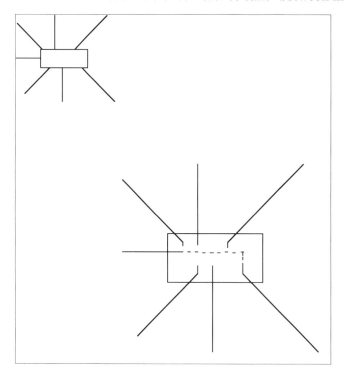

*Figure 4.1. Star topology, showing either many-to-many, or point-to-point connections—e.g. PBX.*

Vendors of private PBXs include Ericsson, Fujitsu, Northern Telecom, Siemens, and AT&T (Dimension).

The *Central Offices* of the local telephone company use sophisticated and more powerful versions of the concepts found in the PBX. Among these are AT&T's #1 ESS, #5 ESS and #4 ESS and Northern Telecom's DMS 100 switches.

Figure 4.2 features the representation of a hierarchy or cascade of stars. Each node depicted by a rectangle is a switch (e.g., a PBX). Its star topology provides a point-to-point connection between stations attached to the node, and between the node itself and the next node in the hierarchy. As an example of this, prior to the breakup by the Justice Department of AT&T in 1984, a call between stations in two AT&T regions may have been switched upwards in a multilevel hierarchy and then down again as follows: A station first connects to a PBX, the first tier in the hierarchy. The next higher tier is the telephone company's Central Office. Then the switch connects to a Toll Center, then to a Primary Center, then to a Sectional Center, finally to a Regional Center. This Regional Center may be laterally connected to another Regional Center from which the call is cascaded downward in a second hierarchy. This means moving down through the corresponding different layers: Sectional Center, then Primary Center then Toll Center then Central Office then PBX, then finally to the other station.

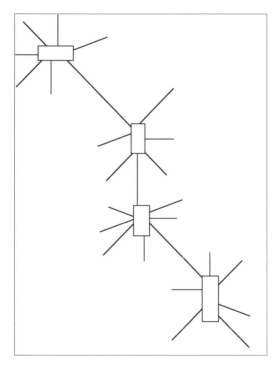

*Figure 4.2. Cascade of stars such as connecting PBXs or telephone company central offices.*

The star topology is preferred for *network management*. Network management includes responsibilities for ensuring that all links are operational. It is easier to perform these functions from a single geographical node point than at the dispersed stations.

## BUS TOPOLOGY REACHES ALL ALMOST AT ONCE

Figure 4.3 shows a schematic of a cable—the bus—to which multiple stations may gain access, not only (perhaps) at the end-points of the cable, but at tap points along its length as well. With the bus topology, when any station transmits, all stations receive the message. The network is quiet if no one is transmitting. (As we shall see later, this is different with ring networks.) Ethernet is an example of bus topology.

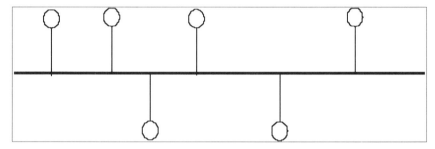

*Figure 4.3. Bus topology. Any station's signal transmissions are propagated on a bus in both directions, so all stations can "hear" them at the same time.*

A bus topology has the advantage that if a single station fails (or loses power) it does not necessarily disable the entire network.

Earlier, we introduced the four major topologies: the star, bus (*or tree*), ring, and mesh. Interestingly, the *tree* is a "star" construed to operate like a bus! How can an implementation of a geographical star (as found, for example, in the StarLAN networks created by AT&T) act topologically like a bus? The answer is that in this case each star electrically connects stations *multipoint*-to-point or point-to-*multipoint*. Hence, the tree connotation, and bus functionality. The electrical connection may or may not be permanent.

In Figure 4.4, consider the boxes as stars in a cascade and the lines connecting the nodes as electrical signal carriers. Transmissions from stations and nodes toward a node that is called the *head end* are defined as *reverse*. Transmissions away from the head end are defined as *forward*. So, in the figure, the reverse signal flow is upward, toward the uppermost link and box labeled *HEAD END*. Viewing this reverse signal flow, the circuit signals are logical ORd together at each node. The signal emerging at the top of the head end is the aggregate of all the signals coming up to it. Alternatively, the signal flowing in the forward direction is split among the lower tributaries. The word "split" here is used in the logical rather than the electrical power sense.

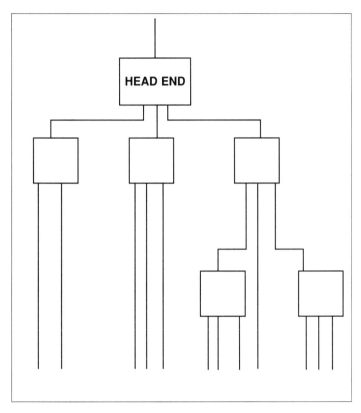

*Figure 4.4. Head End. "Forward" transmissions are copied (split) among down-stream subordinates; "reverse" transmissions, towards the Head End, are con-solidated (ORd).*

In networks such as StarLAN (see Figure 7.3), each cable link between nodes at different layers contains two circuits, i.e., two pairs of conductors. One pair is for the reverse transmission, the other for forward transmission. Multiple reverse signals received in a node are logically ORd together and form the single (reverse) output from it. Like other nodes, the head end accepts signals that are inbound to it and aggregates these reverse transmissions received by performing a logical OR. But, the head end node's output circuit is the first leg of all forward transmissions. Except for the head end, each node receives one (and only one) forward transmission circuit. This forward signal is copied to each of its lower tributaries.

## RING TOPOLOGY

A *ring* network, (Figure 4.5), features a number of stations and links, each station connecting to exactly two links. The station always receives any messages on the one link and transmits on the other. An *n*-station ring is connected together with a total of *n* links. Each link is a distinct circuit. The station itself is a repeater between its two links, repeating the signal received, and amplifying it. This is done bit by bit—i.e., digitally. If a station is disabled, the network is disabled until the two stations surrounding the failed one can be connected together.

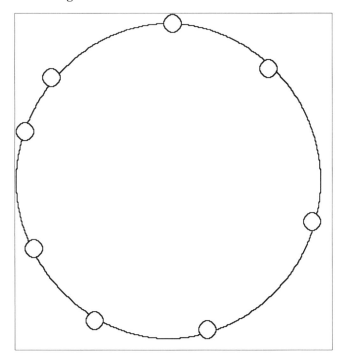

*Figure 4.5. Ring topology. Each station is a repeater.*

A ring network is always busy. Data are always circulating in the network on one or more of the links. When no user messages are on the network, network management "tokens" are being circulated. These are special frames that solicit the token-receiving station to transmit.

For ease of network management, some ingenuity is required to configure a ring topology network into a geographical star. In Figure 4.6, each of the eight repeater stations shown is connected to a central site (Multistation Access

Unit) with two lines. Each line is (a pair of wires) brought to a single geographical site such as a wiring cabinet. Here, the pair of wires that carries the output from one station connects to the pair of wires input to another station. Physically the configuration is a star, but the topology remains a ring.

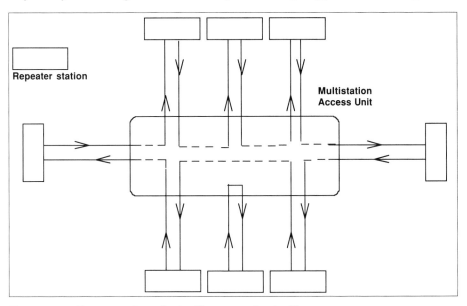

*Figure 4.6. Ring topology logically, star physically.*

### Making a Ring Look Like a Star

A number of devices are available to implement this concept. IBM's Multi-station Access Unit (MAU) Model 8228 and Controlled Access Unit (CAU) Model 8230 are two such devices. Illustrated in Figure 4.7, with no station cables connected to it, the MAU's internal relays connect port $n$ to adjacent ports $n$-$1$ and $n$+$1$. To complete the ring, a *patch cable* connects RO, the ring's *OUT* port to RI, the ring's *IN* port. RI connects internally to port 1. Port 8 connects internally to RO. The MAU is a passive wiring concentrator: it does not have a power supply. The boxes labeled RI and RO are "ports" for connecting MAUs to other MAUs, or to repeaters that extend the ring size. Boxes numbered 1 through 8 in the figure are ports that accept repeater stations' cables. Each cable end has a special connector. Inserting this into a MAU's port permits a 5 volt DC current provided by the station to open a relay within the MAU that otherwise keeps the ring intact. (In Figure 4.8, we see station A just prior to its insertion into the ring, or subsequent to its removal from the ring. On the right, station B has connected onto the ring, and is providing the 5V DC.) The MAU itself contains the ring; opening the relay incorporates the new station. The cable is a *lobe* to the station and contains two pairs of wires, a pair each for transmit and receive.

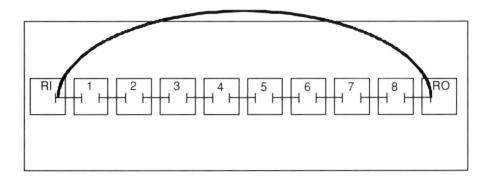

Legend: RI is Ring IN; RO is Ring OUT. Each MAU port has a relay (not shown) that "shorts" its two internal terminals unless a repeater is inserted into the port by means of cable and connector.

*Figure 4.7. An 8-port multi-station access unit.*

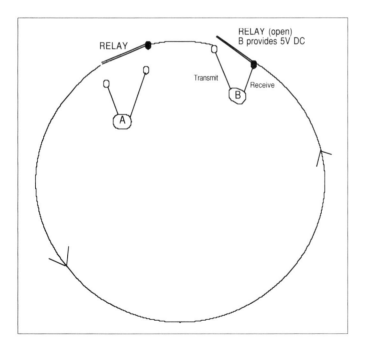

*Figure 4.8. MAU port insertion and removal. Station A has been removed from the ring so relay completes the ring.*

## Cable Quality Dictates Number of Stations

If the network is larger than eight ports, two or more MAUs are needed. The RO of one connects to the RI of the second, etc. The RO of the last MAU connects to the RI of the first. As many as 33 MAUs can be interconnected in this daisy-chain, allowing up to 260 stations on the ring. The maximum number depends not only on the number of ports but also on the type of medium chosen in the cabling between the stations and the MAU, and between MAUs. *Shielded data-grade twisted pair* for example, allows for nearly four times the number of connectable stations than *unshielded telephone twisted pair*. (In the latter case, a maximum of nine MAUs may be linked together, yielding a maximum of 72 attached stations.)

## CAUs are Powered, MAUs are Not

The other IBM product mentioned previously is the Model 8230 Controlled Access Unit (CAU). The CAU has a power supply. Its *Lobe Attachment Module* is able to support 20 stations as opposed to 8 in a MAU. Four 20-port modules may be stacked together to provide a total capacity—in one CAU—of 80 stations. A feature of the CAU not offered by the MAU is *automatic ring configuration* whereby faulty stations may be logically removed from the ring without physically disconnecting them.

## MESH AND COST

The final type of topology we discuss is the *mesh*. We introduced the concept of a mesh in Chapter 2. Figures 2.9 and 4.9 are diagrams of mesh networks. The mesh is characterized by many stations possessing point-to-point connections to other stations. In the figures, some stations have more than two connections to other stations. In general, we note that it is impractical or too expensive for a mesh network to provide direct connections between every pair of stations. Making direct links available makes economic sense only if there is continuous traffic between the stations involved. This is unlikely for most applications: data traffic is *bursty* in nature. File transfers or image transfers between two computers are followed by relatively long periods of quiet. Transaction processing is also subject to the quiet between initial data entry or "query" and the response. Voice communications—i.e., telephone conversations—do not endure interminably, certainly not between the station and *every* other station in the network.

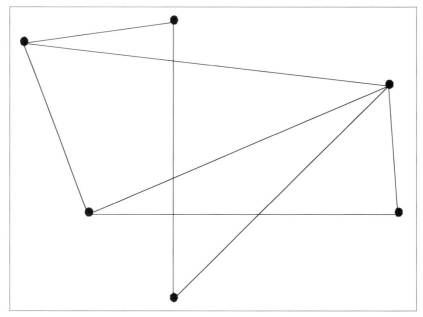

*Figure 4.9. Mesh Topology.*

## PAY NOW OR PAY LATER?

When deciding on one of the network topologies, it is important to consider not only the initial installation costs but also the ongoing maintenance requirements. Since every network will change at some date, the costs of making changes should be considered when evaluating the initial installation alternatives. One may pay less at the outset only to be confronted by prohibitive costs or charges later. Alternatively, perhaps a slightly more expensive investment up front may allow for lower overall life cycle costs. In practical terms, it may be prudent at the outset to lay redundant cable, or to lay cable making it possible to later connect currently unused stations or station sites. Labor costs are higher than material costs, particularly at change time when walls or floors may need to be opened up.

Earlier we mentioned that a physical star network is preferred for network management. We noted that networks can be implemented using any of the three topologies—star, bus or ring. What then are the issues that bear on the choice of topology?

## MEDIUM ACCESS CONTROL

A major issue is that of *Medium Access Control*. A problem arises when a station sends a message on a shared medium at the same time as another station. Both stations' messages can be destroyed. There are six generic solutions to avoid this problem. These are:

1. Centralized, sequential control

2. Reservation-based

3. Multiplexing the medium

4. Contention (unconstrained)

5. Contention (collision detection)

6. Sequential right-to-transmit

### *Traditional Centralized Sequential Control*

The first solution is centralized, sequential control. This is epitomized by *unbalanced* networks such as hierarchical host-terminal systems. In Figure 4.10, the (computer mainframe, say) host and its communications controller together are the *primary* station. It controls access to the bus medium shared by the *secondaries*, stations A, B, C, and D. The host sends special messages that all stations hear concurrently. One of these messages is a sequentially sent *poll* that solicits transmission from a specific station. The poll gives the identified station the right to transmit on the medium any message it may have ready. Another message type also heard by all the stations but heeded by only one is a *select*. This host transmission is a message destined for the selected station.

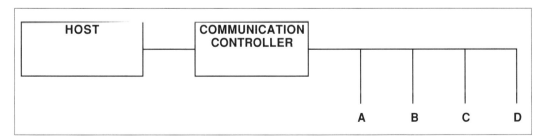

*Figure 4.10. Centralized control. Secondary station A, B, C or D is polled (soliciting transmission) or selected (told to receive host transmission) with priority decided by host.*

One advantage of centralized control is that the host may recognize a particular station as having more importance, providing it preferential or more frequent access to the medium than others. In Figure 4.10, stations A, B, C and D would normally be polled sequentially in a *round robin* fashion, A then B then C then D then A again and so on. But if station A is preferred, the host may use a polling sequence such as A B A C A D A B A C A D ... effectively raising A's priority.

Centralized control can be disadvantageous in that a host-centered operation may not be desired. With LANs, a characteristic is that the stations are equal in status. All are combined *primary/secondary* stations. As a primary, any or all of them may initiate transmissions without permission from some "host"; as a secondary they defer to any peer that has asserted its primacy, albeit temporarily.

## Time Division Multiplexing

The second mechanism for allowing more than one station to share a communication line is reservation-based *time division multiplexing*, TDM. A time period is divided equally among the stations sharing the medium. Each station is granted a time slot every period. The station only transmits in its time slot, and has exclusive use of the medium for that time. Usually, the function of placing multiple messages in time slots on a medium is performed by a node such as a switch that simultaneously receives *n* inputs from *n* stations. Otherwise, if an individual station places its message in an assigned time slot, it must synchronize its access using one clock with all other participating stations in the network. The clock synchronizes the start of each time slot.

## T1 Uses TDM

An example of time division multiplexing is the telephone company's (or privately acquired) *T1* capability. The basic unit of transmission, the T1 frame, occurs every 125 microseconds. It contains 8 bits each of data placed on the medium on behalf of 24 stations. The amount of time available per station is about 5.2 microseconds. The second station's 8 bits are placed 5.2 microseconds after the first time slot started; the third station's slot starts 5.2 microseconds after the second slot started and so on. In Figure 4.11, the T1 frame is seen to consist of 8 x 24 or 192 bits from the 24 stations, plus a framing bit used by the network, totaling 193 bits in all. Every 125 microseconds, or 8,000 times per second, 193 bits are transmitted. This totals 1,544,000 bits per second.

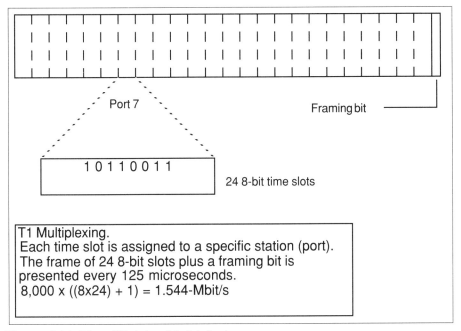

Figure 4.11. Time Division Multiplexing.

The device that receives input from the 24 original stations on separate circuits and places 24 messages in T1 format on a medium is a multiplexer or switch.

### Frequency Division Multiplexing for Broadband

The third method allowing multiple stations simultaneous access to a shared medium is multiplexing the medium. In contrast to the time division multiplexing just discussed, this approach uses *frequency division multiplexing*. *Broadband* is another term given to frequency division multiplexing. Figure 4.12 illustrates how multiple channels appear on the same medium, using broadband. This method is used in commercial television, where the medium is either the unbounded atmosphere or coaxial cable from the local *Cable Television* company. A channel occupies an assigned *pass-band* of frequencies.

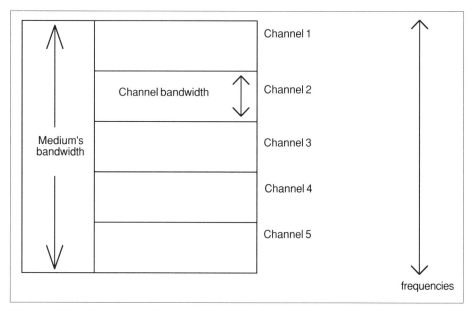

*Figure 4.12. Frequency Division Multiplexing. Different channels occupy different pass-bands of frequency.*

## Defining Pass-band and Bandwidth...

The *bandwidth* of a channel is the difference between its highest and lowest frequencies. A TV channel's bandwidth is about 6 MHz. The difference in concept between pass-band and bandwidth is that pass-band is the location of the frequencies in the spectrum. For example, the 6-MHz bandwidth may be placed in the 202-Mhz to 208-MHz pass-band, or in the 160-Mhz to 166-MHz pass-band, etc.

The function of placing a message in a pass-band on the medium is not time sensitive, and so can be done by stations that are dispersed, without needing any synchronization between them.

## Radio Frequency May be on Cable

*Radio frequency* (or *RF*) equipment—capable of tuning in to certain frequency pass-bands—is needed at each broadband station. Note that using radio frequency does not necessarily imply use of the unbounded medium (through the atmosphere). For example, cable TV channels are transmitted to the consumer through radio frequency multiplexed coaxial cable. The tuners that select these are RF. RF equipment is expensive.

Beside expense, a disadvantage of broadband may arise from the fact that the frequency pass-bands are allocated centrally. For the case of the unbounded medium, the Federal Communications Commission is the authority responsible for assigning pass-bands to particular applications. In practice, the pass-bands for bounded media e.g., coaxial cable, while not subject to Federal regulation in this context, are assigned by a central arbitrator such as the corporation or organization itself. And, once set, these assignments are more-or-less permanent.

Some networks have the ability to assign resources on an as-needed basis. As transmission needs arise, the communicating station is advised (through some other communication channel) which pass-band is assigned to it from the multiple pass-bands that are available. The station adjusts its RF equipment, tuning into the allocated pass-band. Either a human operator turns dials or switches, or *frequency agile modems* automatically select the channel through programmable software.

### Contention for the Medium

There is a network management ramification to the above scenario. By what mechanism does a station alert the allocator of pass-bands that it needs one? The station may lack "some other communication channel." Techniques, described next, use the medium as needed without incurring network management difficulties for dynamic resource allocation. These are the *contention*-based techniques, "unconstrained" and "collision detection."

### A 1970s Solution—Quick ALOHA Tour

In one approach, stations simply transmit packets of data when ready, then check to see if problems arose. This was done in the ALOHA system developed in the early 1970s at the University of Hawaii. ALOHA was developed as a radio alternative to underwater cabling communication between a computer center and seven sites on different islands. The ITU's International Frequency Regulatory Board assigned two 100-kHz pass-bands for ALOHA. The first was used for messages outbound from the computer center. The second was a shared band for data traffic inbound to the computer center from the sites. All sites used the same 100-kHz band for reception of data from the computer center, and all shared the second band to transmit. After transmitting, a site waited for positive acknowledgment from the computer center. If the computer center received the message without any transmission problems (in other words, if the checksum in the message was valid), it broadcast (on the first channel), an acknowledgment identifying the source. But had a checksum failure occurred, caused by collision, perhaps, of two or more messages, no ACK was generated. Consequently, the site (or sites) would re-transmit.

## Slotted ALOHA Mixes CA and CD for Results

A variation of ALOHA, *Slotted ALOHA* is more efficient. All sites initiate the transmission of their messages on the same "pulse" beat. Timing cues are taken from synchronizing messages issued by the computer center. Packet transmission time is shorter than the interval between pulses. Figure 4.13 shows station A transmitting four packets labeled a1, a2, a3 and a4. In ALOHA, (upper diagram), station A's packets merely follow one another. The start time for submitting packets is not synchronized between stations. Station B places its packet b1 on the medium at a random time. In so doing, b1 destroys not only itself and the tail end of a1, but the first part of a2 as well. In Slotted ALOHA (bottom diagram), packets are transmitted at synchronized intervals. Because station B submits packet b1 at the same time as A submits a2, only b1 and a2 are lost. The technique doubles the effective packet-carrying capacity of an ALOHA network.

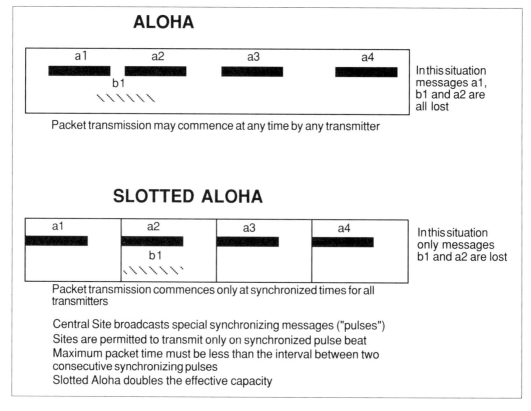

*Figure 4.13. Collision Avoidance as used in Slotted Aloha. Aloha is shown for comparison.*

In both ALOHA and Slotted ALOHA, stations transmit first, then check to see if it was successful. ALOHA and Slotted ALOHA are precursors to the *Carrier Sense Multiple Access* medium access method made popular by Ethernet. There are two CSMA approaches: *CSMA/Collision Detect, CSMA/CD,* and *CSMA/Collision Avoidance, CSMA/CA.* Because of the popularity of *Ethernet* that essentially uses CSMA/CD, CSMA/CD is found in many more networks than CSMA/CA.

## Collision Avoidance

CSMA/CA is a hybrid of time division multiplexing and CSMA/CD. It is found mainly in the interconnection of computer mainframes with devices such as mass disk storage where transmission delays cannot be tolerated. It derives its collision avoidance name from the fact that all stations have pre-assigned time slots during which they may transmit a packet. In some CSMA/CA systems one of the time slots is dedicated for acknowledgments. This cannot itself be subject to a collision since the receiver has exclusive use of the channel for a defined period. If none of the stations uses its time slot, this is sensed by all stations and *CSMA/CD,* described next, applies during the next time frame. After that, the network reverts to CSMA/CA.

## CSMA/CD

CSMA/CD is a contention approach in which stations sense the medium *beforehand* to check if it is busy. It involves stations listening to the medium and only attempting transmission if it is quiet. If the medium is busy, stations delay for a period of time before attempting to re-transmit.

If the medium is quiet, a sender transmits. Senders listen to the medium while transmitting. If another station also happens to start sending, their messages will collide. Different algorithms vary the delay of the re-transmission so that senders do not attempt to re-transmit simultaneously. On busy networks it is possible for a succession of collisions to occur to the same packet. For this reason, CSMA/CD is known as a *stochastic* access method: the actual time at which a packet will be transmitted cannot be guaranteed. In practice, this is not a problem if the network is rarely congested.

### *Sequential Rights to Submit*

By contrast, *deterministic* access methods are available. These are found in the *sequential* class of access methods. This class grants access in ring topologies, for example. The deterministic quality follows from the predictability of when a message will gain access to the medium. A common approach taken involves the use of a *token*, a special frame that circulates from station to station on the network. Possessing the token gives permission to transmit. Amount of transmission time is limited. Thereafter, the token is relinquished to the next station. The system is fair with stations generally gaining access in "round robin" order. However, a priority mechanism may impart higher importance to some stations. These gain access either more frequently or sooner than others.

## Token Passing Bus

*Token passing* is not restricted solely to ring networks. In IEEE 802.4, the bus medium is accessed by passing tokens as well.

## Side Notes on Register Insertion and Slotted Ring

Token passing rings may seem obvious today as the approach to implement a ring network. However, other methods were invented to solve the sequential medium access requirement, including *register insertion* and the *slotted* or *Cambridge* ring. As a side note, we describe these lesser known access methods.

Figure 4.14 illustrates the operation known as *register insertion*. The register insertion ring is initially made up of a number of bit repeaters, connected together in series. When a station has information to transmit, it loads its message into a register. Usually, this is a shift register with a limited capacity of a few dozen bits. The shift register momentarily takes the place of one of the repeaters that is in series with other ring connections, i.e., repeaters (and other shift registers). While the shift register is part of the ring, it increases the bit carrying capacity of the ring. (The shift register is seen as part of the ring in the lower half of Figure 4.14.) During the message's journey round the ring, it gets copied by the target station. When it reappears in the shift register, the register itself is switched out of the circuit, and the original repeater is reinstated. We observe that while the principle is simple, the procedure is complex in practice, due to the high speeds needed for switching.

In the *slotted ring*, advantage is taken of the finite time taken by bits in moving from station to station. Electromagnetic signals propagate through copper medium at about 200 million meters per second. A signal takes

$$\frac{10}{200 \text{ x } 10^6} = 0.05$$

microseconds to propagate from one end of a 10 meter cable segment to the other. If the ring is operating at 10 million bits per second, the number of bits transmitted in this time is 0.5. So, each 10 meter cable segment may be viewed as a 0.5 bit buffer. Additionally, since each node in a ring is a repeater, there is a one bit delay per node. A 100 node ring containing 100 segments, therefore, has a bit capacity of 100 x 0.5 + 100 = 150. This allows four frames, of 37 bits each, to circulate continuously round the ring.

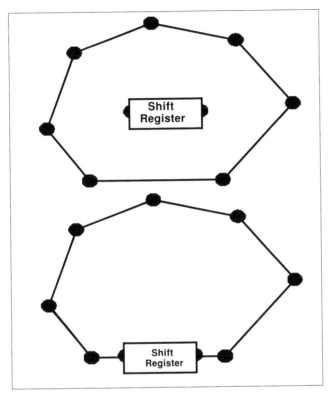

*Figure 4.14. Register Insertion. Shift register contains message. When register is inserted, it increases bit capacity of ring.*

The following may describe their format. Each bit of the slotted ring frame is repeated at a node. Bit 1 is simply a start frame flag. If the next two bits are 00, the slot is available. If the slot has been seized, bits 2 and 3 are "repeated" as 11.

256 unique station numbers may be identified on the ring. 8-bit destination address and 8-bit source address respectively occupy the next two octets of the slot.

Sixteen bits of payload data follow these address bits in the slot.

Trailing the payload are a couple of bits for flags. Set by the sender to 11, they are changed by the destination node to reflect the status as follows: busy (00), slot was accepted (01) or slot was rejected (10).

# 5

## Media

In Chapter 4, we looked at the different configurations of network topologies and the various medium access methods. Star, bus, ring, and mesh topologies were described, and what one needs to consider for gaining access within them. These include reserving facilities, allotting time to each user for the different resources, and the different policies applied to dedicating or sharing facilities among users so as to avoid message collisions. It examined the considerations of managing resources from a central point or permitting distributed, or peer-management.

### WHAT TO LOOK FOR IN A MEDIUM

In this chapter, we proceed to examine the characteristics of the communications *media* themselves in more detail. Our objective in studying the media is to equip us to compare the benefits that their different attributes accord for transporting data, voice, image or video. At the same time, we need to be aware of each medium's limitations. All applications share the same general criteria for communications effectiveness. But some capabilities are unique to certain media, and can bring more important—even critical—benefits to a specific application.

Of primary interest for most applications is the *communications capacity* of the medium. Sometimes (loosely) referred to as bandwidth, this is the measure of the medium's digit carrying capacity. By definition, it is the number of bits the medium can transport in a unit of time. *Optical fibers*, at the top of the list of bounded media, outperform copper wire in this respect.

*Delay* may refer to the time that a message takes to transit to its destination across a segment of the medium. This is known as *propagation delay*. Or, it could be the time that the user waits, contending for access to the medium (*access delay*).

In applications such as video or voice conversations, delay and, in particular, *varying* delay, is not only annoying, but beyond certain bounds it is unacceptable. Here, delay may be a function not only of the medium itself but of the intermediate routing and switching devices or nodes within the network. Such applications demand little or no delay or delay variance. As an aside, most of these applications need, therefore, isochronous transmission.

The attribute of *quality* is always critical. Does the medium reliably separate signal from noise, and retain the differentiation from the point in geography it is sent from through to the destination? How immune from—or prone to—noise is it? Do certain types of noise pose more of a problem for this medium than others? What is the impact of noise on performance?

Since segments of any and all media are subject to noise, how does this affect the physical dimensions of the network? What is the maximum segment length beyond which signals are lost because they are overwhelmed by noise? Can the range of the signal be extended?

*Signal attenuation* refers to the weakening of a signal's strength or power over distance. Certain ranges of frequencies of the signal may attenuate more than others: generally, the higher the frequency, the greater the signal loss. Some media are more vulnerable to this than others. How capable is the receiving equipment in recovering an attenuated signal?

Media costs should be weighed against the benefits sought. Cost/benefit ratios to be considered include cost/performance, cost/reliability, cost/privacy, and cost/security. But, not always easily measured, one medium may offer functions not available to others. For example, the ability to transmit *single to many* broadcasts is intrinsic to radio. The benefits from this are weighed in a cost/functionality measure.

Sending signals requires energy. Mechanical energy is used in everyday speech as we describe below. However, we are concerned with transmitting signals over distances that may possibly be measured in miles or hundreds of miles. Signals, for these purposes, are sent using either electrical or light energy.

## BOUNDED AND UNBOUNDED

A convenient taxonomy of communications is by how the signals are bounded in the media. A *bounded* medium is one that conducts signals from transmitter to receiver within a wire, conduit or fiber. Copper wire is the element of choice for the bounded transmission of electrical signals; transparent glass fibers for light signals. Copper wire is implemented in *twisted pair* and *coaxial* forms discussed next. The glass fibers are a product of the *fiber-optics* which will also be discussed.

Signals from transmitter to receiver are not limited to propagation via bounded media only. Examples of *unbounded* media include those penetrated by means of radio transmission, such as the atmosphere, ocean, outer space or the "ether." Besides radio, (including television transmission), other forms of communication that use the unbounded media include infrared radiation over local areas and human speech through the air. For speech, the larynx alternately compresses and decompresses air molecules causing pressure waves to move through the air. At the ear, the pressure variations are sensed and interpreted as sound.

Radio is transmitted either via directional beams, or omni-directionally. Spread spectrum radio, microwave, cellular radio, and satellite transmission are applications of the unbounded medium.

One advantage of using unbounded media is that communications may be directed to or shared by many recipients simultaneously. With an unbounded medium operating omni-directionally, it is easy to *broadcast* one-to-many messages.

By contrast, the advantage of using a bounded medium derives from the intrinsic one-to-one state of connection of the communicating parties where *privacy* and *security* are both features and benefits. (Notwithstanding this, security may be attained with an unbounded medium, as we shall see with spread spectrum radio. And, as can be attested to by anyone exposed to spy tales, privacy and security within bounded media may be compromised by the "tapping" of telephone connections!)

## COMMUNICATIONS CAPACITY

Let us look now at a primary attribute of interest for many applications, the *maximum communications load* that a medium is capable of handling in unit time. The difference between the lowest and highest frequencies carried on a medium is its *bandwidth*. Bandwidth and digit carrying capacity of a medium are correlated: the higher the bandwidth, the greater the number of bits the medium is capable of transporting per unit time. Table 5.1 lists the typically maximum frequencies of different media today. A similar ranking would follow for bandwidths and for bit carrying capacities.

| Medium | Typical Frequency (MHz) | Comments |
|---|---|---|
| Unshielded Twisted Pair | 1 to 10; but may be as high as 100 | Higher frequencies require EIA/TIA Categories 3 through 5 |
| Shielded Twisted Pair | 20 | Good for 16-Mbit/s token ring |
| Coaxial Cable | 400 to 600 | Cable TV; about 80 to 100 channels |
| Spread Spectrum Radio | 3 bands: 902 to 928; 2,400 to 2,483 and 5,725 to 5,850 | Low power |
| Directional Radio | 10,000 and up e.g., terrestrial at 18,000 Ku-band satellite at 12,000 and 14,000 | Microwave |
| Fiber optics | 100 to 100,000 | No EMI |

*Table 5.1. Typical maximum frequencies of different media.*

In practice, communication channels that use lower frequencies are transported within bounded media while applications with channels that use higher frequencies are typically carried by unbounded media. This is not a hard and fast rule: some applications have ranges of frequencies equally suitable for both bounded and unbounded media. Indeed, communicating via unbounded media requires an *antenna* at the point of inception, or reception; the antenna itself being the interface between the bounded nature of adjacent equipment and the unbounded radiated medium.

Very High Frequency (VHF) signals—in the range 100 MHz (100 megahertz or million cycles per second) to 300 MHz—while communicable by cable are also communicated through the air.

Figure 5.1 lists the names of radio bands and their frequency ranges. For example, C band and Ku band used with satellites for commercial television and for Very Small Aperture Terminal VSAT (data) applications are at 4 GHz, and 12 GHz respectively (that is, 4 and 12 gigahertz or billion cycles per second).

| DESIGNATION | LATER DESIGNATION | PASS-BAND |
|---|---|---|
| VHF | A | 100 MHz — 300 MHz |
| UHF | B and C | 300 MHz — 1 GHz |
| L band | D | 1 – 2 GHz |
| S band | E, F | 2 – 4 GHz |
| C band | G, H | 4 – 8 GHz |
| X band | I and partly J | 8 – 12 GHz |
| Ku band | partly J | 12 – 18 GHz |
| K, Ka | partly J, K | 18 – 40 GHz |
| millimeter | L, M | 40+ GHz |

*Figure 5.1. Radio Frequency Allocation. Designations in the left-hand column are in general use within the U.S.A. communications and radar industry (World War II vintage).*

## COAXIAL CABLE FEATURES

Among the *bounded* media, we first examine *coaxial* cable. Figure 5.2 illustrates a coaxial cable. It features an inner conductor, usually a solid, non-stranded copper wire, or copper covered steel wire, surrounded by a dielectric medium—insulation made from material such as polyvinyl chloride, fiberglass, or polyethylene, the latter, if present, in a solid, foamed or semi-solid form. Braided around the insulation is a woven copper mesh which forms the outer conductor. A polyethylene, polyvinyl chloride, or sometimes, aluminum jacket surrounds the entire cable.

The energy of the higher frequencies of electricity carried in a metallic wire tends to be conducted on the surface. This is known as the "skin effect." Since thicker wires have more surface area than do thinner wires, they allow for larger bandwidths of signals. Also, at higher frequencies, conductors tend to radiate their surface energy. The outer braided conductor of coaxial cables acts as a shield. Because of this, coaxial cables allow higher frequencies than conventional "twisted pair" cables.

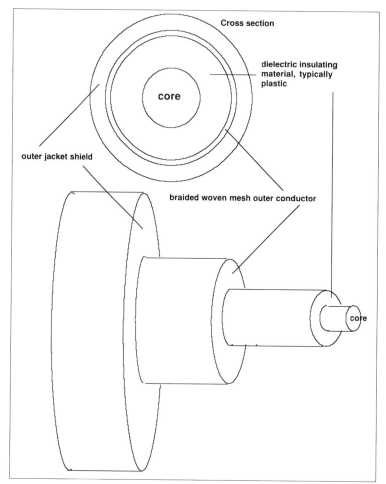

*Figure 5.2. Illustration of a coaxial cable.*

## RG Numbers

Coaxial cables are frequently designated by military origin "RG" numbers; the letters denote Radio Government for reasons now obscure. Over a hundred different types of coaxial cable exist. The more common ones are listed in Table 5.2.

Costs are shown for rough guidance only; for current, more accurate numbers, vendors should be consulted.

| RG Name | Description | Characteristic Impedance (Ohms) | Cost (cents per foot) |
|---|---|---|---|
| RG-6 | Broadband, standard CATV; also ARCNET | 75 | |
| RG-8 | Standard (Thick) Ethernet | 50 | 95 |
| RG-9 | same as RG-8 but with plenum shielding | 50 | |
| RG-11 | Broadband Trunk/ feeder | 75 | 5 |
| RG-58 | Thinnet ("Cheapernet") | 50 | 25 |
| RG-59 | dual Wang broadband | 75 | 15 |
| RG-62 | IBM 3270; ARCNET | 93 | 20 |
| Twinax (not coax) | IBM 5250 | 78 | |

*Table 5.2. Common types of coaxial cable.*

### Backbone and Riser Cables

RG-8 and RG-9, standard thick Ethernet cable, is useful in environments where the cable will not be relocated frequently; the configuration of equipment being static. Its thickness and bulk (weight and volume per foot) make it difficult to handle. Certainly in comparison with RG-58 (Thinnet or "Cheapernet") it is cumbersome and awkward. However, it is ideal installed in risers between floors of a building or in environments where it is the *backbone* link between facilities and where, once again, the cable does not need to be moved. Also, it supports a segment length of 500 meters, in contrast with the 185-meter limitation of "Cheapernet."

#### Thick Ethernet Adapters and Connectors

End-points of segments of coaxial cable use connectors for interfacing to *adapters* or *terminators*. Figure 5.3 shows a cable with "Type N" end connector. This is available from vendors for connecting segments of RG-8, or RG-9, the standard thick "Ethernet" coaxial cable. The connector itself is male with a threaded inner cavity. It connects the end of the cable segment to either an *adapter* which effectively elongates the segment or a *terminator* which is a device housing a resistor that is the sink for electrical energy on the cable. Adapters link two segments together. As an example, the Type N barrel connectors are adapters. These are physically symmetrical barrel shaped devices, female/female at either end, threaded on the outer surface and mechanically compatible with the Type N connector. Likewise, threads on the outer surface of the terminator mechanically couple it to the cable.

An adapter is not a *repeater*. Repeaters need power to actively regenerate and reshape pulses. Adapters have no power.

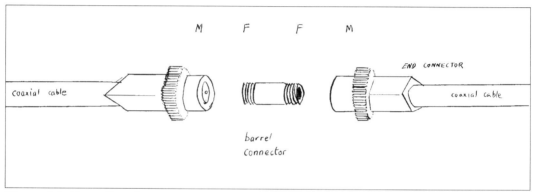

*Figure 5.3. Type N end connector cable.*

## Tapping into the Ethernet Cable

Electrical access to the conductors in thick Ethernet cable is made through taps along its length, not at the ends. To make a tap, a small hole is pierced through the cable's protective jacket at a point that is distant by a certain number of meters from adjacent taps. "Vampire clamp" aptly describes the device that mechanically attaches and pierces the cable. At each such point, one connecting wire is supplied to touch the outer braiding while a second wire, itself insulated from shorting with the braiding, penetrates through the dielectric to make contact with the inner conductor. The distance separating taps is 2.5 meters. (Vendors mark in ink the cable tap places.) This minimizes unwanted echo that is caused by differences in the electrical impedance of the cable at the tap points.

The two conductors are under the control of a *transceiver*, an electronic device implemented on a printed circuit card housed in a small box on or near the cable. Connecting a PC to a LAN, whose medium is this standard thick RG-8 or RG-9 Ethernet cable, is done by means of another cable connected to this transceiver. This is called a *drop* cable, *Attachment Unit Interface* cable or *transceiver cable*. It is not coaxial. Its 8 individual wires serve four circuits on four twisted pairs. Signals in these wires are activated by the transceiver. Via the 8-wire drop cable, the transceiver communicates to and from the PC's adapter card what transpires on the two conductors within the thick Ethernet cable.

## A Note on Notation

Ethernet is almost the same as the IEEE 802.3 standard described as "10Base5." The latter's notation illustrates a popular way for distinguishing or specifying different CSMA/CD LANs. The notation is in three parts. In the first part, (here "10"), the speed of the LAN is indicated in Mbit/s. In the middle part, the word (here "Base") is a clue to the nature of the signaling method used by the LAN (here "baseband" which we describe in Chapter 6). The third, final part describes a key cable characteristic (here the numeral 5 indicates the maximum cable segment length in hundreds of meters). So, 10Base2 is a specification for a CSMA/CD LAN also operating at 10 Mbit/s with baseband, but using 200-meter long (thin, coaxial) segments. (Actually, to be precise, 10Base2 is the same as Thinnet or "Cheapernet" with maximum cable segment lengths of 185 meters!) Let us look at 10Base2's cabling characteristics now.

## *Adapters and Connectors for 10Base2*

Like Ethernet, the thinner 10Base2 Cheapernet cable also has male connectors. Also like Ethernet, it features terminators at both ends of a cable segment. However, in contrast with that on a thick Ethernet cable, the Cheapernet cable connector is "BNC" or bayonet-type, with small studs that protrude orthogonally to the cable's length. The two studs are diametrically opposite each other on the connector. To engage its mating receptor, the studs slide within the latter's grooves and lock with a twist action. See Figure 5.4. Two types of adapter are available for Cheapernet. One is the barrel female/female adapter that connects two segments together. More useful, perhaps, is the "T" adapter that also connects two segments together but connects them to an adapter card (in a PC usually). PCs attached to a Cheapernet LAN do not need drop cable connections; the transceivers are part of the adapter cards themselves.

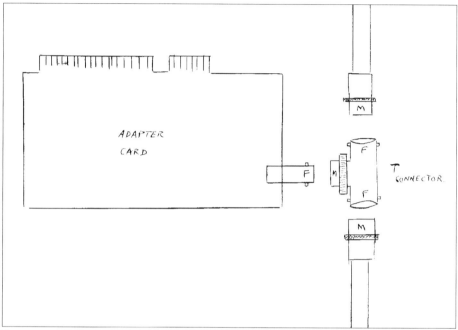

*Figure 5.4. Thin "Cheapernet" cable connectors and terminators.*

## TWISTED PAIR

The second bounded medium we consider is *twisted pair*. This medium—shown in Figure 5.5—is the most common type of signal cabling found today for commercial, or private use. As a comment on its ubiquitousness, it is the cable that throughout the world connects telephones at businesses or residences with local telephone company's exchanges. Thus, it is the medium of the *subscriber loop* (although in some areas, experiments with optical-fibers for this purpose have begun). Most of the telephone twisted pair installed is unshielded.

The name twisted pair derives from the mutual twisting of two insulated conductors around each other's length, while essentially preserving their longitude. The twisting is not a tight coiling. Twist rate is two to twelve twists per foot.

As an example, the transceiver cable, referred to above, contains 8 individual wires that are paired to form four twisted pair circuits: transmit, receive, collision, and power. The wires are either #20 or #22 AWG.

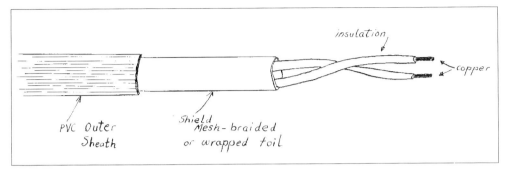

*Figure 5.5. Example of shielded twisted pair.*

## AMERICAN WIRE GAUGE

AWG is the *American Wire Gauge* rating, a classification of wires by diameter that differentiates current carrying and therefore heat capacities. With AWG, the larger a wire's diameter is, the smaller is its AWG number; the narrower a wire's diameter, the larger its AWG number. AWG #22 is wire of diameter 25 thousandths of an inch. AWG #24 is narrower, at 20 thousandths of an inch, while AWG #26 is even narrower at 16 thousandths of an inch.

## TWISTING CANNOT SOLVE ALL THE PROBLEMS

Twisting a pair of adjacent conductors is done so that any electromagnetic interference (EMI) noise picked up by one conductor will probably be picked up by the other conductor too. This tends to preserve the signal levels in the wires relative to each other. But EMI is only one source of signal impairment. Another is attenuation, which twisting abates only marginally. In fact, frequencies on twisted pair (such as AWG 19 which is thicker than "normal" telephone grade wire) attenuate at 1 decibel per mile. This means that signal strengths received are only fractions of what was transmitted. (The signal strength at 10 miles is 10%, at 20 miles 1% and at 30 miles 0.1% of what was transmitted.) For this reason, repeaters are installed in twisted pair circuits to reinforce, or regenerate the signal.

Twisted pair is not as versatile for the handling of high frequency transmissions as is coaxial cable. Generally, higher frequencies are demanded by higher bit rates of transmission. In practice, the highest frequency that unshielded twisted pair accommodates today is 50 MHz to 100 MHz depending on distance. This is about 20% of the maximum frequency that coaxial cable can accommodate. Error free data transmission on twisted pair is more easily attained for high speeds when the distances are less than 100 meters.

### Maximum Distances vs. Impairments

Four main factors determine the range of wire length for transmitting error free bits at high speed over twisted pair. These include the frequency range of the signal carried, the degree to which the wire is shielded from electromagnetic interference, crosstalk, and the return loss. Higher bit rates of transmission demand shorter lengths of wire. Shielding may be used to push the performance higher, but shielding may present other problems. As the transmission rates increase, the shield capacitance to ground increasingly acts as a short circuit for the signal. The third and fourth signal impairments which we describe in more detail now are *crosstalk* which becomes an issue when the cable contains multiple pairs, and *return loss*.

### Crosstalk

*Near end crosstalk* or *NEXT* is an undesirable side-effect of the assembly of multiple pairs of conductors within a single cable. NEXT is noise interference caused by the physically adjacent isolated circuits coupling electro-magnetically. Each circuit's magnetic field induces unwanted voltage to appear in the other's signal. Also, capacitance imbalance between the four conductors of two pairs causes mutual capacitive coupling which, with impedance mismatch, also affects the signal.

#### How is NEXT Measured?

For most twisted pair applications, NEXT is capacitive. Consequently, NEXT can be reduced if the sets of paired conductors in a cable are manufactured in such a way as to reduce or eliminate capacitance differences. The quality control specifies the maximum allowable NEXT using one of two measures depending on the number of pairs in the cable. These are the *pair-to-pair* measure or the *power sum* measure. The pair-to-pair crosstalk measure is typically used for 4-pair cable; power sum for 25-pair.

#### Differences in Measure Apply by # of Pairs

If the pairs of 4-pair cable are numbered #1, #2, #3, and #4, the crosstalk in the cable is measured for each of the six possible combinations of pairs: #1 with #2; #1 with #3; #1 with #4; #2 with #3; #2 with #4; and #3 with #4. The pair-to-pair measure selected for the cable is that of the "worst" pair, the pair suffering most noise.

The crosstalk in a 25-pair cable is defined by the power sum, a more demanding measure. Again, one measures noise for every combination of two pairs. Note that if the pair A to pair B crosstalk is measured positive, the pair B to pair A crosstalk is the same, but negative. So, for the 600 pair to pair values, only 300 physical measurements are needed. Examining any specific pair, its 24 measurements with other pairs are "added" together in a special way to give a sense of the total crosstalk experienced by or caused by that pair. The largest (worst) of the 25 results becomes the power sum.

The special way of adding the crosstalk is necessary because half of dBs are negative; simply summing the numbers may yield anomalous measures. For example, in a three-pair cable if pair #1's crosstalk with pair #2 was x dB and its crosstalk with pair #3 was -x dB, simple summation would ascribe pair #1 a 0 crosstalk! The formula resolves this by squaring each of the 300 terms. For any pair, its 24 squares are summed. (At least) one sum of the 25 won't be less than any other; its square root defines the *power sum* for the cable. For the mathematically inclined, note that:

$$\text{powersum} = \max_{i=1}^{25} (f_i) \qquad \text{where} \qquad f_i = \sqrt{\sum_{\substack{j=1 \\ j \neq i}}^{25} \text{pair}_{i,j}^2}$$

The second signal impediment to consider is *(Structured) Return Loss*. This measures the variation of impedance between two end-points—either within the cable itself, or, more likely, between the cable and its connectors. Any mismatch in impedance that the signal encounters causes it to be reflected; the greater the mismatch, the more severe the undesirable echo.

### EIA/TIA Category Cable

Network administrators of telephone, LAN, MAN, and WAN connections, while attracted by the ease-of-use and economy of unshielded twisted pair need to be aware of the medium's limitations, since different applications will demand different levels of performance. The Electronics Industries Association and Telecommunications Industries Association have rated different quality unshielded twisted pair in five categories based on attenuation properties and NEXT and return loss limits:

- **Category 1** is plain old style used for voice applications and low speed data transmission up to 20 kbit/s.

- **Category 2** is telephone wire rated to 1 MHz. It is acceptable for T1 (1.544 Mbit/s), or ISDN Basic Rate (144 kbit/s). With baluns, it can be used instead of coaxial or twinax cable to connect terminals to computers e.g., IBM 5250s to System /34, /36 and /38, and AS/400. Category 2 cable is also defined by Underwriter Laboratories (UL) "Level II" specifications of maximum allowable attenuation, impedance and mutual capacitance.

- **Category 3** accommodates frequencies to 16 MHz. It is suitable for speeds up to 10 Mbit/s. A common application is the "10BaseT" Ethernet. 4-Mbit/s Token Ring is fine on this category cable. Category 3, of course, supports terminal connections like Category 2. Parameters for Category 3 cable are the same as for UL "Level III."

- **Category 4** is suitable for voice and data applications up to 20 MHz. 16-Mbit/s Token Ring and 10BaseT are the applications. To meet near-end crosstalk (NEXT) maxima demanded by EIA/TIA, this category cable tolerates numerically more pairs in it than does Category 5. Category 4 cable conforms to UL's "Level IV" specifications.

- **Category 5** is suitable for voice and data applications up to 100 MHz. In addition to 16-Mbit/s Token Ring and 10BaseT, the 100-Mbit/s TP-PMD ("FDDI over copper") and 155-Mbit/s ATM are target applications. Maximum allowable NEXT and Return Loss are lowest and most stringent for this category of all. UL Level V applies.

LANs, once the sole province of coaxial cable, still to a large extent today use coaxial cable. But, unlike in the past when Ethernet LANs exclusively used coaxial cable, many of today's Ethernets are implemented using twisted pair. The other popular LAN, Token Ring, exclusively uses twisted pair. IBM, a protagonist of the Token Ring, proposes its own cabling system for copper wire in different *Types* of twisted pair cable as follows.

### IBM Cabling System

IBM Types 1, 2, and 3 cables all use 22 AWG solid conductors. Types 6, 8 and 9 use thinner gauge AWG 26 conductors.

For support of the 16-Mbit/s Token Ring, IBM advocates its Type 1 or Type 2 cable. Type 1 contains two pairs i.e., four conductors. Each 22 AWG pair is individually twisted and wrapped in a braided metallic shield. *Type 1* cable comes in two forms: indoor cable and outdoor cable. To reduce hazards resulting from insulation subjected to fire (rapid spread of fire along cable lengths, accompanied by the release of toxic fumes), indoor cables drawn through air ducts or room-to-room conduits and interstices need flame-retardant non-toxic materials in the insulation. Such cable is certified for plenum installation ("plenum" means duct or pathway). Users should be aware that some local fire codes may not recognize the plenum rating; in such environments metallic conduits are mandated. Outdoor Type 1 cable is equipped with a rugged weatherproof jacket. It can be procured in two forms, depending on whether the cable will be buried or aerial. Buried cable needs an armored or metallic outer jacket. Aerial cable is equipped with metallic wire for structural strength.

IBM *Type 3* cable consists of four unshielded twisted pairs. These are used for telephone connections, and indoor applications only.

IBM *Type 2* cable combines Type 1 and Type 3 in one cable. It contains six pairs, two pairs of which have braided shields equivalent to Type 1. Type 2 cable is available for indoor use only.

IBM *Type 6* cable consists of two pairs of flexible, stranded 26 AWG conductors for use as jumper cables in indoor patch panels and wiring closets. Segment lengths of 8, 30, 75, and 150 feet are used to interconnect Type 1 or Type 2 cables.

IBM *Type 8* cable consists of two pairs of 26 AWG unshielded twisted pair for indoor under-carpet use.

IBM *Type 9* cable contains two pairs of 26 AWG twisted pair, overall shielded with a tinned copper braid. This indoor-only cable's advantage (relative to Type 1) is its lower cost.

---

## OPTICAL FIBER

The medium with by far greatest capacity and greatest potential for bit carrying is optical fiber. The medium itself consists of thin strands made from glass of exceptionally high quality, giving it a transparency much higher than ordinary glass. If the ocean were as transparent, one could see the ocean floor at its deepest point when looking over the side of a ship.

### Light Sources are LEDs and Lasers

The source of light is either a *Light Emitting Diode* or a *Laser Diode*. LED sources cost less; lasers on the other hand cost more but they feature higher performance. Both LEDs and lasers convert electrical energy into light pulses or photons that are beamed into the fiber end. LEDs produce light that is spread over a wide range of frequencies. Lasers emit coherent light, or light with a narrow range of frequencies. We shall see below that these characteristics bear on the pulse rate and speed of transmission.

## Optical Receivers

The receiver devices are light sensitive diodes known as *photo-diodes*. These convert the optical signals to electrical currents. Once again, there are two receiver types, one costly and the other not. The *avalanche photo-diode*, while relatively expensive compared to the normal positive-intrinsic-negative PIN *photo-diode*, is more capable of detecting low light intensity signals. It is capable of generating currents that are 10 dB through 30 dB (one to three orders of magnitude) stronger than the PIN photo-diode. As a consequence, the avalanche photo-diode is superior for receiving transmissions over long distances. However, the PIN photo-diode does enjoy an advantage apart from lower cost—it is not as sensitive to variations in the operating temperature.

## Infrared Light

Although light is the energy form carried through the optical fiber, it is not visible light. The frequency of light used for communication purposes is in the *infrared* part of the spectrum. We explore why below. (As an aside, to avoid retinal injury one should never look into the end of what may seem to be a "dark" fiber. It could be emitting harmful infrared radiation.)

### Absorption is a Light Enemy

To provide a high degree of transparency, the optical fiber needs to pass the light rays without *absorbing* or *dispersing* them. In turn, the amount of light that gets absorbed depends partly on its wavelength, certain wavelengths being more prone to absorption by the glass than others. Experimentation has shown that, in glass, the 1300 nanometer wavelength enjoys the lowest loss due to absorption. Another "good" waveband is found from 1500 to 1700 nanometers. Both are in the infrared part of the spectrum.

At lower wavelengths, the absorption is due to random atomic or "Rayleigh" scattering; at higher wavelengths, the materials that were added to control the refractive index of the glass are impurities that add to the absorption.

## Dispersion Hurts Performance

Dispersion refers to any reshaping of a precisely shaped pulse. A pulse that starts square shaped, of duration $T$, is dispersed if it arrives at its destination somewhat bell-shaped. The pulse time measured at the destination is $T + d$, reflecting the flattened pulse. As we shall see later, this is because some rays of the original pulse do not arrive at the same time as the bulk of those simultaneously sent. If $d$ is 0, there would be no dispersion, and the optical fiber could accommodate as many pulses as the transmitter were capable of emitting.

To illustrate the impact of dispersion on performance, consider this example: if $d$ were 0.5 seconds, then even if the pulses were infinitely "thin," (i.e., T almost equal to 0), at most two pulses per second could be detected by the receiver. One can see, then, that the theoretical maximum bit rate depends inversely on the dispersion: it is 1/d bits per second. In practice, the maximum bit rate is 70% of the 1/d value.

## Lasers—More Capability, but at a Cost

Lasers offer less dispersion than LEDs. They emit light within a narrower band of wavelengths than do LEDs, and this leads to them shipping more parallel rays, accounting for their ability to deliver higher pulse rates and speeds of transmission.

Dispersion increases with distance. Higher bit rates are possible only with corresponding shorter distances for the fiber-optic segment. Using optical fiber of a certain quality, the number of "bits per second per kilometer" is constant. With the same quality cable, users needing longer segments must settle for lower numbers of bits per second. Alternatively, users can obtain higher-rates with shorter fiber-optic segments.

Fiber-optic products with ratings of 100 gigahertz per kilometer are commercially available. Materials capable of 1000 Ghz per km have been demonstrated in the laboratory.

### *Inside the Fiber—A Quick Overview*

How is the medium constructed? Figure 5.6 shows cross-sections of three types of fiber. The top sketch illustrates the *step-index* type. This consists of a long thin *core* of glass with a refractive index of 2. (We discuss refractive index in Appendix E). Its diameter is generally 62.5 microns i.c., 62.5 millionths of a meter. Other diameters are notably 50 and 80 microns. The core is "wrapped" inside *cladding*, effectively a transparent, hollow glass tube whose inner diameter matches the core's diameter (typically 62.5 microns) and whose outer diameter is typically 125 microns. The refractive index of the cladding is 1.5.

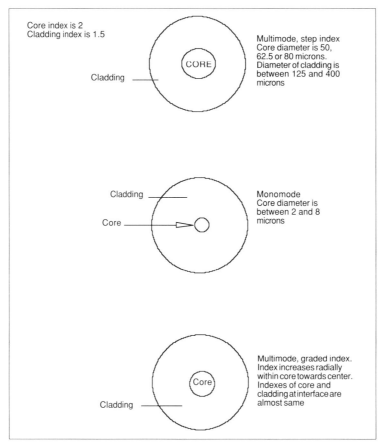

*Figure 5.6. Cross-sections of three different types of fiber-optic cable.*

If the refractive index within the core is not uniform but decreases continuously radially from the core's center, the fiber is said to have a *graded index*. This is illustrated in the bottom diagram of Figure 5.6.

Both step index and graded index fiber are used in *multimode* applications. In these applications the light is dispersed, and therefore causes some degradation in performance. By contrast, in *monomode* applications (characterized by the use of fiber with a core diameter between 2 and 8 microns), there is zero dispersion. Monomode fiber is more expensive than the other types and is capable of supporting much higher bit rates.

To better understand the difference between monomode and multimode in more detail, and for a description of the overall principles of fiber-optics, *Appendix E—How Optical Fibers Work* is suggested.

## Dispersion

Rays of light that are reflected on their path from source to destination will take more time to make the journey than rays of parallel light, because of the greater distance traveled. This variance is a major performance limiter; it defines dispersion.

The dispersion may be abated with the use of a *graded index* fiber. For example, let us consider fiber, where the center of the core has a refractive index of 2. The core is manufactured using materials with different optical qualities so that, radially, its index differs gradually from slightly more than 1.5 at the outer diameter to 2 at the center. The cladding has index 1.5.

Using these graded index fibers, rays of light in the central core that are not parallel to the length of the fiber will depart the central core at some point. There the refractive index reduces slightly, and the rays react to the diminishing refractive index by bending a little away from the "normal" and speeding up a bit. The bend is not enough to cause reflection until the rays reach the cladding. This is because the indices at these core "surfaces" are almost identical; of course, were the indices identical there would be no bending of the light whatsoever.

Eventually, at the core-cladding surface, a ray's angle of incidence reaches a critical angle causing it to reflect back within the core towards the center. As the ray makes its way through increasing refractive indices it bends gradually towards the "normal"—and slows slightly—until it reenters the high, uniform refractive index part of the core.

The rays move straight through this to the diametrically opposite point in the core. There again the refractive index begins to decrease, and the angle of incidence for the ray is the same it had prior to its first refraction. Symmetrical repetition of what we have just described occurs. Thus,once reflected, light in the core does not escape.

## Stepped vs. Graded Index

Let us compare the time taken for a ray to traverse a given length of fiber using stepped index verses graded index fiber. Light propagates proportionately faster through materials with lower refractive index. Rays that move in a fiber's core parallel to its length do not reflect. Since the index in the cores of both types of fiber is the same, the travel times of the parallel rays through either type of fiber are identical. But non-parallel rays do incur reflections, travel longer distances, and thus arrive later than parallel rays. In graded index fiber, however, non-parallel ray reflections occur less frequently than in stepped index. Between reflections, rays are propagated faster because of the lower refractive index of the material through which these rays traverse. Hence, rays arrive sooner than they would in the stepped index fibers.

For this reason, graded index fibers enjoy lower dispersion qualities than stepped index. But, they are more expensive.

## When Monomode is Called For

If there were only parallel rays transmitted with no reflection, the problem of dispersion would not exist. By using a fiber whose core is only a few times wider than the wavelength of light, the physics of coherent light comes into play and puts this "ideal" state in reach. Here, any light that enters the core is only capable of moving parallel to the length of the fiber. We call this type of fiber *monomode*. It is the most expensive to make, and it demands the use of laser diodes for transmitters. But, because of the zero dispersion qualities of the signal, the monomode fiber exhibits the highest performance.

## UNBOUNDED MEDIA

The use of *unbounded* media is dominated by various applications of radio communications. *Infrared* applications take a distant second place.

A major consideration that pertains to the use of radio (and also, but not as severely, to bounded media) is governmental regulation. With some exception, the use of a radio transmitter requires a license from the Federal Communications Commission (FCC) for the chosen communication channels. This is because of the scarcity of frequency bands within the electromagnetic spectrum that are usable by today's technology.

Figure 5.1 tabulates some of the popular frequency bands and their designations.

### A Note on Antennas

Antennas are either *directional* or *omni-directional*. Antennas such as horns, parabolic dishes and grids are used for directional point-to-point beams for applications such as *microwave transmission*. Conventional microwave radio transmitters require licenses from the FCC. The bands used operate typically at 18 and 23.2 GHz. Microwave antennas are usually mounted on high towers or atop buildings, with clear views to the communicating partner's equipment. In general, use of the higher frequencies requires line of sight between antenna and receiver. (Use of the higher frequencies refers to the pass-band in which the communication channel exists. It does not mean that the data transmission rate is consequently high—low bit rates are often communicated in the higher frequency bands.)

Infrared "beamers" are directional. A universal example of the use of IR in directional applications is the remote control used with TV or stereo equipment.

By contrast, omni-directional radios, with rod-like antennas, radiate in all directions, and do not necessarily have line of sight with the other communicator. Applications of these types typically use frequency bands at or below UHF, approximately 1 GHz.

Line of sight applications are vulnerable to temporary obstructions to the line of sight. Perhaps the worst offender here is water vapor. Mist, fog, rain or cloud can impair a clear signal. Particles of water are able to absorb the energy of microwaves causing signal loss.

### Impairments—Fading and Reflections

Problems of *fading* and *reflections* may affect line of sight applications, but generally they are more severe for omni-directional applications. In omni-directional situations, structures between the source and receiver may block or tend to attenuate the signal strength. Some signals may reflect, particularly if the structures contain metal. Reflections of a signal may create echoes finding more circuitous paths to the receiver. This manifests itself as a dispersion of the received signal, making it more difficult for the receiver to discern the transmitted signal.

Reflections are taken advantage of in the omni-directional application of *diffuse infrared*.

### Satellite Communications

One of the more conspicuous applications of radio involves communications via satellite. In this application, a geosynchronous satellite acts as a repeater, receiving signals beamed directionally to it from a (usually) several meter-diameter dish located at a corporate headquarters. It relays them back earthward to a wide "footprint." The satellite's position in space is 22,300 miles away, in the equatorial plane. Its orbital speed exactly matches that of the earth's rotation so that it appears to be stationary (*geo-stationary*). Most satellites have more than one *transponder*, equipping them to deal with multiple inbound "uplink" channels. The satellite's transponder is a set of electronics that amplifies the received signal when it repeats it. While doing so, it shifts the pass-band of received frequencies by a fixed bandwidth. Whereas a single satellite is the target of the directed *uplink* transmission, the *downlink* transmission from the satellite to earth is characterized by a footprint of coverage. Therefore, satellite transmission is suited (among other things) for one-to-many broadcasting.

Another of the unique advantages from using satellite circuits is the independence of terrestrial distance coverage and cost. A signal can be transmitted as cheaply across the country, ocean, or continent as across the street. Consequently, satellite transmission is cost competitive for some long distance applications.

## VSATs

Very Small Aperture Terminal satellite applications usually operate in the "Ku" band. (See Figure 5.1). VSAT Ku-band applications usually involve the transmission of low to medium speed data (1200 to 64000 bit/s). *Uplink* Ku band earth stations send data to the satellite in the 14- to 14.5-GHz pass-band; *downlink* earth stations receive in the 11.7- to 12.2-GHz range. The VSAT derives its name from the diameter of a representative earth station dish, which is small (1 meter or less) compared with say a "C"-band antenna (typically 5 meters).

Ku band signal reception is impaired by intervening water particles. Potential VSAT procurers should be careful to stipulate a minimum signal level that would be acceptable under worst-case conditions, e.g., particularly heavy rainfall.

C-band applications include commercial television. The C-band uplink pass-band is 5.925 to 6.425 GHz; the downlink pass-band is 3.7 GHz to 4.2 GHz. Because they are presently manufactured in greater volume, C-band earth stations cost less than Ku band equipment. Also, C-band transmissions are not as sensitive to rain attenuation as are those in the Ku band.

## Licensing Needed

Whether operating in the Ku or C-band, uplink earth stations (transmitters/antennas) require licensing by the FCC; an FCC license is not mandatory for downlink receivers.

Although the transmission from the satellite may be received by multiple earth stations, not all transmissions are intended for all earth stations. The communications protocol allows for a specific earth station to be selected.

## Allow for Delay

Because the satellite is 22,300 miles from earth, a signal beamed from earth via satellite takes about a quarter-second to reach its terrestrial target from the time of departure. This inherent delay makes satellite transmission less attractive for isochronous applications, e.g., voice and video conversations. In particular, if more than one satellite is in the communications path, as in a multi-hop circuit, the delay is exacerbated.

### Spread Spectrum Radio

Spread Spectrum Radio (SSR) technology, once a military technology, is now receiving considerable attention from commercial developers. The newer applications made possible by SSR include wireless local area networks, and personal communications networks. SSR is also likely to be effective in the area of private metropolitan area networks. An example may be taken from the area of *Advanced Traffic Management Systems*. Here, information from and to the roadside (intersection signal coordination, traffic conditions, distress and hazard alerts, advisories etc.) may be communicated by radio equipment without the installation problems or delays inherent in laying communications cables.

### SSR and FCC Licensing

One major advantage that spread spectrum radio enjoys is that no FCC license is required to install or operate it. As long as the radio complies with certain rules (Part 15.247 of the FCC Rules and Regulations), it can operate freely in the same frequency bands as other independent SSRs causing them minimal interference, and, reciprocally, being subjected to acceptably low-levels of intrusion from other transmitters.

The rule stipulates that any spread spectrum radio operating with less than one watt of output power and radiating in the following pass-bands does not need a license:

$$902 - 928 \text{ MHz}$$
$$2.4000 - 2.4835 \text{ GHz}$$
$$5.725 - 5.850 \text{ GHz}$$

The rule was enacted by the FCC in 1985 to stimulate the development by the private sector of non-military, commercial uses for SSR. One such use is the wireless local area network, enabling data transfer among personal computers in offices. Other applications now appearing include communication between mobile end devices such as laptops or Personal Digital Assistants and base computers.

### Wireless Standards—The Status

The IEEE 802.11 committee is chartered with the responsibility of drafting a wireless standard so that all these devices can operate concurrently within the same area. The 802.11 committee's standards for OSI physical layer 1 were expected in 1994 for two types of spectrum spreading methods, described below, as well as for infrared.

What are the capabilities and how does spread spectrum radio work? Data transmission takes place from low-to-high speeds. The low is below 64 kbit/s; the high is 1.544 to 2.048 Mbit/s. The high ends correspond to the T1 and the European E1 rates, respectively.

## How SSR Operates—Direct Sequence

Radios communicate with each other using one of two spectrum spreading techniques, *direct sequence* and *frequency hopping*. In the direct sequence mode, a narrow-band signal's energy is spread over a wide range of frequencies and noise is interspersed. Only receivers equipped with a decoding "key" know what frequencies to tune to in order to receive the message. Figure 5.7, read from top to bottom, illustrates the concept, showing the coding of the transmission sequence implemented in three steps. In the figure, the horizontal axis is frequency; the vertical axis represents the energy of the signal.

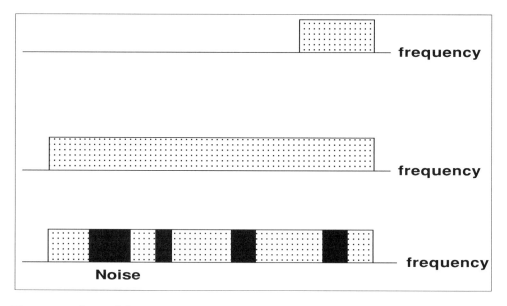

*Figure 5.7. Spread Spectrum (direct sequence). Takes a narrowband signal and spreads it over a wider frequency range, interspersing noise. Receivers need a "key" to decode.*

## Frequency Hopping

The other spread spectrum technique is known as *frequency hopping*. As illustrated in Figure 5.8, the frequency hopping signal is active at a particular frequency for only a brief interval of time. After a few milliseconds, it will be positioned at some other frequency. Here, it will not dwell necessarily for the same amount of time as it did at the first frequency position. This process continues, with new frequency positions being occupied by the signal for new dwell times. In other words, the signal dynamically relocates. Only a receiver that has been programmed to know when to look for a signal at a particular frequency can decode the transmission. Two IEEE 802.11 standards are expected for SSR, one covering 1-Mbit/s dual mode (direct sequence and/or frequency hop), the other standard 2-Mbit/s single mode.

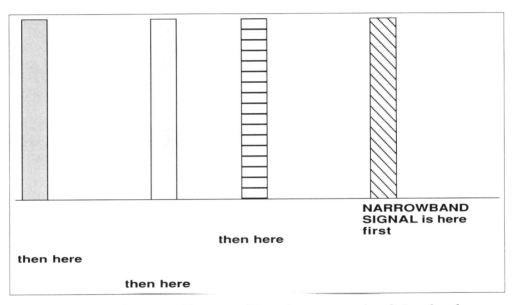

**NARROWBAND SIGNAL is here first**

**then here**

**then here**

**then here**

*Figure 5.8. Spread Spectrum Frequency Hop takes a narrowband signal and dynamically repositions it to a new band for a short time duration—then hops to another band, etc. Only receiver knowing when and where next to look for the signal can decode it.*

## SSR is Deployed Quickly

A major advantage from using SSR is that equipment can be deployed in a short period of time. By contrast with 18.2-GHz or 23.2-GHz microwave radios, the SSR does not need time-consuming and costly planning and coordination delays, nor the lengthy FCC license-filing process before equipment can be installed.

SSRs operate with either directional or omni-directional antennas. Generally, the radios supporting higher numbers of bits per second use directional, line of sight antennas. They cover 10 miles or less, since power is constrained to less than 1 watt.

## Encoding and Terrestrial Interfaces

The radios use B8ZS or AMI encoding. We discuss these in the next chapter. Many radios are equipped with standard DTE/DCE interfaces. Thus, they appear as would standard "modems" to terminals or personal computers, using V.35, EIA-530 or EIA-232 interfaces. These concepts are described in Chapter 9.

## *Cellular Radio*

We now discuss the use of *cellular radio* for data transmission. Figure 5.9 is a schematic aerial view of a geographical area segmented into cells within which radios are capable of reaching or being reached by one or more *base-stations*. Each radio uses two frequency bands, one for reception of signals from the base-station, the other for sending to the base-station. At any point in time, these frequencies are available to only one radio; no other users in the cell share the same frequencies at the same time. The radios themselves are said to be *frequency agile*: they are able to dynamically reassign the frequency bands used. They reassign frequencies on directive from the base-station.

One band is said to be forward, for the receipt of transmissions sent from the base-station to the user. The other, so called reverse channel, is for the user transmissions to the base-station. Radio communications between any two cellular users is done with the base-station acting as a switching hub. With both users in range of the same base-station, four frequency bands are used.

Base-stations are connected by conventional land-line or microwave links to adjacent base-stations and to the local telephone company. This enables a radio user in a cell to communicate with another user beyond the scope of the local base-station, or to anyone in the public wide area network.

The cellular application most commonly used is mobile data communications. Here, a user is in a moving vehicle equipped with a radio. The base-station monitors the signal strength coming to it from the user's radio. If the signal strength weakens (probably because the vehicle containing the radio is moving out of a base-station's range), the base-station hands the user over to an adjacent base-station, where the user's signal is stronger.

The communications frequencies used by cellular radio are assigned by the host base-station. As the radio moves from one base-station's coverage into another's, it is assigned a new pair of transmit and receive frequency-bands.

The period during which old frequencies are superseded by new is one during which transmitted bits may be lost. This impacts the quality of data transmission. The (OSI Reference Model) transport layer 4 communications protocol in place should ensure that recovery takes place in the event of errors from lost or destroyed data caused by the break. Cellular radio operates in the 800- to 900 MHz part of the spectrum.

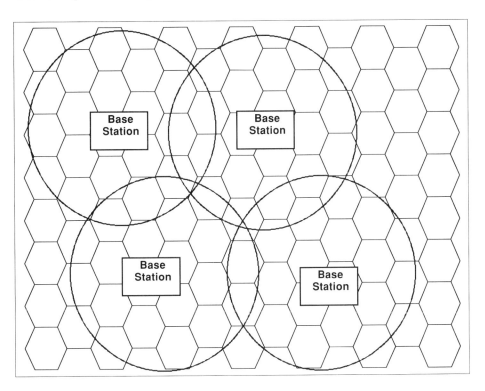

*Figure 5.9. Cellular radio. A mobile communicator traversing multiple cells during a conversation or communications session may be supported by more than one base-station. Each base-station dynamically assigns the customer a new pass-band.*

# 6

# Signaling

In the previous chapter, we discussed the various types of media and their characteristics. In this chapter, we discuss different types of *signaling*. Signaling refers to the method used for communicating data to a remote location by converting 1s and 0s at the source to some form of energy (electricity or light), and then doing the converse at the destination.

Of major concern to all signaling technologies is the reliability of signal reception. Therefore, it is important to understand the various impairments that any chosen medium is prone or vulnerable to. We describe these below. Better signaling methods either eliminate, overcome, or ameliorate the deficiencies.

Computer memories contain 1s and 0s. At any point in time, the value, 1 or 0, of a single computer memory bit is determined by an electrical voltage associated with it. The voltages chosen are arbitrary and depend on the design of the computer. In some computers the voltage associated with a particular bit may be $n$ volts, ascribing to it the value 1; while the voltage associated for a bit's 0 value may be zero volts. Different computers use different conventions and values of $n$.

Communicating a byte of information (from one computer to a remote other), we frequently represent the transmission of each bit of the byte by a *pulse train*. In a graph of voltage versus time, voltage for each bit of the byte is typically shown by a histogram bar for one bit time. In Figure 2.7 for example, the letter V, encoded in ASCII with odd parity, is a binary 11010110. Remember that, by convention, the least significant bit of the byte is transmitted first, the parity bit last.

## WHY DO SIGNALS DETERIORATE?

When voltage is applied to any circuit, it gradually weakens or *attenuates* in relation to the distance between the points of voltage application (i.e., whence the signal is sent) and voltage measurement (i.e., where it is received). In bounded medium transmissions, the length of conductor between transmitter and receiver is a major determinant of the degree of attenuation. Another factor is frequency. The signal strengths of higher frequencies attenuate more readily.

Figure 6.1 illustrates the strength of voltage of a signal as sent (on the left of the figure) and as received (on the right, lower curve). Depending on how much amplitude is lost, the voltage of the original signal may not be correctly recovered and if the circuit is being used for data, errors may occur.

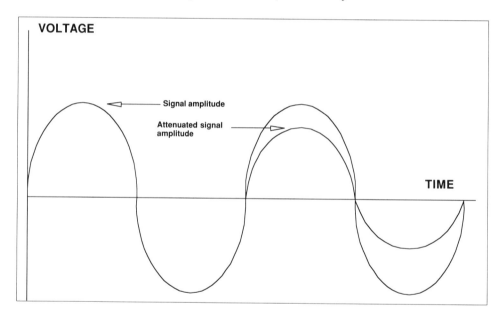

*Figure 6.1. Signal deterioration by attenuation.*

### *Analog Circuits Model Speech*

Plain old telephone (voice-grade service) circuits are called *analog* circuits because the spectrum of frequencies used and their respective amplitudes electrically model the mechanical energy of human speech. The electrical analog circuit is created using a mouthpiece at one end and a speaker at the other.

The mouthpiece consists of a bed of carbon granules beneath a flexible diaphragm. The loudspeaker contains a flexible membrane which responds to voltage fluctuations in an electromagnet.

Human speech causes air pressure variations. These pressure variations impinge on the mouthpiece diaphragm. Since the electrical resistance of the carbon granules as a whole varies with the tightness or looseness of their packing, the less the diaphragm compresses them, the greater is the resistance, and vice-versa. Thus, reaction to air pressure variations by the diaphragm causes different voltages at different frequencies in the circuit.

In turn, the current in the circuit affects the loudspeaker. Here the circuit's wire is coiled around a solenoid to form an electromagnet. As the current through its coils varies, it alternately attracts and repels the magnet attached to the loudspeaker's membrane. The membrane moves the air, recreating mechanical energy that our ears equate to sound.

## Bit Cell

In digital transmission, a single bit is sent during a *bit cell*. Depending on transmission speed for its duration, the bit cell is a time interval during which the signal represents the value of the bit. Single bits are recovered during each bit cell at the receiver.

The bit cell at the receiver starts a fixed amount of time after the *corresponding* bit cell commenced at the sender. The time lag depends on the length of the conductor between sender and receiver and the speed with which electromagnetic energy of its signal propagated through it (in copper, about $2 \times 10^8$ meters per second). Depending on the network configuration, this could be measured in the order of nanoseconds, microseconds, milliseconds or even, in the case of communication via satellite, about 1/4 second.

## Jitter

Start times of successive bit cells must remain perfectly synchronized between sender and receiver. A transmitted bit's signal not arriving in sync with the timing of the receiver's bit cell, introduces an impairment known as *jitter*. This affects signal reception since the contents of the receiver's cell may contain parts of adjacent bits, not corresponding to the cell contents as sent. The upper right of Figure 6.2 illustrates phase jitter, showing the original signal with no phase jitter and one whose phase in time is slightly delayed.

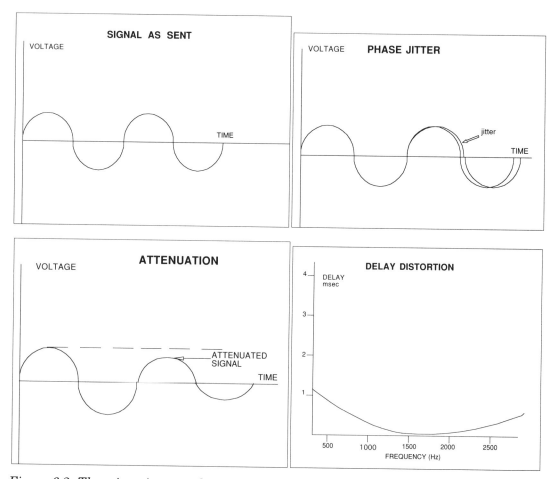

*Figure 6.2. Three impairments that may affect the signal as sent.*

In certain applications, signals are sent using composite or multiple frequencies. Higher frequencies generally propagate faster through the medium than do others. This results in their earlier arrival at the destination. The graph at the lower right of Figure 6.2 illustrates *delay distortion* where frequencies between 1500 and 2000 Hz arrive at their destination with less delay than others.

As indicated earlier, a signaling method may help eliminate, overcome, or ameliorate the deficiencies suffered by the various media. These include impairments such as attenuation, phase jitter and delay distortion.

First, let us examine how attenuation is normally handled. Attenuation may only be ignored if the signal loss is always acceptable by the time the signal reaches the receiver.

## SUBSCRIBER LOOP COILS REDUCE ATTENUATION

As one example of how attenuation is addressed, consider the telephone company's solution for plain old telephone voice-grade service circuits. The *subscriber loop* connecting a single subscriber (residence or business) to the telephone company's central office is, on average, two miles long, or less. The attenuation of the signal strengths of the range of frequencies between 300- and 3300 Hz is minimized by using an inductance coil in the circuit. Circuits using coils are *loaded circuits* (see Figure 6.3). In loaded circuits higher frequencies are attenuated. However, for voice applications this is not a hardship. Despite the human ability to use and recognize frequencies as low as a few hertz and as high as about 20,000 hertz, we comfortably identify speakers and accept the quality of voice limited to frequencies in the 300- to 3300 hertz pass-band.

Otherwise, attenuation must be abated by either amplifying or repeating the signal using equipment located between source and destination. *Amplification* is an *analog* boosting. All the frequencies received by the amplifying equipment are re-transmitted with higher amplitude (loudness). The disadvantage of this approach is that noise energy is amplified, too. After enough relays, the signal to noise ratio can worsen to the degree that data may be lost.

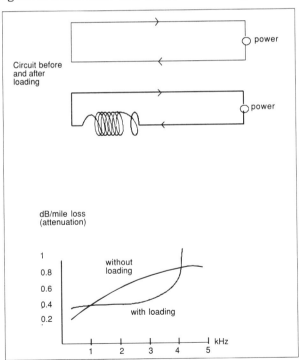

*Figure 6.3. Effect of loading on attenuation. An 88-mH AWG 19 coil at 6,000 ft distance is typical. It provides inductance with same power (more voltage less current).*

## REPEATERS

A *repeater* deals with digital 1s and 0s. It decides whether it has received a 1 or a 0, and re-transmits a corresponding, perfectly reshaped 1 or 0. This means that after a number of relays, the shapes of the 1s and 0s as received are identical to those originally transmitted. Any intermittent noise introduced at any stage during the transmission is eliminated on the repeating.

An example of a repeater is a station in a Token Ring. With IBM Type 1 or Type 2 cable, the repeaters are separated by a maximum distance of 2525 feet, about one half mile or three-quarters of a km. Another example is repeaters used for T1, 1.544-Mbit/s, or European E1 at 2.048-Mbit/s digital circuits. These are positioned 1 to 2 miles apart (1.6 to 3.2 kilometers).

## BASEBAND AND BROADBAND—WHAT THEY ARE

Signals are transmitted on media in *baseband* or *broadband* fashion. A medium or cable is operating in baseband mode when the entire bandwidth of the medium is dedicated to carrying the signal of a single channel. Baseband operation implies dedication to one and only one channel regardless of the range of frequencies used. The medium is baseband even if it uses just a single frequency for the channel. Note that in transmitting square shaped pulse signals for the solitary channel, the baseband medium typically uses all available frequencies. (According to the French mathematician, Fourier, any wave-form, including that of a square shaped pulse, can be represented by the sum of enough sine and cosine waves of different frequencies.)

By contrast, *broadband* shares the bandwidth of the medium among a number of channels. Here, frequency division multiplexing is used to share the circuit capacity of a single transmission line. To abate attenuation, at various relay points between sender and receiver, the broadband signals are amplified rather than repeated: the amplitude (loudness) of all frequencies received is simply boosted. Prior to relaying it, broadband amplifiers do *not* interpret the received signal energy into the 1s and 0s of the individual channels. They do not recompose the original signal.

When a medium is used in broadband fashion, different bands of frequencies are dedicated to different channels. Commercial television is an example of broadband channel spectrum usage. Special equipment at both the sender and the receiver isolate the TV channels into 6-MHz pass-bands. For commercial TV reception this is the tuner. The broadband medium may be unbounded; for most data applications, it is bounded in the form of coaxial (RG-6, RG-11 and RG-59 75 ohm) cable.

In data transmission using broadband, two pass-bands of frequencies are dedicated to each sender-receiver pair. The outbound data channel from a station uses one pass-band; its inbound data channel the other. Equipment in the station transmits at the one set of dedicated frequencies and receives at (the other set of) dedicated frequencies. Even when used with cable, the equipment is referred to as *radio frequency (RF)*.

## Broadband and Head Ends

Broadband sharing of a medium may be considered when $n$ stations simultaneously need to communicate, one with any other. A total of $n$ x $(n-1)$ pass-bands is needed, two pass-bands for each pair of stations, as indicated before. If all $n$ stations communicated continuously, this use of bandwidth would be recommended. But, since data communications is bursty, (as is true for most terminal-to-computer, and computer-to-computer communications), dedicating pass-bands to channels is wasteful because of the periods of channel inactivity.

For this reason, many broadband configurations feature exactly *two* channels whose use is *contended* for by the stations as they need them. We discuss contention mechanisms in the next chapter. Limiting the number of pass-bands to two, all the stations receive at frequency band $b_r$ and transmit at frequency band $b_t$. A special device called a *head end* is needed. This device "listens" at frequency band $b_t$, shifts all the frequencies and re-transmits them at frequency band $b_r$. (In so doing, the head end also helps counter any attenuation.) Figure 6.4 illustrates two cases of a head end up-shifting a $b_t$ "reverse channel" received at the head end between 53.75 to 71.75 MHz. In the top diagram, the up-shift adds 138.25 MHz; in the middle diagram, 175.25 MHz. These new frequencies create the "forward channel" band $b_r$.

In *dual cable* applications, illustrated in the bottom diagram of Figure 6.4, the head end receives frequency band $b_t$ on one cable, and re-transmits them at frequency band $b_r$ on the second cable. (If there were no other channels on the inbound and outbound circuits, each of the two cables is being used in baseband fashion.)

Figure 6.5 illustrates this concept from the point-of-view of terminals using the services of a head end. Two terminals, A and B, are each identically equipped to share two channels. Both transmit on the same "reverse" channel, and both receive on the same "forward" channel. The head end up-shifts frequencies received on the reverse channel, transmitting them on the forward channel. (Recall, by so doing, the head end also helps counter any attenuation.) The same principle applies when there are $n$ terminals. The advantage is that they are all identically equipped.

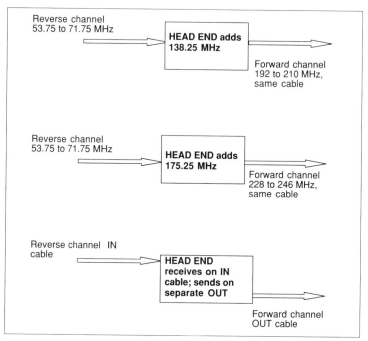

*Figure 6.4. Head end shifting frequencies within same cable (top, and middle); or relaying to separate cable ("dual cable" configuration).*

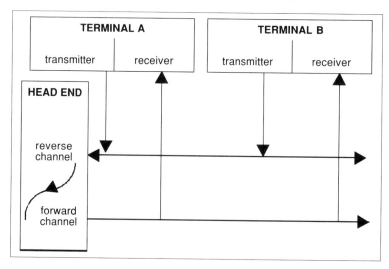

*Figure 6.5. Head end station receives frames on its incoming "reverse" channel. It transmits frames on its "forward" channel either using a higher frequency on the same cable or using another cable (dual cable).*

## Low-, Medium- and High-split Bands

When different head ends are used in different broadband applications, one may find the bandwidth of about 400 MHz divided differently between forward and reverse channels. Since broadband segments often inter-operate within a network of segments, care should be taken to ensure the compatibility of these head end conventions. One broadband application may *center split* the bandwidth with half the frequencies, 0 to 200 MHz, used for reverse channels, and the remaining half, 200 to 400 MHz, for forward channels. Another may be *low split* with 0 to less than 200 MHz (say 50 MHz) allocated for reverse channels. The *high split* uses 0 to some number greater than 200 MHz (like 350 MHz) for the reverse channels, with, therefore, a relatively smaller bandwidth remaining for the forward channels.

Some Ethernet LANs are implemented on broadband. Here, three adjacent 6-MHz pass-bands are used by stations to transmit the reverse channel. Separately, three adjacent 6-MHz pass-bands are also used for receiving the forward channel. While each 18-MHz channel certainly can support the 10 Mbit/s data rates of the *IEEE 802.3 CSMA/CD 10Broad36*, (essentially broadband Ethernet), a minimum of two adjacent 6-MHz channels can deliver 10 Mbit/s. With another standard, one solitary 6-MHz channel delivers 5-Mbit/s. On yet another, one 1.5-MHz channel is needed for 1 Mbit/s. Figure 6.6 lists commonly used pass-band frequencies occupied by the 18-MHz or 6-MHz reverse and forward broadband channels.

| Bandwidth MHz | Stations Transmit on "Reverse" Channel | MHz Added by Head end | |
|---|---|---|---|
| | | 156.25 | 192.25 |
| | | Stations Receive on "Forward" Channel | |
| 18 | 53.75 - 71.75 | 210 - 228 | 246 - 264 |
| 6 | 65.75 - 71.75 | | 258 - 264 |

*Figure 6.6. Common Broadband Frequency Allocations. Broadband CSMA/CD needs two channels totalling 36 MHz. Each 18-MHz channel supports 10 Mbit/s throughput, one for transmit, one for receive. (For 5 Mbit/s, at minimum 6-MHz is needed. At least two adjacent 6-MHz channels are needed to deliver 10 Mbit/s and at least one 1.5-MHz channel is needed to deliver 1 Mbit/s.)*

## NRZ AND RZ ENCODING

Returning now to baseband, let us compare the *Non Return to Zero (NRZ)* and *Return to Zero (RZ)* signaling methods shown in Figure 6.7. As shown in the figure, a 0 ("space" in "telegraphese") is transmitted by the bit cell containing a positive voltage, a 1 ("mark") by negative voltage. RZ differs from NRZ. In the second half of every RZ bit's time, the voltage returns to zero volts (ground).

Both the examples shown are bi-polar encoding schemes since they feature distinct positive and negative voltages. By contrast, *uni-polar NRZ* is an NRZ scheme where only one of the polarities, say +3V, is chosen for one of the binary values, with zero volts representing the other. Such a system is typical in computers.

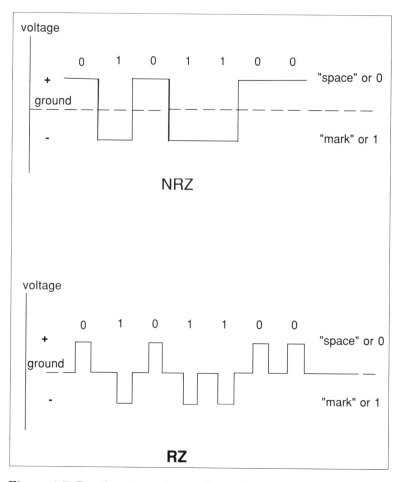

*Figure 6.7. Baseband encoding schemes Non Return to Zero (top) and Return to Zero.*

## *How Can One Get Self-clocking Data?*

With NRZ encoding a possibility exists that long sequences of bit cells of the same polarity could cause miscounts at the receiver. $n$ identical bits could be interpreted as n ± 1 bits. This could occur if the receiver's timing devices such as crystal oscillators have tolerances that despite specification are slightly different from those in the sender's equipment. Also, any jitter that may occur is not remedied with this encoding system, and could cause the loss, or insertion of bits.

By contrast, RZ is *self-clocking*. Every bit cell *must* return to zero. Consequently, even with long sequences of the same binary value, the sender and receiver will be able to always stay in sync because there is a predictable voltage transition in every bit-cell.

## *DC Charge Build-up*

A problem of a different nature that is not bit-by-bit timing related needs attention. This is the problem of cumulative electrical charge on a circuit. In NRZ, a sequence of $n$ 0s without 1s places positive voltage on the circuit for $n$ bit cell times. Likewise, a string of $n$ consecutive 1s without 0s causes the voltage on the line to be negative for $n$ bit times.

Because of this, it is possible to see the build-up of undesirable charge on the circuit.

Charge build-up is a problem even for RZ encoding. An unbroken sequence of 1s, say, causes a sequence of positive and zero voltages. With no offsetting negative voltages, the positive charge builds up.

Figure 6.8 illustrates two techniques whereby self-clocking achieves bit cell synchronization while avoiding DC charge build-up: Manchester encoding (showing two conventions) and Alternate Mark Inversion or AMI.

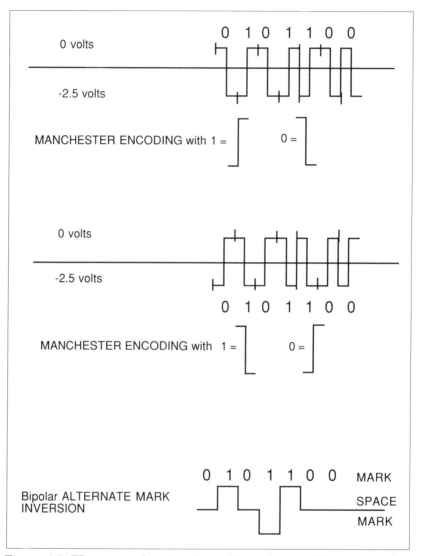

*Figure 6.8. Three more baseband encoding schemes. The top two show conventions for Manchester encoding. Bottom figure shows bipolar Alternate Mark Inversion.*

## MANCHESTER ENCODING

In *Manchester encoding*, a binary value is transmitted by presenting, successively, two voltage polarities within a bit cell. Thus, a *polarity transition* always occurs mid-cell. Two conventions apply. The encoding convention shown by the top diagram in Figure 6.8 ascribes a 0 to a bit cell whose voltage starts high or positive and ends low or negative; a 1 starts low and ends high. The other, equivalent, convention shown by the center diagram, interprets low to high as 0, and high to low as 1. Self-clocking is derived from the receiving equipment being able to synchronize its bit cells with those of the sender by using the reliable mid-cell voltage transitions. This helps eliminate the problem of jitter. As an aside, we note that when a bit is followed by an identical bit (as is the case with two 1s, or two 0s), the signal's phase changes 180° at the cell border between the two bits.

Manchester encoding, and a variant of it, *Differential Manchester* encoding are used in local area networks for their accurate bit recovery and jitter handling at high bit rates (to 100 Mbit/s).

Should a polarity transition be lacking at mid-cell, a *violation* is said to have occurred. Senders and receivers may use violations, deliberately, to signal special events such as the start and end of frames. The "J" and "K" non-data symbols are violations of 0s and 1s.

## DIFFERENTIAL MANCHESTER ENCODING ALSO SELF-CLOCKS

*Differential Manchester encoding*, (see Figure 6.9), is similar to Manchester encoding. Once again, both voltage polarities are found to occupy a bit cell, and the polarity always switches at mid-cell. However, the way 1s and 0s is ascribed is different. The interpretation occurs at the cell border between two bits. There, a change in phase, or no change, are the two criteria that signal the binary value for the second bit. Once again, two conventions are possible. In the first, a 1 is signaled by the signal's phase not changing between the bits. Conversely, a 0 is signaled by a 180° change. Using the second convention, a 0 is signaled by no phase change, and a 1 is signaled by a 180° phase change between bits.

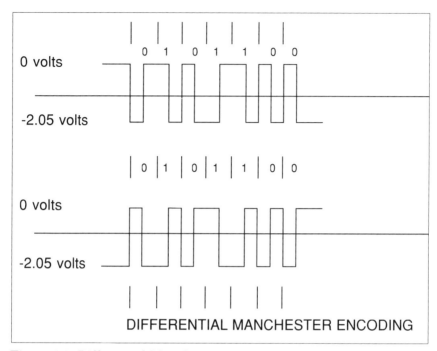

*Figure 6.9. Differential Manchester encoding scheme. Polarity always switches at mid-cell. Bit cell has a value 0 if polarities of cell's start and preceding cell's tail-end differ, value 1 otherwise.*

## AMI

An encoding scheme popular with wide area networks is *Alternate Mark Inversion (AMI)* shown in Figure 6.8. This uses ground or zero voltage to signal 0s, and the bipolar positive and negative voltages to signal 1s. AMI also has the advantages of a self-clocking encoding system in which the DC charge does not build up. Each 1 ("mark," in telegraphese) in a bit cell is denoted by the occupancy of voltage opposite in polarity to that used for the preceding mark. Hence the name. Note that the polarity inversion applies regardless of how many 0s ("spaces," in telegraphese) intervene between successive marks.

If the receiving equipment sees two consecutive 1 bits with the same polarity, a "bipolar violation" has occurred. This indicates that either an intermediate 1 bit was lost between the two, that an erroneous extra 1 bit was picked up, that equipment has malfunctioned, or, as we shall later, that the sending equipment deliberately wished to draw the attention of the receiver for some special purpose.

Because every positive voltage is followed sooner or later by an equivalent offsetting negative, the circuit using AMI is inherently DC neutral.

AMI's self-clocking derives from the reliance by the receiver on regular switches in polarity of 1s. Any drift to the timing of bit-cells that the equipment may suffer is continuously adjusted because when any 1 arrives, its accompanying voltage transition can be used to re-synchronize. The transition defines the start of a bit-cell. Note that while most receivers can ride out short intervals between successive re-synchronization, too much time, i.e., too many intervening 0s, could cause receivers to go out of sync. This is because there would then be no transition on which the receiver may re-synchronize its bit cell timing.

### B8ZS Foils the String of Zeros

The problem is resolved by using a technique known as *Binary 8 Zeros Substitution*, *B8ZS* in conjunction with AMI. B8ZS assumes that the receiving equipment can always remain synchronized with the sending equipment provided at least one voltage polarity transition appears every eight bit-cells. A sequence of eight consecutive AMI 0s contains no transitions. The sender, using B8ZS, has to replace any 00000000 by a special 8-bit pattern that does contain transitions—the pattern contains two deliberately inserted bipolar violations. Figure 6.10 illustrates this. Instead of the receiver getting eight bit-cells with zero voltage, the receiver sees 000v10v1 where each v is a 1 violating the alternate mark inversion rule. The receiver interprets this string as a healthy 00000000, and synchronizes on the 1s within the special pattern.

Note that the problems of jitter and DC content are overcome with encoding techniques such as Manchester or Differential Manchester, or AMI with B8ZS. Furthermore, the effects of attenuation are minimized since these techniques rely on the detection of discrete events like phase or polarity transitions to discern 1s from 0s.

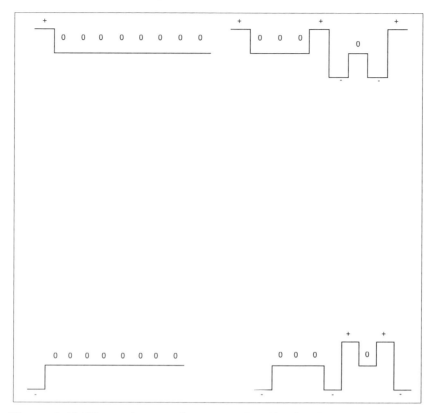

*Figure 6.10. Binary 8-zero substitution (B8ZS). Sender substitutes sequence of three 0s, then an AMI-violation bit (if polarity of last "1" before the string of eight 0s was positive, this is another positive; else a negative), "1," "0," another violation, and finally a "1." Note that AMI's DC neutrality is retained.*

## NRZI

*Non-Return-to-Zero-Inverted* (NRZI) is a bipolar encoding scheme in which each bit-cell is entirely possessed by only one of the two polarities. Pairs of cells are compared in order to define the binary value of the second cell. One binary value (chosen, by convention to be 1 or, by another convention 0) is indicated if the cell's polarity differs from its predecessor's; the opposite binary value applying if they are the same. A convention of NRZI that we see below used in conjunction with FDDI, is illustrated in Figure 6.11. Here a polarity transition between cells signals a 1.

Provided enough of the digits that require polarity transition are in the data, the receiver can use cell-to-cell transitions to synchronize cell-times.

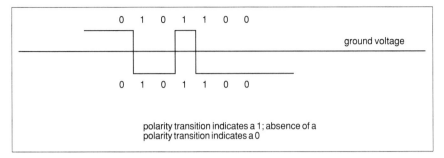

*Figure 6.11. NRZI (Non-Return-to-Zero with inversion for ones).*

## 4B/5B

The *Fiber Distributed Data Interface (FDDI)* and its derivative for Category 5 copper wire, *Twisted Pair, Physical Medium Dependent (TP-PMD)*, are standards developed by ANSI for 100-Mbit/s communications. They use the NRZI encoding system (with inversion for 1s) in a scheme that assures that the bit stream transmitted has no more than three consecutive 0s in it at any time. FDDI achieves this by mapping each hexadecimal nibble (half-byte) of user data into a 5-bit code that is actually transmitted as follows:

| 0 | 11110 | 4 | 01010 | 8 | 10010 | C | 11010 |
|---|-------|---|-------|---|-------|---|-------|
| 1 | 01001 | 5 | 01011 | 9 | 10011 | D | 11011 |
| 2 | 10100 | 6 | 01110 | A | 10110 | E | 11100 |
| 3 | 10101 | 7 | 01111 | B | 10111 | F | 11101 |

No quintet has more than two consecutive 0s within it, and no matter how one juxtaposes any two quintets together, there are never more than three 0s in a row.

An advantage of using this *4B/5B* mapping is that non-data characters such frame delimiters, and control characters such as Reset and Set can be incorporated in the transmission. Eight non-data characters may be encoded as follows:

| Line State Quiet | 00000 |
|---|---|
| Line State Idle | 11111 |
| Line State Halt | 00100 |
| Delimiter J | 11000 |
| Delimiter K | 10001 |
| Delimiter T | 01101 |
| Control Reset | 00111 |
| Control Set | 11001 |

At the receiver, the quintet is re-mapped to the original hexadecimal nibble. In practical terms, FDDI transmits and receives 5 signals for each 4 bits of user data; the *baud rate* of 125 megabaud yields a *bit rate* of 100 Mbit/s.

NRZI, coupled with the 4B/5B mapping of FDDI, provides sufficient transitions to permit the receiver to remain in synchronization with the sender.

## FSK WITH PHASE COHERENT OR PHASE CONTINUOUS

Two other types of signaling appear in the IEEE 802.4 standard, used for Token Passing Bus applications. These are called *Phase Continuous Frequency Shift Keying* and *Phase Coherent Frequency Shift Keying*. In both cases, the phase of the signal remains the same, in contrast to the Manchester and Differential Manchester encoding systems, where the phase possibly shifts 180° at the start of any bit-cell. Both these FSK techniques are usually referred to as *carrier band* rather than baseband, since they involve the frequency modulation of a carrier signal.

The 1-Mbit/s Token Passing Bus specification uses *Phase Continuous Frequency Shift Keying*. In a sense, like Manchester or Differential Manchester encoding, Phase Continuous Frequency Shift Keying is characterized by bit-cells containing one of two states in their first half, and the other state in the second half. Instead of using a signal's voltage polarity, the "high" or "low" state is defined by *frequency* in the bit-cell, high being 6.25 MHz and low 3.75 MHz. A basic 5-MHz carrier is frequency shifted by 1.25 MHz either up or down to do this.

0s are denoted by cells containing high-low, 1s by low-high. The (frequency) transition always occurs mid-cell. Receivers synchronize bit-cells on the reliability of this transition.

Manchester and differential Manchester cells containing only one frequency are violations. The standard uses deliberately encoded violations to delimit frames, creating the "J" or "K" non-data characters referred to earlier.

For 5- and 10-Mbit/s Token Passing Bus applications, *Phase Coherent Frequency Shift Keying* applies. This encoding technique differs from the last in that the signal in each bit cell is entirely at one frequency. For 5-Mbit/s applications, one finds either 5- or 10 MHz in the cell; for 10-Mbit/s applications, 10 or 20 MHz. Thus, the signaling frequencies are integrally linked to the bit rate, being identical to or double it. This is illustrated in Figure 6.12. By convention, the presence in a bit-cell of exactly one complete cycle of the lower frequency signal defines a 1; a 0 is two cycles of the higher frequency.

Regardless of whether the bit-cell is at lower or higher frequency, as can be seen in Figure 6.12, the receiver of Phase Coherent FSK signals can always rely on a signal crossing the zero-voltage state from negative to positive at the start of a bit-cell. This enables the receiver to continually re-synchronize.

Phase Coherent FSK cells containing more than one frequency are violations. Once again, deliberately encoded violations may be used to create the "J" or "K" non-data characters used to delimit frames.

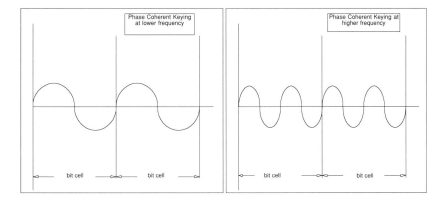

*Figure 6.12. Phase Coherent Keying.*

# 7

# Local Area Networks

In this chapter, we discuss the major local area networks, Ethernet and Token Ring. We also discuss Token Bus. StarLAN, MAP and TOP are also described.

Local area networks are high-speed communication networks characterized by limited geographical coverage. Figure 1.8 reveals that the span or reach of a LAN extends from less than 5 kilometers in a high-rise or single level building to 10 (or a few 10s of) kilometers for a campus.

A key consideration affecting the LAN user is that its ownership, operation and management are private. This distinguishes LANs from wide area networks such as the public switched telephone service, where the operative word is "public."

## ETHERNET

Ethernet was developed in the 1970s by the Xerox, DEC and Intel corporations. Based on a bus topology where physical dimensions were constrained, Ethernet was a technology that allowed data terminals or workstations access to a common medium without requiring a centralized controller. All participating equipment on the Ethernet bus monitored the action on it "cooperatively" and as peers.

Furthermore, it was the first attempt to allow for relatively high data transmission rates—measured in megabits per second rather than the kilobits per second that characterized the then level of performance for data communications, using modems on voice-grade circuits.

In the early days of its existence, Ethernet's advantage was that it allowed users to share expensive computer peripherals such as printers and disk drives among distributed computer systems.

Today, peripheral sharing is still sought, but the major use to which LANs such as Ethernet are put is the sharing of data resources. The problem and cost of providing multiple communications channels was made easier by the observation that most data applications at a terminal are intrinsically *bursty*. Periods of transaction activity follow periods of inactivity. Multiple terminals could, therefore, share a single medium.

Ethernet's origins may be traced to work done by Metcalfe and Boggs in 1976 on a 3-Mbit/s network at Xerox Corporation's Palo Alto Research Center in northern California. The *IEEE 802.3 Carrier Sense Multiple Access with Collision Detect CSMA/CD* standard was developed afterwards; it incorporates features of Ethernet in the same sense, perhaps, as Ethernet itself incorporates features of ALOHA (see Chapter 4).

The backbone of Ethernet is traditionally coaxial cable, although now EIA/TIA Category 3, 4 or 5 twisted pair cable is becoming popular. A workstation, such as a PC, is equipped with an adapter, or "network controller." This is a printed circuit card with either a "T" connector to Cheapernet (RG-58 cable), or a modular jack connector to standard unshielded twisted pair cable, or an edge connector conforming with the *Attachment Unit Interface* to a four-twisted-pair transceiver cable. Figures 5.4 and 7.1 show two of these connections respectively: one to Cheapernet, the other to the (four twisted pairs in the) transceiver cable. In the latter case, the transceiver electronics, in turn, connect the transceiver cable to the coax (thick RG-8 cable). The transceiver communicates to the adapter the data *received, transmitted, collisions and signal quality* (*heartbeat*) sensed on the thick cable. In Cheapernet and unshielded twisted pair configurations, the equivalent transceiver functions are incorporated within the adapter card itself.

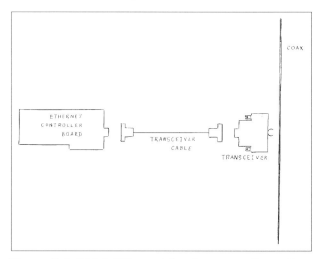

*Figure 7.1. Thick Ethernet hardware configuration.*

We now focus our attention on the mechanism by which stations gain access to the medium. The *Carrier Sense* attribute of the access method allows a station to transmit only if the medium is initially quiet. If a station listens on the medium and finds that it is not quiet, it defers from transmitting. But, transmitting only when the medium is quiet is itself no guarantee that a collision will not occur. Firstly, it is possible that another station will also start transmitting at the same time. Both stations monitor their own transmissions and recognize a collision, should one occur. There is a remedy for this eventuality which we describe below. However, there is a scenario in which the station or stations may be unaware that a collision has taken place (or, more accurately, *will* take place). We discuss this first since it provides some insight as to the importance of minimum frame length and slot time.

### The Unknown Collision Scenario

Figure 7.2 illustrates the scenario of an unknown, or undetected collision. Station "A" listens on the medium—it is quiet. It transmits its first bit. Assume a bit sent from station "B" is already on its way to A and is scheduled to arrive $n$ bit times later. If the number of bits in A's packet is not greater than $n$, A could send all its bits successfully and deduce immediately thereafter (but wrongly) that the transmission was successful. Every time A sent a bit it listened on the medium, heard no collision and so concluded that all was well. But in fact all was not well: A's and B's packets will collide on the medium. Their frames will mutually damage each other's by the time they arrive at their respective destinations.

*A listens—hears nothing,*
*assumes medium is free*
*  so transmits bit a*
*0.1 μ sec. later, it sends bit b*
*0.1 μ sec. later, bit c*
*A listens—hears nothing*
*assumes no collision*

*B listens—hears nothing,*
*assumes medium is free so*
*  transmits bit 1*
*0.1 μ sec. later it sends bit 2*
*0.1 μ sec. later bit 3*
*0.1 μ sec. later bit 4*
*0.1 μ sec. later bit 5*
*0.1 μ sec. later bit 6*
*0.1 μ sec. later bit 7*
*  and 0.1 μ sec. later bits 1, 2,*
*  a, b collide*

| A |   |   |   |   |   |   |   |   | B |
|---|---|---|---|---|---|---|---|---|---|
|   |   |   |   |   |   |   |   |   | 1 |
|   |   |   |   |   |   |   |   | 1 | 2 |
|   |   |   |   |   |   |   | 1 | 2 | 3 |
|   |   |   |   |   |   | 1 | 2 | 3 | 4 |
| a |   |   |   |   | 1 | 2 | 3 | 4 | 5 |
| b | a |   |   | 1 | 2 | 3 | 4 | 5 | 6 |
| c | b | a | 1 | 2 | 3 | 4 | 5 | 6 | 7 |
|   | c | X | X | 3 | 4 | 5 | 6 | 7 |   |
|   | X | X | X | X | 5 | 6 | 7 |   |   |
| X | X | X | X | X | X | 7 |   |   |   |
| X | X | X | X | X | X | X |   |   |   |

*Figure 7.2. "Unknown Collision" Scenario. In this hypothetical example, successive rows show the progression of bits on the medium 0.1 µ second later in time. Here, stations A and B are physically 10 "bit-times" apart, i.e., the distance an electromagnetic signal can travel in 1 µ second. For these stations then to know definitely that messages have not collided, message lengths should be at least 20 bits (twice 10).*

## Importance of Frame Length

*Minimum frame length* (equivalently, "*packet*" length) is a key concept in CSMA/CD, providing a solution to the above problem. Under IEEE 802.3 CSMA/CD, the maximum distance between any two nodes is 2,500 meters. Now, electromagnetic signals travel in copper at about $2 \times 10^8$ meters per second. The leading bit of a transmitted signal will, therefore, take 12.5 µseconds to travel between the furthest points of the network, the distance of 2500 meters. In 12.5 µseconds, at 10 Mbit/s, 125 bits can be transmitted. So, by the time the first bit reaches the furthest point, 125 bits could be on the medium.

If all senders agreed on a minimum frame length of at least twice this number of bits, then no frames could be launched simultaneously or nearly simultaneously by two stations without both stations being able to detect at least one bit colliding. In fact, IEEE 802.3's minimum frame size is 512 bits, which is more than double. Thus, the CSMA/CD minimum frame length is a factor of the maximum distance, speed of signal propagation and the speed of the LAN. It is large enough to detect any collision possible should two stations attempt to transmit simultaneously.

## Collisions

We saw that the Carrier Sense and Collision Detect functions of CSMA/CD come into play prior to and during transmission, and detect or prevent "obvious" collisions. Using a minimum frame length helps assure the detection of all potential collisions, including the "not-so-obvious" ones described earlier.

Collisions occur when two stations (unknowingly) transmit simultaneously. The methods of detection of a collision depend on whether the medium is used in baseband or broadband fashion. Baseband collisions are revealed by a direct current (DC) level greater than that of a single transmitter. Broadband collisions are detected by the transmitter comparing what it sent on reverse channel $f_1$ with what it receives on forward channel $f_2$ and finding the two different.

While CSMA/CD's protocol allows shared access to the medium, it is *not deterministic*. As can be seen from the following explanation, it is difficult to predict exactly when an intended transmission will take place.

Firstly, the station wishing to transmit "senses" the carrier, i.e., listens to, the communication medium. If data are presently being carried, the station defers until silence is detected. The amount of wait is variable, although the message can occupy the medium for no more than about 1.2 milliseconds. (This is a factor of the maximum message length which, in CSMA/CD, is 1,500 octets). Only then does the waiting station transmit, listening to the medium and, of course, hoping to hear no collision.

If a collision is detected, the station transmits a 32-bit jamming signal on the medium for a short time. This is long enough to guarantee that other stations will recognize that a collision has occurred. The station "backs off" or waits a random time interval. Then, as before, it listens and waits for the medium to become silent before trying to re-transmit.

## Exponential Back Off Longer When Busy

The random interval is calculated using an *exponential back-off algorithm*. On the first occurrence of a collision, the wait is 0 or 1 *slot time*, chosen with equal probability. Slot time is the time taken to transmit a minimum length frame. After the next consecutive collision, where "consecutive" implies that no frame was successfully transmitted since the last collision, the wait is randomly chosen from a list that contains twice as many choices of wait times as the previous time. The entries in the list are choices of wait times that start with 0 and increase by one slot time per entry. In this case (after two consecutive collisions), the list of waits is 0, 1, 2 or 3 slot times. Note that the probability is 50% that the wait chosen will be longer than the one that just occurred, since half of the choices (here, 2 or 3 slot times) involve longer waits. This pattern repeats. With the third consecutive collision, the wait is selected randomly from a list that has twice again as many choices, namely eight. These are 0, 1, 2, ..., 6 or 7 slot times, and the probability of a choice resulting in a longer wait than the preceding one is again 50%, or 4 in 8. While consecutive collisions are occurring, this process continues until ten consecutive collisions occur. Then the wait is selected from one of 0, 1, 2, ..., 1022 or 1023 slot times, where again the probability is 50% (512 in 1024) that the selected wait will be longer than the one immediately preceding. The eleventh (and beyond the eleventh) consecutive collision is treated as for the tenth. But, after 16 collisions, any further attempt to re-transmit is abandoned.

## TOP

In typical office environments, the non-deterministic nature of the access is not found to be a hardship, particularly with lightly loaded networks. The *Technical and Office Protocol* or TOP uses the IEEE 802.3 standard specifications for its bottom two layers of functions, corresponding to the data link and physical layers of the OSI Reference Model. Initiated and sponsored by a user, Boeing Computer Services, TOP is a protocol suite made up of various standards listed in Table 7.1. One of the objectives of the TOP configuration is to free users from dependence on proprietary vendor products. There are a number of standard OSI protocols incorporated in TOP.

| Layer | Protocol |
| --- | --- |
| 7 | ISO FTAM (DP) 8571 File Transfer Protocol |
| 6 | null; uses ASCII and binary encoding |
| 5 | ISO Session (IS) 8372 Basic Combined Subset and Session Kernel; full duplex |
| 4 | ISO Transport (IS) 8073 Class IV |
| 3 | ISO Internet (DIS) 8473 Connectionless and for X.25—Sub-network Dependent Convergence Protocol |
| 2 | ISO Logical Link Control (DIS) 8802-2 (IEEE 802.2) Type 1, Class 1 |
| 1 | ISO CSMA/CD (DIS) 8802-3 (IEEE 802.3 CSMA/CD 10Base5) |

*Table 7.1. TOP standards.*

# 1BASE5

The IEEE CSMA/CD 1-Mbit/s standard is referred to as 1Base5. Prior to the advent of EIA/TIA Category 3, 4 and 5 twisted pair, it offered a lower-cost Ethernet alternative to coaxial cable, albeit at a slower bit rate. The cable is operated baseband. After EIA/TIA Category 3, 4 and 5 appeared on the market, users could obtain 10BaseT, a full 10-Mbit/s twisted pair implementation of CSMA/CD.

The original developer and promoter of the 1Base5 standard was AT&T. AT&T marketed it under the name StarLAN. It was made available to and marketed commercially by other vendors as well.

1Base5 networks physically resemble a star topology in the way stations and hubs (nodes) are linked together and to other hubs. Two twisted pairs connect a station to a hub, one pair for receiving, the other for transmitting to it. Using 25 AWG twisted pair, the stations are located a radial distance of up to 250 meters (800 feet) from a hub. Hubs in turn are linked hierarchically. Two twisted pairs are also used for the hub-to-hub connections. At the top of the hierarchy, the head end node receives "reverse channel" transmissions from stations and hubs. Prior to reaching the head end, signals received from multiple stations at a hub are logically ORd together and form a single output from it. Like other hubs, the head end logically ORs signals inbound to it and aggregates them. Its outbound circuit or circuits define the first leg of the forward transmissions (see Figure 7.3). A hub receives only one forward transmission input. It copies that onto each of its lower tributaries.

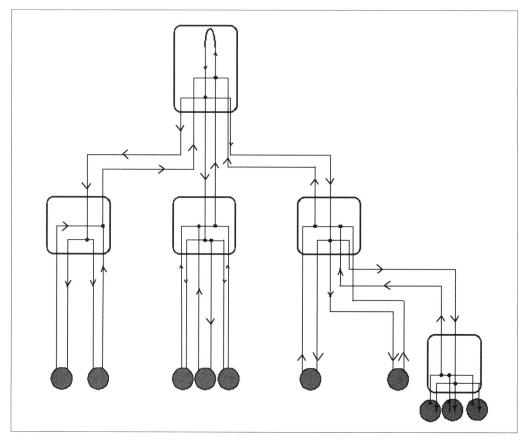

*Figure 7.3. 1Base5 topology. At each hub from the bottom moving up, each terminal's signal is ORd with others. If more than one signal is present simultaneously, the hub generates a "collision" signal. From the top, the head end, then each hub, forwards and shares the consolidated ("ORd") signal among downstream hubs.*

In this topology, single station failures do not disable the entire network. The electrical topology is bus-like. Each hub performs an electrical "OR" combination of its inputs. Table 7.2 describes the output from the hub for various combinations of input signals:

| INPUT | OUTPUT | | |
|---|---|---|---|
| | IDLE | VALID MANCHESTER CODE | COLLISION (MANCHESTER VIOLATION) |
| All pairs IDLE | X | | |
| One pair valid Manchester code, all other pairs IDLE | | X | |
| Two or more pairs not IDLE | | | X |

*Table 7.2.*

A disadvantage of the 1Base5 is that, at 1-Mbit/s, it is incompatible with 10-Mbit/s 10Base5 products. An advantage, however, is the low cost of its cabling and of connectors such as the standard RJ-45 telephone connector. Given a choice in today's environment, the user should opt for 10BaseT.

## RINGS, NOTABLY TOKEN RING

*Ring* topologies present three implementation choices—token ring, register insertion and slotted ring.

Register insertion and slotted ring were described in Chapter 4. In practice, these ring approaches have not proven popular or practical for commercial application.

*Token Ring*, however, has a sizable share of market. The essence of token passing is that a special frame—the *token*—circulates among contenders for access to the medium, and possession of it permits access to the medium. Token passing has the advantages of no contention—there are no collisions. One may predict exactly when a user will gain access to the medium. For this reason, token passing is said to be *deterministic*.

In the *Token Passing Ring* standard defined by the IEEE committee 802.5 (and, equivalently, by ISO 8802-5), stations are connected together in a ring. Messages circulate in a single direction from station to station round the ring. Transmission rates are either 4 or 16 Mbit/s. Stations receive messages from their *nearest active upstream neighbor*. Each station acts as a repeater and sends messages it receives to the next station downstream. The last node downstream is the first node upstream.

The two formats for IEEE 802.5 frames are shown in Figures 7.4 and 7.5. One format is for the token and one for the information frame. The station receiving an information frame from its upstream neighbor re-transmits it (repeats it, bit-by-bit) to the downstream station. If it is the addressee—recognizable from the *Destination Address*—the station simultaneously copies the data into its memory for its own use. It sets "Address Recognized" and Frame Copied" bits in the Frame Status byte. The repeating process continues round the ring until the frame arrives at the station that originated it—recognized from the frame's *Source Address*. That station removes the frame simply by not re-transmitting. Instead, the station sends a token.

**TOKEN**

| Physical header | MAC header | Physical trailer |
|-----------------|------------|------------------|
| SD | AC | ED |

SD   Start Delimiter octet JK0JK000
"J" and "K" are not natural bits; instead they are violations of Differential Manchester code.
The "J" is the first "bit " of the octet to be transmitted

AC   Access Control octet RRRMTPPP with Ps transmitted first

PPP   Priority, from 0 through 7
T     0 = Token in use. ( Otherwise, 1 = Information Frame in use)
M     1 = Monitoring
RRR   Priority level of token requested by waiting station, from 0 through 7

ED   Ending Delimiter octet JK1JK1IE
(As for SD,  "J" and "K" are not natural bits; instead they are violations of Differential Manchester code.
The  "J" is the first "bit " of the octet to be transmitted)
I = 1 last frame in sequence
I = 0 more follows
E = 1 error
E = 0 no error

*Figure 7.4. Structure of token in IEEE 802.5 (Token Passing Ring).*

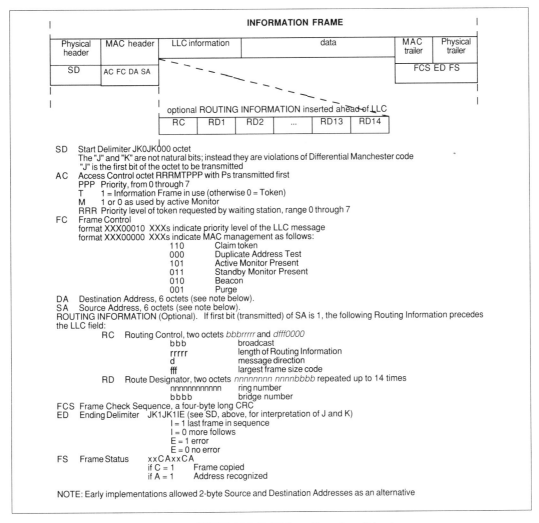

*Figure 7.5. Information Frame IEEE 802.5 (Token Passing Ring).*

## Priority in the Ring

Priority is supported in the Token Ring by according stations priority numbers. The token itself carries two fields within it to manage priority. Receipt of the token is a permit to transmit provided the priority of the station receiving it is high enough. If the station receiving the token does not have a message to transmit, it re-transmits the token downstream. If it does, and the *priority* of the station is equal to or greater than that indicated by the three priority bits in the token, the station *seizes* the token. It removes the token from the ring, by changing it into an information frame (by changing the token's T bit from 0 to 1 and by appending its message in the frame).

If the station does not have high enough priority to seize the token, it must pass it on. In so doing, however, it may request that a token of its priority be released. It does this by amending the "requested" field of the token, (RRR bits in the diagram of Figure 7.4), with its own priority. Note that the station may only do this if its priority is greater than these three "requested" bits. In either event, it then repeats the amended-or-not token. Stations that generate the token after removing an information frame, set its priority equal to the requested bits.

### Monitor Functions Keep the Ring Operating

Once a token has completed a circuit of the ring without being seized, a *monitor* station will reset the token's priority and requested fields to the lowest level.

How does a station become a monitor? Normal operational stations perform standby or active monitor duties. One duty of a *standby monitor* is to start a 7-second timer. If the station receives a special network management "Active_Monitor_Present" frame before the timer elapses, it sends a Standby_Monitor_Present frame. But if no Active_Monitor_Present frame is received prior to the expiry of the timer, the station transmits an Active_Monitor_Present frame instead. It then restarts the timer. A station receiving its own Active_Monitor_Present frame (after a full-circuit of the token ring) becomes the active monitor.

What are active monitor functions? Only one operational station may be the active monitor: it assures that there is no more than one! Its prime responsibility is to ensure that there are no missing or duplicate tokens, and no endlessly circulating information frames.

The active monitor sets the maximum interval timer for a token to return. It releases a new token if it determines that the token is missing, as indicated by the timer elapsing without the monitor having received a token.

By setting the "Monitor" bit in an information frame, lost, or endlessly circulating messages are avoided. The active monitor does this by removing incoming frames with already-set Monitor bits.

The monitor issues frequent "Active_Monitor_Present" frames. It broadcasts "Nearest_Active_Upstream_Neighbor" NAUN frames every 7 seconds. This is used for the Beaconing procedure. Each active station maintains two key addresses: its own and the address of its NAUN. These are used in the Beaconing procedure to repair a network when a station fails. If a station suspects that its NAUN has failed, it sends a beacon frame to it. The suspect station must go off-line and do a self-test.

## Physical Addresses

There is only one physical address per node. This is present in the adapter card and is a 6-byte field. Three bytes (or, strictly speaking, 22 bits) of the field are allocated by the IEEE, the second half by the adapter's manufacturer. The field begins with a hexadecimal 10 and is followed by a 2-byte manufacturer's code in firmware. For example, IBM is hex 005A and DEC hex 00D4. Locally administered addresses (software) are recognized by the first 2 bytes being in range hex 4000 to 7FFF.

## Functional Addresses

Physical station addresses are not the only addresses needed to operate the network. There are also *functional addresses* used, for example, to identify the station that is the active monitor. To signal these functional addresses, the first four bytes are hex C0000000, while the next 2 bytes address the different functions (see Table 7.3):

| Hex | Function |
|------|----------------------|
| 2000 | LAN Manager |
| 1000 | MAU |
| 0100 | Bridge |
| 0080 | NETBIOS |
| 0010 | Config Report Server |
| 0008 | Ring Error Monitor |
| 0002 | Ring Parameter Server |
| 0001 | Active Monitor |

*Table 7.3.*

## TOKEN PASSING BUS

Possibly the lowest cost LAN, in terms of the costs of adapter cards and cabling, is that of the IEEE 802.4 or ISO 8802-4 *Token Passing Bus*. The archetype of the network is represented by the 2.5-Mbit/s ARCNET, developed by the Datapoint Corporation in the late 1970s.

Token Passing Bus combines the good features of 802.3 (the bus) and of 802.5 (the deterministic access method). The cabling is a simple, passive bus. No repeater functions are required of the stations as in 802.5.

Like the token in 802.5, the 802.4 token is a frame with no user data, but in this case the token does contain destination and source addresses. Figure 7.6 illustrates the format of the 802.4 frame.

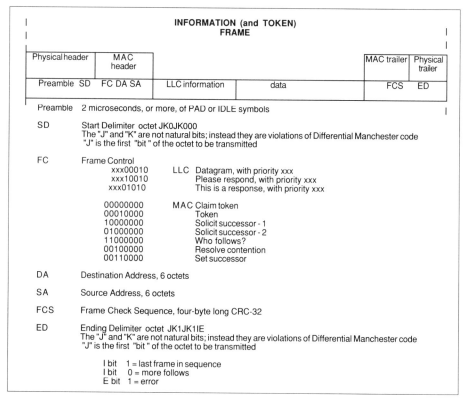

*Figure 7.6. Information/Token Frame IEEE 802.4 (Token Passing Bus).*

All stations receive the token at the same time—only the identified destination station acts on it, however. Stations are uniquely numbered from 0 to 255 using hardware switches on the adapter card. The token is passed in a logical ring fashion from station to station in a numerical sequence. The station with the next lowest number is the destination. Figure 7.7 shows a logical ring with stations 50, 40, 21, 19, 06 and 01.

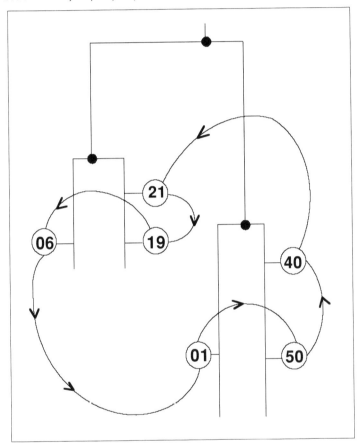

*Figure 7.7. Token Passing Bus 802.4. Each station maintains three addresses. In addition to its own number, it knows its successor station's number and its predecessor station's number. A station transmits an information frame only after receiving a token from its predecessor. After sending the information frame, the station sends a token frame to its successor.*

## Maintaining a Ring in 802.4

Each station maintains three addresses: its own station number, its successor's number, and its predecessor number.

On receipt of the token, a station with an information frame to transmit may do so. After transmitting, the sender transmits the token to its successor. Two advantages of the protocol are that no collisions are possible and that it is not possible to lose a token. The last sender of the token re-transmits it if it does not hear its successor transmitting either an information frame or a token. It listens again. If there is still silence, it assumes that its successor left the network. Using the *who-follows?* procedure as described below, it solicits the identity of a new successor. The solicitor and new successor splice together a new logical ring with the other stations. The token is sent to this new successor.

### How Logical Ring Breaks are Patched

*Who follows the departed successor?* To find out, the soliciting station sends a "who follows?" frame, naming its non-responding successor number. All stations hear this (as they do all transmissions). Only the station with the matching predecessor number responds. It sends a set_successor frame, naming itself as the follower, to the solicitor. The solicitor, in turn, amends its successor number to be this responder. It then sends the token to this new successor. The latter amends its predecessor number to be the solicitor, thereby completing the splice.

If the solicitor receives no "set_successor" frames, it repeats the "who follows?" If there still is no response, the *solicit a successor* procedure ensues. We examine this procedure to see how any new station may be added to the logical ring.

### How to Add New Names

The *solicit a successor* procedure enables new stations to be added periodically to the logical ring. Every station periodically issues solicit_successor frames. All stations hear this solicitation and compare their own station numbers to the two in the frame: the solicitor's station number and that of its current successor. (The only time that both numbers in the frame are the same, i.e., where the solicitor's station number itself is duplicated in the field marked "successor," is after a non-responsive *who follows?* has happened—see prior paragraph). If the station's number is between the two, it sends the solicitor a set_successor frame. The solicitor records the new successor number and sends it the token. For the new successor, its predecessor now is the solicitor, and its successor is the solicitor's previous successor number.

## Collisions Can Occur

If two or more stations simultaneously send set_successor frames, the solicitor gets a garbled response. The solicitor issues a *resolve_contention* frame. Using the lowest order two bits in its address to define a number, each colliding station first waits that number (0, 1, 2, or 3) of slot times before re-sending its set_successor frame. The delays helps the responders to get their messages to the solicitor in a non-overlapping time slot. If yet another collision occurs, the solicitor repeats its issue of the *resolve_contention* frame. Now, using the next two higher bits in its address to find the number of slot times it must first wait, a responder again sends set_successor frames after 0, 1, 2, or 3 slot times. This process continues interactively, moving up the address until no more collisions occur.

To delete a station from the logical ring, the exiting station, on receipt of the token, sends a set_successor frame to its predecessor. On receipt of this set_successor frame, the predecessor splices to the exiting node's successor by replacing its successor number with the successor number of the exiting station.

## MAP

One of the better known implementations involving the use of IEEE 802.4 is *Manufacturing Automation Protocol*, or *MAP*. It is a standard initiated by a user for use in manufacturing and industrial environments. Initial leadership for its development and support came from the General Motors corporation. Later, responsibility for the administration of the MAP standard was taken over by the Society for Mechanical Engineering, SME.

MAP offers 802.4 in either a broadband, or carrier band Token Bus implementation. For broadband use, the encoding is known as Multi-level Duo-binary AM/PSK. Multiple non-MAP applications may coexist on the broadband cable.

The encoding used for carrier band depends on the speed of MAP chosen. For the 5- or 10-Mbit/s single channel use, Phase coherent encoding is used. Phase continuous applies to the 1-Mbit/s system. No application other than MAP is on the cable.

Like TOP, MAP identifies specific ISO and IEEE standards at all the 7 layers of the ISO Reference Model; see Table 7.4.

| 7 | ISO FTAM (DP) 8571 File Transfer Protocol, Manufacturing Messaging Format Standard (MMFS), and Common Application Service Elements (CASE) |
|---|---|
| 6 | null; uses ASCII and binary encoding |
| 5 | ISO Session (IS) 8372 Basic Combined Subset and Session Kernel; full-duplex |
| 4 | ISO Transport (IS) 8073 Class IV |
| 3 | ISO Internet (DIS) 8473 Connectionless and for X.25—Sub-network Dependent Convergence Protocol |
| 2 | ISO Logical Link Control (DIS) 8802-2 (IEEE 802.2) Type 1, Class 1 |
| 1 | ISO Token Passing Bus (DIS) 8802-4 (IEEE 802.4) |

*Table 7.4. ISO and IEEE Standards for MAP.*

# 8

# Metropolitan Area Networks

In this chapter we discuss Metropolitan Area Networks. These networks evolved primarily to permit LANs to interconnect across a metropolis or a county. There are two major technologies we look at: DQDB and FDDI. The Bellcore-defined Switched Multi-megabit Data Services are predicated on using one of these technologies, DQDB.

While SMDS is discussed in this chapter, the extent to which MANs interconnect with each other via wide area capabilities such as SONET, ATM, and broadband ISDN is discussed in the next chapter.

## DQDB AND FDDI ARE THE MANs

*Distributed Queue Dual Bus (DQDB)* is the technology adopted in 1990 by the IEEE 802.6 committee, and by ISO 8802-6, as the MAN standard. DQDB has its origins in a technology called QPSX, Queued Packet and Synchronous Exchange, developed in the mid-1980s in Western Australia by university researchers cooperating with the Australian telecommunications industry.

*Fiber Distributed Data Interface, FDDI* was developed in the United States and standardized by the ANSI X3T9.5 committee. Motivation for its development was not only the interconnection of LANs but the need for a high-speed network to transfer complex images, and for the internal transfer at high-speed of huge volumes of data by computer systems with peripherals such as DASD disk storage systems not physically adjacent to the host.

Since DQDB is a multiplexing method, its medium is not limited to any one type. It operates either on fiber-optic facilities or on copper using 44.736-Mbit/s T3 facilities (described in *Chapter 9—Wide Area Networks*).

Of course, FDDI operates on a fiber-optic medium. But FDDI has a copper-wire counterpart called TP-PMD, Twisted Pair—Physical Medium Dependent. This uses EIA/TIA Category 5 cable.

Let us focus now on DQDB and return later to FDDI.

### DQDB for both Isochronous and Delay Insensitive Data

DQDB is a communications technology that supports both *connection-oriented* and *connectionless* message transfer. As a LAN-to-LAN transport it supports the *connectionless* links of LANs. The transfer of data messages between stations on two LANs is handled by DQDB to appear as if they were on the same LAN. These messages do not mandate prior establishment of circuits or virtual circuits, as is the case with voice calls, or packet-switched X.25 calls.

However, DQDB does have the potential for carrying *isochronous* data such as voice or video. As we shall see, there are two modes in which users may gain access to the DQDB transport: by *pre-arbitration* for isochronous voice/video and by *queued arbitration* for non-isochronous applications. The pre-arbitration mode is *connection-oriented*.

### DQDB Architecture

The architecture of DQDB is illustrated in Figure 8.1. The "dual bus" part of its name alludes to the two buses (named Bus A and Bus B in the figure) accessible to every node or station. These buses do not pass through each node; they pass *by* them. From a reliability viewpoint, this means that the failure of an individual node cannot incapacitate the network.

While the buses are physically identical and symmetrically installed, they will not be transmitting the same identical data.

Empty data frames (slots) are continuously generated by the two *frame sources*. The frame sources are stations at the head of each bus. At the *sink* tail-end of each bus, the frames are annihilated.

Note that the diagram illustrates DQDB's logical structure. Physically, one may see three implementations. The first of these is known as the *open dual bus* and looks the same as the logical structure shown in the diagram. The other two are known as the *point-to-point bus*, and the *folded*, or *looped dual bus*. Of these, the second configuration, point-to-point, features exactly two stations, each symmetrically acting as frame source on the one bus, and as sink on the other. The folded, or looped dual bus, is the third; it places the frame sources and sinks of both buses within the same station. The two buses appear to form a counter-rotating ring.

The open dual bus configuration is the most general configuration. It offers a modicum of recovery should the buses between any two nodes be severed. Two islands of nodes will then be formed. The stations immediately to either side of the break become frame sources and sinks servicing their respective islands. Of course, in this scenario there is no communication between the two islands.

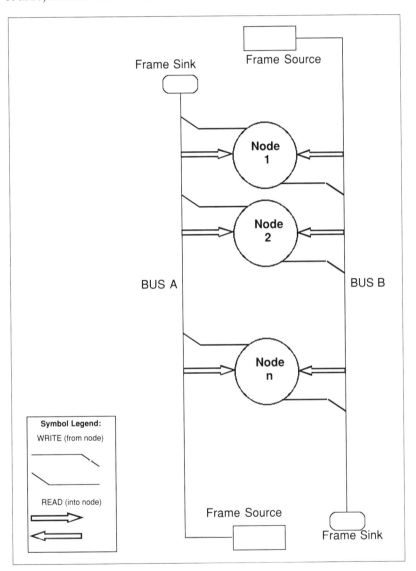

*Figure 8.1. 802.6 MAN DQDB.*

Addressing the reliability question again, an advantage of the folded, or looped dual bus configuration is that should one of the buses be severed, messages can still get to their destinations on the other bus, if not directly then via the head end station. Isolation into islands is averted.

## How DQDB Works

The frames generated by the sources are empty "containers" for messages to be placed in by stations on the bus. Messages may be read by any of the stations downstream: the empty frames and messages travel down each bus uni-directionally from their source to a *sink* where they terminate. In the diagram, Bus B's frames first travel past node 1, then past node 2 and so on until finally past node *n*; Bus A's frames travel in the opposite direction starting first at node *n* and arriving last at node 1.

Each node may peek non-destructively at the frames as they go by on either, or both buses, and examine their headers. A header contains indicators that the frame (synonymously "slot" or "cell") is vacant or not. If the slot has been occupied by a message from an upstream node, the header indicates this fact and also what node is its destination. The destination node copies the message to its own memory. Copying does not destroy the message on the bus.

Whether or not the node is the message destination, the node uses information from all passing headers to record the source addresses of the messages. Each node keeps an updated table to use for locating stations it may later want to send messages to—noting on which bus they are, downstream of it.

Nodes read and write. To write, a node logically "ORs" its message with, and replaces the contents of, an empty frame. But DQDB is "fair": a node may not acquire an empty frame that has been "reserved" by another node downstream. This is the essence of the *queued arbitration* access described next. The access method applies to non-isochronous data traffic only. (By contrast, all *pre-arbitrated* frames appear busy to most nodes: only isochronous data nodes may act on them).

### Reserving a Frame

How does a node know that nodes downstream of it have reserved frames? The answer is "via the other bus." Each time a node needs an empty frame to send a message downstream on Bus A, it requests a frame (by setting a bit in the header of a frame) on Bus B. (Depending on the node's priority (see below), the bit is placed in a 3-bit sub-field of the header, provided that bit position was previously unused! Failing that, the node must wait for a frame with a 0 in the sub-field. See Figure 8.2 to refer to the 3-bit sub-field of the header's Access Control Field, titled "Request Priority Level.")

The DQDB frame is 53-octets long. It is prefaced by a header. The payload is in the last 48 octets.

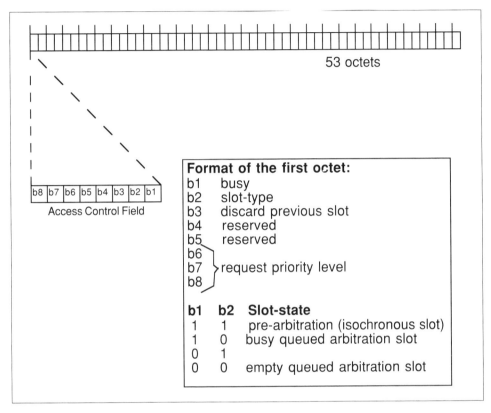

*Figure 8.2. Slot structure in DQDB.*

## First Come First Served

We describe now how DQDB is a fair *first-come-first-served* access method for non-isochronous, queued arbitration applications. We noted above that stations may be accorded different levels of priority. DQDB supports three levels. The priority gives the network manager flexibility. For example, some stations may be more critical for network survival. Traffic requests from stations of the highest priority must be satisfied first, then all stations of second priority, before, finally, any stations of the lowest priority.

A set of three request counters, one for each priority level, plus a countdown counter are maintained by the node for each bus. Thus, there are eight counters in total. The header passing on Bus B may include a request. If so, the node increments one of the three request counters. The requests were made by nodes upstream of it on Bus B. Those nodes are *downstream* of it on Bus A and are requesting empty Bus A slots to enable them to send messages downstream of *them* on that Bus.

Symmetrically, requests in headers passing by on Bus A, cause the node to increment the applicable counter of requests (at the priority level requested) for Bus B empty slots.

A slot is empty, or not, as indicated by (bits in) its header. As each empty slot passes a node, the node decrements the counter of the highest priority requests for the slot. If that counter was zero, the node decrements the counter of requests for the next highest priority.

## Getting on a DQDB Bus

What does a node do to send a message downstream on Bus A? The node must obtain an empty frame that had not been reserved earlier by any Bus-A nodes downstream of it. It examines the counters for higher or equal priority requests; if these counts are zero, the node may seize the next empty frame. Otherwise, the node must alert nodes (upstream of it on Bus A) of its request and its priority level. (To do this, it waits for a slot to appear on Bus B with an unused "Request" bit (0) in its header sub-field. One of these 3 bits corresponds to the node's priority level. The node sets it to 1). Then, the node sums up the contents of all request counters for Bus A, except those of lower priority. The result becomes the start of a *countdown* counter.

In addition to maintaining the request counters as before, the node *decrements* the countdown counter every time an empty frame passes the node on Bus A. But the node also increments it any time it sees a request made by a *higher* priority node upstream of it on Bus B. After the countdown counter reaches zero, sufficient empty frames have been passed to satisfy all the requests from nodes of higher priority downstream on Bus A, plus any requests made earlier in time by nodes of the same priority. This node's turn to use the next empty frame will have arrived.

## Isochronous Messages

*Isochronous* messages are those for which the user cannot tolerate delay, or variations in the delay. Voice and video are two applications that suffer should there be delay greater than a few milliseconds between transmission and reception, it being worse, or even unacceptable if it varies with every transmission. DQDB has a capability for delivering isochronous messages. This is a *connection-oriented* service. Prior to the communication, a call is established. To do so, the node initiating an isochronous connection first communicates with a frame source. The frame source assigns a virtual channel indicator (VCI) to the node and its partner. The VCI is a 20-bit field. The frame source thereafter generates *pre-arbitrated frames* for this particular virtual circuit number, at the rate of one every 125 microseconds. The frame source will have advised the node which octet (or octets) within these frames it should use for its voice or video message.

A pre-arbitrated, isochronous frame is recognized by bits in the frame's header (1s in the first two bits). The 20-bit virtual channel identifier appears within the first 5 octets of the frame.

Unlike the procedure followed for non-isochronous messages described earlier, nodes do not request slots to communicate on their assigned isochronous virtual channel. First, to provide voice, as we shall see in the next Chapter, a technique called *Pulse Coded Modulation* may be used. As in today's telephone networks, voice is sampled (creating octet samples) 8,000 times per second. PBX nodes using DQDB may be assigned any or all of the 48 octets in each pre-arbitrated frame for up to 48 voice circuits. Once again, a frame source must have assigned the octet-locations.

## FIBER DISTRIBUTED DATA INTERFACE (FDDI)

*Fiber Distributed Data Interface*, developed by the ANSI X3T9.5 committee, uses the architecture of IEEE 802.2 Logical Link Control above the physical Medium Access Control layer. Because of this, FDDI is similar, although not identical, to the IEEE 802.5 Token Passing Ring standard. The frame format is similar to that of 802.5 shown in Figure 7.4, incorporating a preamble for synchronization similar in function to the preamble of the 802.4 frame (Figure 7.7).

## FDDI'S FEATURES

Physically, the Fiber Distributed Data Interface supports a ring of stations with a maximum circumference of 100 kilometers. The optical fiber used has typically a 62.5-μm core diameter with 125-μm cladding diameter (also 50-/125-μm and 100-/140-μm are supported in the standard). The source for the 1300-nanometer wavelength light is a light emitting diode if multimode fiber is used. The standard also supports monomode fiber; in this case a laser is the light source.

## FDDI High-Performance Low Error Rate

The data transmission speed is 100 Mbit/s. The maximum frame length is 4,500 octets. Prior to actual transmission, each 4 bits or "symbol" of user data is mapped to a 5-bit quintet using the 4B/5B encoding method described in Chapter 6. At the destination, the received quintet is inversely re-mapped to the original symbol. *Non-Return-to-Zero-Inverted* coding, also described in Chapter 6, is the encoding technique used on the medium. Delivering 100 Mbit/s, the network actually operates at 125 megabaud.

With optical fiber, the bit error rate is low, at 1 in $10^{12}$.

Figure 8.3 shows FDDI's topology consisting of dual counter-rotating rings. For this reason, although the maximum circumference of the ring is 100 kilometers, the maximum total length of fiber is 200 kilometers. Messages generally circulate on the outer ring, with the inner ring remaining idle, and standing by for back-up.

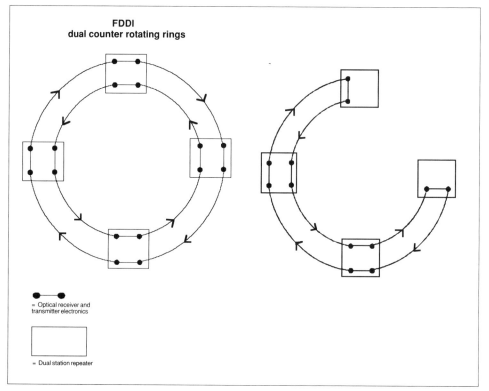

*Figure 8.3. FDDI, illustrating self-healing feature. In the right-hand sketch, the link between the station at "noon" and that at "3 o'clock" has been severed.*

### Similarities to Token Ring

Each FDDI station is a repeater. As in Token Ring, it outputs the messages it receives, except if the input was originally created by the node. FDDI's Medium Access Control is similar, but not identical to that of IEEE 802.5, token passing ring. One difference is in the timing of token releases. The sender releases a token at the end of the transmission rather than after removing the circulated, original message. Token privileges vary with the degree of network load, as measured by the station itself. According to this load, some stations may avail themselves of more transmitting time.

### Single or Dual Attachment Stations

Each FDDI station is either a Class A or Class B station. Class A stations are called *dual attachment stations* since they connect to both rings; Class B stations, *single attachment stations*, only connect to one ring, the primary, "outer," ring. The lower cost of the Class B station is reflected in its lower reliability when compared to Class A.

In fact, for reliability reasons, each Class B station is usually configured physically as a point in a star with a Class A station at its hub. In this case, the Class B's input and output fibers both emanate from and terminate in the same Class A station. A Class A station may, therefore, be used as a wiring concentrator, connecting one or more than one Class B station. The primary cable threads through the wiring concentrator, then through a single Class B station, returning to the wiring concentrator before threading through the next Class B station, then back to the wiring concentrator and so on.

### Handling Failures; Self-healing

Breaks in the fiber can be handled in three ways depending on where they occur, and how many rings are affected.

If the primary ring is severed on a "lobe" to a star-configured Class B station or if the Class B station itself fails, this does not necessarily incapacitate the ring; the faulty station or lobe may be patched around at the Class A station or concentrator. If the primary ring alone is severed on any other link (e.g., between two Class A stations), the network could switch to the remaining functional ring. However, access would then be lost to all Class B stations. As an alternative, FDDI offers a "*self-heal*"ing feature. This is also the remedy if both rings are jointly severed. Referring to the right-hand sketch in Figure 8.3, the two (Class A) stations on either side of the break heal the ring by patching (optic-electrically within each station) between the two rings to make a single new ring, almost twice as long as the primary. The entire complement of stations is still reachable, (except for any Class B stations on the segment of the failed primary ring that had previously linked the two healing stations).

An FDDI network may contain a maximum of 1000 physical ring connections. At most 500 Class A or 1000 Class B stations may be in the network. Class A stations, of course, have two connections, one per ring. The maximum distance between any two repeaters is 2 kilometers.

## FDDI II

An extension to FDDI called *FDDI II* is underway but does not appear to be drawing much support from the industry. FDDI II capabilities permit isochronous services such as voice, video and compressed video, to be multiplexed with packet data. FDDI stations measure the time between successive appearances of the token. Every station compares the measured token rotation time versus a target. If the ring was lightly loaded, the token appears sooner than expected. The station then may avail itself of any extra time. Thus, an advantage of FDDI is that it makes its network resources available as the capacity varies. The *target token rotation time* is derived at by a process that polls all the stations in the ring. TTRT is set at the initialization of the network. In practice, FDDI's isochronous class of service is little used.

## SWITCHED MULTI-MEGABIT DATA SERVICE (SMDS)

The major commercial offering for DQDB type public services is *Switched Multi-megabit Data Service*. Strictly speaking, as a service, SMDS is independent of technology; however, it appears to have been designed with the capabilities of DQDB clearly in mind. Within metropolitan domains, it enables common carriers to offer an alternative to *Frame Relay*, with higher throughput rates that extend to 34 Mbit/s and 150 Mbit/s. (Frame Relay is described in the next Chapter). In terms of "service roll-out," the equipment for which SMDS interface cards will be initially available include devices that today use Frame Relay services, e.g., routers, gateways, and minicomputers.

SMDS operates on either copper-based T3 facilities or optical fiber. T1 or T3 access lines link the service to equipment on the customer's premises. Usually, the customer premises equipment is a router shared by multiple stations on a LAN.

The driving application for SMDS is LAN interconnection within a metropolitan area. In the same way as it is for Frame Relay, the business attraction is lower costs than private lines.

In terms of the ISO Reference Model, SMDS services are offered primarily at the physical layer and the data link layer. To the extent that the service provider may (transparently to the user) also link several DQDB networks together, and, therefore, does inter-network message routing, functions of the network layer are included. Higher level protocols such as TCP/IP of the *Internet* network (or TCP/IP for private non-Internet networks), SNA in IBM networks and IPX/SPX in Novell *NetWare* networks may all be found co-existing with SMDS's lower layer functions in forming protocol suites.

## SMDS AND LANs

SMDS is based on the open bus configuration of DQDB. SMDS frames may contain up to 9,188 octets of data. This is large enough to accommodate the largest frame sizes of the standard LANs. Just prior to transmission, SMDS frames are fragmented into DQDB 53-octet cells using 44 octets for payload. Just after transmission, the frame is reassembled.

SMDS currently offers only connectionless (datagram) packet transfer. As such, each SMDS frame contains a full 60-bit address of the message destination. The structure of the 60-bit network address is defined by ITU-TS Recommendation E.164. It resembles the familiar country-area-exchange-subscriber codes used in the POTS system. Each digit is expressed in hexadecimal. An advantage of the connectionless mode of operation is that calls do not need to be established prior to transmission; each SMDS frame contains the full, unique address of the destination. The first DQDB cell contains not only this unique address; it also contains a 10-bit temporary number that roughly resembles a Virtual Channel Indication used in isochronous DQDB applications. The downstream node addressed by the 60-bit address notes the associated 10-bit number; later, it will recognize itself as a cell destination by this number's appearance in subsequent cells.

Datagrams are reassembled from at most 209 44-octet cells (209 x 44 = 9196). After the datagram has been reassembled at the receiving end, the 10-bit number may be reused by another station.

Bellcore has defined a *Subscriber Network Interface*, *SNI*, whereby users access SMDS. (Users may also access SMDS through "ATM switches," via routers equipped to support ATM. Here, instead of the SNI interface, the User Network Interface UNI is used.) Equipment at the customer's premises connects to the SMDS-service i.e., the latter's switching systems, via full-duplex T3 lines at 44.736 Mbit/s. The CPE is typically a router which is described in *Chapter 11—Bridges and Routers*. The protocol obeyed by both parties is called the *SMDS Standard Interface Protocol*, *SIP*. This makes available to the user the various DQDB functions for queue-arbitrated messages.

## Segmentation and Reassembly

Segmentation of the user's data into multiple 53-octet (44-octet payload) cells for transmission, with reassembly at the destination, is an example of one of the SIP functions.

Multiple customers are supported on the same SMDS network by the provider. Each customer needs his or her own access line or lines.

The SMDS service provider may use and switch between more than one DQDB network. An interface different from SNI is used internally by the service provider between switches connecting these networks. The *Inter-Switching Systems Interface, ISSI*, is transparent to the user, however.

## Migration Towards ATM

Because SMDS uses the fixed-size 53-octet cell of DQDB, the MAN switches benefit. Switching may be done by hardware, and different buffer sizes do not have to be allowed for. As we shall see in the next chapter, ATM (broadband ISDN's cell-relay technology), also uses 53-octet, identically sized, cells. This allows for SMDS to ATM migration, or at least makes it easier to co-exist and later migrate.

## SMDS Access

The user may access the service with different speeds, depending on whether T1, E1, T3 or DS3 is selected. Different speeds define access classes. The user negotiates with the service provider, selecting one of six access classes. On a T1 facility, this would be 1.17 Mbit/s; or, on a T3, one of 4, 10, 16, 25 and 34 Mbit/s. The correlation with major LAN speeds is intentional.

## Avoiding Congestion

With SMDS, there is a possibility that, unchecked, the aggregate of user input messages to be transmitted might exceed the capacity of the network. To prevent this, the SMDS user and provider agree, administratively, to a *Sustained Information Rate*. The SIR, expressed as an average of no more than so many bits per time interval on the access line, is what the user expects to submit and transmit over a large interval of time. For short durations, the rate may be higher than the SIR; if the sustained information rate is exceeded, SMDS discards new messages on their submission. For example, a user may have negotiated a 4 Mbit/s access class, to be measured over an hour, and submit a packet at 34 Mbit/s for a few milliseconds. Provided that ensuing message/s are not being submitted uninterruptedly, enough inter-message delay may exist to make the overall rate acceptable when the total traffic transported is measured over several minutes.

Different carriers, such as the Regional Bell Operating Companies, have different rates and tariffs for the service, usually based on the class of access. In a bid to attract new customers, one such tariff offers a monthly SMDS Access fee only, with no charges for usage, distance covered or premiums for busier times of day. Another billing arrangement is based on the number of SMDS frames successfully transported. This gives users the benefit of not having to pay for repeat transmissions where a single cell's failure may cause an entire frame to be re-transmitted—they do not pay for the re-transmission of the many good cells that were in the frame.

# 9

# Wide Area Networks

In this chapter we describe the use of wide area networks. Analog and digital facilities and technologies are discussed, including voice and data, modems, Frame Relay, T1, T3, SONET, ISDN, and ATM.

## LATAs, LECs AND IXCs

When we think of wide area networks, we generally think of communications over long distance. "Wide area" implies beyond the confines of the local area, to other counties, states, provinces, or countries. In the United States, *local access* and *transport areas*, LATAs were created after the 1984 break-up of AT&T. These are geographical domains served by one or more telephone companies or *local exchange carriers*, *LECs*, such as the Bell operating companies. For communications outside the domain of the LATA, the facilities or services of a long distance communications carrier such as MCI, Sprint and AT&T are needed. The latter are *inter-exchange carriers*, *IXCs*, or *IECs*.

### Digital Communications and the Subscriber Loop

Data communications takes advantage of the existing voice-grade facilities and infra-structure. The voice telephone network was in place long before the first computer-based data communications were attempted. In the early days (and, equally today), we find copper wire circuits called *subscriber loops* (or "*local loops*") linking users to their LEC's central office. The electrical frequencies in these loops are models, or *analogs*, of the acoustic or air pressure frequencies generated by speech. However, primarily to abate attenuation, the frequencies of signals in the electrical circuits are *bandpass limited*. Frequencies inside a

300-Hz to 3300-Hz range are included while those outside it are dropped. Although this eliminates many frequencies from the sizable spectrum of speech that humans can sense (tones as low as 50 Hz and as high as about 20,000 Hz are producible and discernible), the pass-band mentioned is satisfactory for voice conversations. One may reasonably identify speakers, and interpret the tones, because the majority of voice energy is in the 300- to 3300-Hz band.

### Frequency Division Multiplexing the Analog Circuits

An advantage arising from limiting voice channels to 4-kHz bandwidths is that it enables the common carrier, an LEC or IXC, to simultaneously *multiplex* a number of voice calls on a single trunk circuit between two of its central offices. (Guard bands of 0 to 300-Hz and 3300 to 4000-Hz surround the voice channel). The technique the common carrier uses to do this is called *frequency division multiplexing*. Here, a wide band of frequencies on the trunk circuit simultaneously carries a multiple of 4–kHz wide channels. Unlike local loops, the trunk circuit is not "loaded" with bandpass limiting equipment and, therefore, may support all frequencies. On transmission, the central office raises each call's frequencies so that, on the trunk circuit, its channel may occupy, for example, one of the bands 60 to 64-kHz, 64 to 68-kHz, 68 to 72-kHz and so on. At the receiving central office, the calls are de-multiplexed.

In practice, twelve voice channels form a 48-kHz channel "group" that is positioned between 60 and 108-kHz. The carrier extends this multiplexing procedure in a hierarchical fashion, using higher frequencies and pass-bands in order to multiplex even larger numbers of channels. Thus, a "supergroup" of five groups contains 60 channels, and a "basic mastergroup" consists of ten supergroups or 600 channels (10 x 60= 600).

## THEORETICAL LIMITS TO BITS PER SECOND

Plain old telephone (voice-grade service) circuits, are called *analog* circuits because the spectrum of frequencies used, and their respective amplitudes, electrically model the mechanical energy of human speech. However, these circuits may be used to send digital data. Indeed, other circuits, discussed later, are also used for this purpose.

In 1949, Claude Shannon published "The Mathematical Theory of Communications." He deduced that the information carrying capacity of a communications channel is a product of two factors—the bandwidth of the channel and a measure of its signal to noise ratio. The measure is "entropy," given by the formula:

$\log_2 (1 + \underline{S})$, where S is signal power and N is noise power.
$\phantom{\log_2 (1 + } N$

Since POTS circuits are engineered for a signal/noise ratio of about 1,000, we find that the typical measure for entropy in the above formula is about 10. The typical voice-grade channel has a maximum usable bandwidth of about 3,000 Hz, so the information carrying capacity is

10 x 3000 = 30,000 bits per second.

In practice, 20 to 25 kbit/s is the maximum achievable, due to impairments such as crosstalk and phase jitter.

With the voice bandwidth limited to 3 kHz, the maximum bit-per-second rate can only be bettered by advances or enhancements in equipment and facilities that improve the signal to noise ratio. In practical terms, this improvement allows a wider range of changes to the signal to be made by the sender and discerned by the receiver. We now discuss the nature of these changes.

## MODEMS

The equipment used to enable digital communications over analog circuits is the modem. Named for its ability to **mod**ulate and **dem**odulate a signal, and thereby communicate information, a modem is *data circuit terminating equipment, DCE*. Modems connect the wide area network with the user's *data terminal equipment, DTE,* e.g., PCs, or terminals. Interfaces such as EIA–232, and V.35 are used between the modem and the DTE. The modem's other side connects to the LEC central office by the subscriber loop (twisted pair). From this LEC central office, the circuit connects possibly to another central office, or, via a second subscriber loop, to a modem (with matching capabilities of the first modem) and to the destination DTE.

The sending modem sends its information as variants of a signal whose constant, predictable properties are known to the receiver. Since the signal carries information by changes that are imposed by the sender and detected by the receiver it earns the name *carrier signal*. Modems may communicate more than one bit for each cycle of the signal by generating (and, at the receiver, detecting) more than one signal variant.

Chapter 6 presented an example of the use of frequency *keying* to send information. In the description of Phase Coherent encoding (see Figure 6.14), we saw that any bit cell may contain one of two frequencies, (one of them double the other). By convention, a bit cell occupied by the higher frequency signals a 0; the lower frequency a 1.

If this were the only technique modems could use on analog circuits, the maximum bit rate would be limited to no higher than about 1,500 bit/s since the highest usable frequency is about 3,000 Hz. Fortunately, there are other (some of them ingenious) techniques that may be employed. A common principle applying in all these techniques is that a monotone signal carrier is transmitted (as a sine wave with an agreed on frequency) between sender and receiver. If no change takes place to the phase, amplitude or frequency of the carrier, no information is communicated. Conversely, information is communicated and meaning is attributed when changes occur to one or more of these characteristics. Modems able to make (and, conversely, detect) $n$ changes to the signal per second are said to have a *baud rate* of $n$.

## Phase Change Modems

One type of modem uses *phase changes* to indicate 1s and 0s. Both the sending and receiving modems agree on a benchmark carrier frequency. The receiver deduces information based on the sender's changes to the phase of the carrier. The more sophisticated the electronics (and, concomitantly, the stronger the signal/noise ratio) the more able the modem is to alter the carrier signal's phase by smaller angles, or to detect such smaller angle changes reliably.

Modems making or recognizing $n$ phase changes to the signal per second have a *baud rate* of $n$. As before, a change in the phase of the carrier transmits information. If the menu of phase change angles is two (a choice of say 90° or 180°), 1 or 0 may be associated with each change respectively. Here, a single bit is communicated per baud. The bit per second rate equals the baud rate (in this case).

More sophisticated modems are able to select from a wider range of phase angles per change (say 45°, 90°, 135° or 180°). And, the sending modem looks at two or more bits at a time rather than merely one. (The actual number of bits, however, is the same each time for the modem.) Based on the content values, the modem selects one of the angles. Taking two bits at a time from its buffer, the sending modem may, for example, select a phase change of 45° for binary value 00, 90° for 01, 135° for 10 and 180° for 11. In these cases, two bits are communicated per baud, resulting in a bit-per-second rate of baud x 2

In general, if a phase-modulating modem can handle (generate, or recognize) $2^p$ distinct phase angles per change, $p$ bits are communicated per baud and the transmission rate is p x baud bits per second.

## V.29 Example of a Modem

As an illustration, consider the 9,600-bit/s modem standard, Recommendation V.29 of ITU-TS. V.29 uses phase modulation in conjunction with different amplitudes. The sender assembles four information bits prior to "sending" them as a single signal change. This activity occurs 2,400 times per second. Eight phase angles 45°, 90°, 135°, 180°, 225°, ... , 360° plus two legal amplitudes per angle provide for sixteen possibilities.

Again, if a combined phase-and-amplitude modulation modem can make $2^p$ distinct phase angles per change, and each such change has $2^q$ distinct amplitudes, p+q bits are communicated per baud and the transmission rate is baud x (p + q) bit/s. Another name for the phase-and amplitude modulation is *quadrature amplitude modulation*.

The V.29 circuit uses a carrier of 1,700 Hz, and makes signal changes at 2,400 baud. Thus, the modem makes more than one signal change per cycle.

V.29 is a one pair (2-wire), half-duplex modem. For full-duplex capabilities on V.29, two pairs of wires are required.

## V.32 and Echo Cancellation

For full-duplex 9,600-bit/s operation on one pair of wires, one needs the capabilities of *V.32*. Through the use of *echo cancellation* techniques, the transmitter and receiver simultaneously use the same carrier frequency. Each transmitting station is able to "listen" (as a receiver) to the combined energy at this frequency, and subtracting from it the energy of its own transmission signal (its own "echo") is able to receive the other's incoming message.

## FSK is Fine for Lower Bit Rates

Is it possible to obtain full duplex capabilities on a single pair by the simultaneous use of two carrier frequencies? At lower baud rates, e.g., 300 baud, the answer is yes. The technique used is *Frequency Shift Keying, FSK*. Modems employing FSK may use a benchmark carrier in this way: small increases and decreases in its frequency (about 10%) signal 1s and 0s respectively. At higher baud rates, the answer is no. The harmonics of each carrier tend to interfere with the quality of the other carrier, and so full-duplex is not feasible on a single pair of wires by the simultaneous use of two carrier frequencies.

### FSK in Bell 103 Modem

In slow speed modems such as the early Bell 103 (refer to Figure 2.10), two carrier frequencies are present, one at 1,170 Hz and the other at 2,125 Hz. One modem transmits its 1s and 0s as shifts on 1,170 Hz (to 1,270 Hz, or to 1,070 Hz); and receives its 1s and 0s as the shifts on the 2,125 Hz carrier (to 2,225 Hz, or 2,025 Hz). The other modem of the communicating pair symmetrically transmits at 2,125 Hz and receives at 1,170 Hz. The modems operate at 300 baud. Each baud delivers exactly one bit (a 0 or 1) based on whether the frequency shifts "left" or "right" (i.e., decreases or increases). (The ITU-TS V.21

Recommendation for 300 bit/s transmission uses the exact opposite convention though; its 1s and 0s are frequency shift decreases and increases respectively. Care!)

---

Arguably, the development of *digital* lines arose from a desire for more efficient and reliable multiplexing schemes for voice circuits than the frequency division multiplexing described earlier.

## CODEC; THE INVERSE STEPS TO A MODEM

The first step in the process that leads to the support of digital lines requires the coding of voice into digits. **Cod**er/**dec**oder *codec* equipment does this. Typically, it examines a voice sample from an analog circuit and grades its amplitude at one of 256 different levels. Thus, the codec comes up with 8 bits, an octet that is transmitted. At the receiver, the octet's bits are used as an index to the same scale of amplitudes to reconstruct the signal.

### Companding

In practice, the scale used to specify amplitudes is not linear. In order to replicate soft speech more successfully, the scale is characterized by gradations that are closer together for lower amplitudes and further apart for higher amplitudes. This is known as *companding*. The notation derives from the sender, in effect, **comp**ressing the analog signal, and the receiver, reciprocally, exp**and**ing it. This is done so as to provide the resolution for many more decision levels for soft signals without needing to increase the number of bits per voice sample.

More than one companding scale is accepted universally. The companding scale that is used in Europe is known as the *A-law*. In North America, another companding scale known as the *μ-law* applies. Regrettably, these scales are incompatible.

How many samples (per unit time) are needed to recreate the signal perfectly? For voice, the answer is 8,000 times per second. This result is a consequence of work done by Nyquist. He showed that any analog signal with a particular bandwidth may be recreated from samples of the original, provided that sampling occurs at a frequency no less than twice the bandwidth of the channel. For voice-grade circuits with bandwidths limited to 4,000 Hz, the minimum sampling rate needed is $(2 \times 4000 = 8,000)$ Hz.

# T1 TDM

Using the *T1* approach, voice samples are taken from 24 different users and their octets are *time division multiplexed* onto 24 consecutive time slots. The common carrier's *channel bank* is the equipment used that combines codec functions with multiplexing. Time division multiplexing and the T1 facility were described in Chapter 4.

Each 193-bit frame is transmitted in 125 μseconds. Each channel, therefore, is transmitting a new octet 8,000 times per second. The 64-kbit/s service is often referred to as "digital signal, level 0," DS0. A voice channel is sometimes called a DS0. A "digital signal, level 1" *DS1* service provides 24 DS0s on a T1 facility.

The service provider needs to have a capability to provide "signaling." The word "signaling" here refers to functions such as dialing and call-establishment. As we shall presently see, there is no measurable impact (on the quality of voice received) when the signaling is done *in-band* on T1 facilities. However, if the T1 is intended to transport data across a switched (public) network, the customer must subscribe to a service where the provider offers *56-kbit/s* channels instead of 64-kbit/s. The user's 56-kbit/s (not 64-kbit/s) data stream is multiplexed by the service provider with its own 8-kbit/s signaling channel.

## Bit Robbing

In voice applications, when one of the bits in an 8-bit voice sample is overwritten by the service provider's own signaling, the technique is called "bit-robbing." We note in passing that if the receiving compander ignored the signaling and viewed all 8 bits as constituting a valid sample, the probability of a companding error is 50%. Half the time, on average, the samples have their original values! For the rest of the times, the resulting companding error will not materially affect the quality of the voice call because the bit change simply means the sample is reconstructed from an adjacent notch on the companding scale. The service provider only needs, in fact, every sixth frame to signal a single bit, so five out of every six frames contain 100% accurate samples for the voice channel anyhow.

Of course, such an approach would be unacceptable for data applications. Data applications are accommodated by the user subscribing to a service such as *Accunet Switched 56*, or *Switched 384*, or to *DDS Digital Data Services*. Additionally, the user may subscribe to T1 or *Fractional T1* services. These are digital services featuring signaling that is done by the carrier independent of the user's channel. Typically, the performance offered on these digital circuits is above the speeds associated with popular modems. The latter include 1,200, 2,400, 4,800, 9,600 and 14,400-bit/s.

Physically, the user's access line to the central office of the LEC or IXC is terminated at both ends by a *channel service unit* (*CSU*). As an aside, whenever the customer's DTE connects with a CSU, another piece of equipment is generally necessary. This is the *Digital Service Unit, DSU*. Its main purpose is the conversion of uni-polar signaling of the computer to bipolar and the provision of the required DCE functions. The interface between the DTE and the DSU is typically EIA–232 or V.35.

Sub-rates below 56 kbit/s are offered through DDS using the same digital facilities. To offer these lower rates, redundant pad bits are used and discarded.

## Clear Channel and ISDN

When no in-band signaling is done, 64 kbit/s or multiples thereof are available. For *clear channel* 64 kbit/s capability, either no signaling is provided at all (as in private T1 networks) or signaling is handled by a completely separate network. In the *Integrated Services Digital Networks, ISDN*, with the Basic Rate interface, a 16-kbit/s signaling D-channel accompanies the two (clear-channel) 64-kbit/s bearer channels. For PBX applications, the *Primary rate ISDN* is used. Here, one of the twenty four 64-kbit/s channels is dedicated for signaling.

The user interfaces his or her private T1 via CSUs, (or routers with CSUs) in a manner not unlike that of the multiplexer features of a channel bank. Users of Primary Rate interface of ISDN also use similar facilities, based on T1 technology.

When the service provider offers clear channel 64-kbit/s DS-0 service on the Basic Rate interface of ISDN, the two 64-kbit/s "Bearer" channels and a 16-kbit/s signaling "D" channel are provided on a single twisted pair local subscriber loop called a *Digital Subscriber Loop*, or *DSL*.

By contrast, T1 and ISDN Primary Rate use two pairs of wires, one for transmit and one for receive, respectively.

## Superframe

T1 is a multiplexing technique, transmitting twenty four 8-bit slots 8,000 times a second. The 192 bits are *framed* by an appended frame-bit. When twelve such frames are managed by the network, the group of twelve frames is known as a *D4 superframe*.

Framing bits are used to enable the network to be confident which 192 bits, in an otherwise endless stream of bits, constitute the frame. The framing bit is successively a bit of a unique sequence such as the following: 1,0,0,0,1,1,0,1,1,1,0,0. The sequence repeats endlessly. The sequence is unique because one finds the incidence of exactly one, two or three successive 1s only once in any twelve consecutive bits of the sequence. Likewise, one, two or three successive 0 bits occur only once. The superframe is 2,304 data bits long; or 2,316 inclusive of framing bits.

## Extended Superframe

The *Extended Superframe* manages twenty four 193-bit frames, that is, twice as many as the superframe. Here, 6 of the 24 framing bits are used as a CRC checksum on the 4,608 data bits within the previous frame. The remaining 18 framing bits include a 6-bit repeating pattern used as above for frame synchronization and bits used for maintenance and diagnostics.

## *AMI and B8ZS*

T1 uses Alternate Mark Inversion, combined with Binary 8-Zeros Substitution for encoding. These techniques were described in Chapter 6. With AMI, the single cycle of a sine wave represents two successive 1s. Therefore, a 772-kHz frequency can deliver 1.544-Mbit/s, which is the T1 rate.

## T3

*T3* differs from T1 in the transmission rate, plus it has additional overhead bits. T3's payload is the equivalent of 28 T1s, supporting 28 x 24 = 672 channels. T3 has an additional 1.504 Mbit/s of overhead than the aggregate of 28 T1s. Its transmission rate is, therefore

28 x 1,544,000 + 1,504,000 = 44,736,000 bits per second.

## SONET

The *Synchronous Optical Network, SONET* is a fiber optic technology, and is a transport interface. In Europe and elsewhere, the *Synchronous Digital Hierarchy* is the equivalent, compatible counterpart used by the Post, Telephone and Telegraph (PTT) administrations. SONET networks provide high-speed, wide area, multiplexed transmission that links international carriers, inter-exchange carriers and LECs. It is an alternative for multiple T3 facilities.

The word "synchronous" in SONET's name implies the use of circuit switching approaches and facilities. This distinguishes SONET from "asynchronous" modes which imply packet, frame or cell switching. SONET can support packet or cell switching, however. Thus, as we shall see, the "Asynchronous Transfer Mode, ATM" may use SONET as its transport vehicle.

## SONET's STS-n Building Block

We introduce SONET by reviewing a SONET frame. This is called the *Synchronous Transport Signal, STS* and offers different levels of performance. *STS-n* is a SONET frame with *n* times the number of bits of the basic building block, the STS-1 frame. (In Europe, the basic building block is an SDH-1 frame, which is identical to STS-3.)

The STS-1 string of bits transmitted by SONET may be viewed as sequences of 6,480-bit frames. Each 6,480-bit frame is, in turn, organized into a

$9 \times 90 = 810$ celled matrix of 8-bit cells shown below with their cell numbers:

| 1 | 2 | 3 | ... | 88 | 89 | 90 |
|---|---|---|-----|-----|-----|-----|
| 91 | 92 | 93 | ... | 178 | 179 | 180 |
| 181 | | | ... | | | 270 |
| 271 | | | ... | | | |
| 361 | | | ... | | | |
| 451 | | | ... | | | |
| 541 | | | ... | | | |
| 631 | | | ... | | | 720 |
| 721 | | | ... | 808 | 809 | 810 |

*Table 9.1. STS-1 frame format.*

8,000 STS-1 frames are transmitted per second, yielding a rate of

$8 \times 8,000 \times 9 \times 90 = 51,840,000$ bit/s.

### Path, Section and Line Overhead

Each STS-1 frame contains octets for overhead in addition to the payload. The overhead octets are arranged in specific columns, and cover or manage different parts of the communication. SONET defines *path* overhead as relating to the end-to-end connection between source and destination. The path consists of one or more *lines* and these, in turn, comprise several *sections*. The overhead for the sections appears in the first three rows and first three columns of the matrix. The overhead for the lines also occupies columns 1, 2 and 3, appearing in rows 4 through 9 of the matrix. Thus, the overhead is spread evenly throughout the frame, not only at the start. The layout of the first three columns in the following table shows the sharing between section and line overhead (S octets and L octets):

| S | S | S |  |  | ... |  |  |  |
|---|---|---|---|---|-----|---|---|---|
| S | S | S |  |  |     |  |  |  |
| S | S | S |  |  | ... |  |  |  |
| L | L | L |  |  | ... |  |  |  |
| L | L | L |  |  | ... |  |  |  |
| L | L | L |  |  | ... |  |  |  |
| L | L | L |  |  | ... |  |  |  |
| L | L | L |  |  | ... |  |  |  |
| L | L | L |  |  | ... |  |  |  |

*Table 9.2.*

## SPE Includes Payload and Path Overhead

The user's data is carried in a 783-octet *synchronous payload envelope (SPE)*. The envelope is organized within the STS–1 frame as 9 rows of 87 octets. The *path's* overhead consists of 9 octets and is considered part of the envelope. This overhead is spread throughout the frame, just as are the section and line overheads. Path overhead octets appear in the same column of consecutive rows.

A user may float his or her payload within a SONET frame; its start need not coincide with cell 4. By doing this, SONET eliminates latency. One may visualize multiple networks, each interconnecting to a SONET transport, and each with its own individual clock defining its payload's start. With the ability to float, the user's synchronous payload envelope may start at any cell in columns 4 through 90 of an STS-1 frame. Since an STS-1 frame appears every 125 µseconds, the average 62.5 µseconds latency is averted by the float. Furthermore, SONET equipment does not need buffers while awaiting the output frame.

Unlike the speeds of the T$n$ hierarchy (like T1 and T3, or, equivalently DS1 and DS3) that characterize copper wire multiples of circuits, the STS-n frame speeds are precise multiples of the STS-1's performance. STS-3, therefore, operates at $8 \times 8,000 \times 9 \times 90 \times 3 = 155,520,000$ bit/s. STS-12 is 4 times that, at 622.08 Mbit/s. So, STS-3 is exactly three times STS-1, while DS3, (or T3) is roughly three times DS-1 (or, T1).

The notation OC-1, OC-3, OC-12 etc.—in general OC-n—relates to SONET's optical carrier standards. STS-n refers to the electrical standards. However, these terms are frequently used interchangeably, and without confusion.

## Virtual Tributaries Support Most Standard Transports

SONET supports the standard DS1, E1, DS1C, and DS3 data rates offered by most common carriers. (E1 is the European PTT's equivalent of DS1, with 32 8-bit channels, not 24. DS1C, not a wide-spread service, approximates two DS1s). Because of this, SONET is a relatively easy transport mechanism for these services to migrate to.

How is this done? A payload is viewed as 87 columns of 9 rows. Since one of these columns is dedicated to the path overhead, 86 remain. The 86 columns are viewed as a resource of seven 12-column *Virtual Tributary Groups*. (Two columns are unused). Each Virtual Tributary Group has of course 9 rows.

If the contents of the 9 by 12 octets in a Virtual Tributary Group are for a single destination, then

$8 \times 8,000 \times 9 \times 12 = 6,912,000$ bits

are delivered per second. This capability is called a VT6. It is suitable for accommodating the 6.312-Mbit/s DS2 service.

Hence, a single STS-1 can simultaneously support seven DS2s.

Alternatively, if every *other* octet (or column) of the 9 by 12 octets in a Virtual Tributary Group is delivered to a destination, then only half the capacity of the bits per second of the 6.912 Mbit/s VTG is delivered. This is called a VT3. It delivers

$8 \times 8,000 \times 9 \times 6 = 3,456,000$ bit/s, suited for the DS1C at 3.152 Mbit/s. Two VT3s are possible per VTG, one created by the odd numbered columns in the VTG, the other by the even.

Similarly, the "VT2" delivers every *third* octet (or column) in the Virtual Tributary Group to the destination, with

$8 \times 8,000 \times 9 \times 4 = 2,304,000$ bits delivered per second. At one third the rate of a VT6, the VT2 is suited to the E1 at 2.048 Mbit/s. Three VT2s are possible per VTG.

Finally, selecting every *fourth* octet in the VTG, delivers

$8 \times 8,000 \times 9 \times 3 = 1,728,000$ bit/s.

With one quarter the rate of a VT6 this "VT1.5" is suited for 1.544-Mbit/s T1. Four VT1.5s are possible per VTG. Since there are seven VTGs per STS-1 frame, a total of 28 VT1.5s may be accommodated. This provides the equivalent of a DS3.

## FRAME RELAY

We introduced the subject of Packet Switching in Chapter 2. In what follows, we describe the *fast packet switching* services of *Frame Relay* and, where applicable, contrast them with X.25.

Frame Relay is a standard devised by ITU-TS and ANSI for the interface between the user and the network. More precisely, it is a set of standards including ITU-TS Recommendations I.123 and I.233 and ANSI T1.606. Services using Frame Relay are aimed primarily at LAN interconnection. In a Frame Relay network, as in an X.25 packet switched network involving virtual circuits, a virtual circuit must be established prior to the transport of the user messages. Frame Relay is, therefore, *connection-oriented*. Most Frame Relay customers subscribe to a permanent virtual circuit service by administrative procedures, making it unnecessary for the caller to incur dialing and connection delay—the virtual circuit has already been pre-established, and is the equivalent of a leased line.

### Comparing X.25 and Frame Relay

Like X.25, one of the advantages of Frame Relay is that a single physical connection (i.e., wires connecting the user to the network) can simultaneously support multiple logical connections.

Whereas in X.25, the user's data are presented to the network in packets of 128 or 256 bytes, in Frame Relay the frames accepted *and transmitted* are of variable length. The equipment that interfaces the network to the user is called a Frame Assembler and Disassembler, or FRAD. It affixes a header and trailer to the user's frame. Within the header is the *Data Link Connection Identifier*, for the frame's virtual circuit. The FRAD processes the HDLC-like protocol *LAP-F*, the Link Access Procedures to Frame-Mode Bearer Services. ITU-TS Recommendation Q.922 describes LAP-F. While LAP-F features the familiar $01111110$ flag, plus a 2-octet Frame Check Sequence CRC, no sequencing counts are present. We shall soon see why not.

## Transmission Quality has Improved Enormously

Within an X.25 network, as each packet is forwarded to and received by intermediate nodes, the nodes perform a complex range of functions. These include calculating CRCs, acknowledging or rejecting good or faulty packets, detecting out-of-sequence packets, managing timers, multiplexing logical channels, and generating and responding to the Automatic Request for Repeat (ARQ) functions such as Receiver Not Ready, etc. Note that these X.25 procedures apply to every link in the virtual circuit. They repeat at every intermediate node en route to the final destination.

What all this error control achieves is a high level of accuracy and reliability that was prized in the 1970s when X.25 was introduced, because of the then poor quality of transmission lines (notably voice-grade analog lines, and older switching equipment).

But today's optical-fiber-based networks feature extraordinarily high reliability, by comparison. Error control and acknowledging are unnecessary at the intermediate node level because the overwhelming majority of transmissions display no errors. The error control et cetera, done by intermediate nodes, needlessly slows the overall performance of the network, and limits the amount of traffic that may be handled.

The network manager may rightly ask why this effort should be incurred if the data are found to be right in almost 100% of all instances. In fact, he or she may argue that error control itself has the potential to create errors! Congestion, that might otherwise not have existed, could arise simply because nodes are busy doing (unnecessary) error control. This may force nodes without enough buffers to adequately handle the incoming traffic to drop frames, causing re-transmission which exacerbates the whole situation in a vicious cycle.

Frame Relay takes the posture that the optical medium is reliable, and so the probability of successful transmission is high in the first place. Second, data integrity is still assured by letting error control take place not at the intermediate nodes but rather at the end-points (where it happens anyhow). End-to-end errors that occur are detected and corrected by ISO OSI *Level 4, Transport* mechanisms. Re-transmissions on errors are initiated by these end-points without any node-to-node error control involvement. Third, at the intermediate nodes, frames with any errors (notably CRC failures in the header's DLCI address, or in the Frame Check Sequence, or congestion) are simply dropped without any notification to the sender. Thus, processing is simplified at all nodes making more processing power available for handling the traffic.

### Congestion—the Achilles Heel if Unchecked

The premise of error-free transport is fundamental to the viability of Frame Relay. However, under the best of physical conditions (in terms of signal quality) the network may be vulnerable. The vulnerability arises in conditions of congestion. Per the algorithm above, once congestion accumulates at an intermediate node, it simply drops frames. The receiving end-point detects that a frame is missing (via its functions done at the OSI Level 4, Transport) and signals its partner for a re-transmission. As mentioned above, this process itself aggravates the congestion, causing a cycle of re-transmissions.

To avert the problem, two different approaches may be taken to control congestion, *implicit congestion control* and *explicit congestion control*.

## Implicit Congestion Control

*Implicit congestion control* is the approach where the end-points observe the incidence of errors or degradation in performance, and decide that these problems are congestion related. When the end-points determine that re-transmission is necessary, they back off from requesting or doing any re-transmissions for a random interval of time, until such time as the congestion has eased. Since the end-points have no way of determining empirically that conditions have improved, their resumption of transmission may again occur during congested times.

## Explicit Congestion Control

Alternatively, a form of *explicit congestion control* is adopted. Two steps are necessary. First, when the user subscribes to the Frame Relay service, a *Committed Information Rate (CIR)* for each virtual circuit is agreed to administratively. The user commits to submit no more than an agreed number of bits over a pre-determined time interval. (Reciprocally, the service provider commits to a certain level of service, given the subscriber's compliance with this CIR.) At the ingress to the network, the service provider, through the FRAD device, decides whether or not to accept a frame. It calculates whether, with this frame, the aggregated bit rate conforms with the agreed CIR allowed for the virtual circuit. If so, it passes the frame into the network. If, on the other hand, accepting the frame would mean that the aggregated bit rate exceeds the threshold, the service provider may reject it outright, or it may pass it, depending on the severity of the excess.

If the bits per second demand of a submitted frame exceeded an acceptable threshold by 20%, for example, the service provider may elect to reject the frame outright. The service provider may elect to only accept such frames if the threshold were exceeded by less than 5%, say. Any such accepted frame is marked *Discard Eligible* in its header. Intermediate nodes that are confronted by congestion will discard frames so marked first. Absent congestion, the frame will reach its destination in the normal fashion.

## One Can Exceed CIR for a Short Time

Note that the *instantaneous* demands of the equipment for a particular virtual circuit at the points of entry to, and exit from, the network may be higher than the CIR. Because the network uses statistical multiplexing techniques, the aggregate of CIR loads on the network is less than the aggregate service capacity. Thus, a user may have T1 access to Frame Relay while agreeing to a 384-kbit/s CIR, for example. As long as the average over an agreed interval of time meets the CIR, the submission is acceptable.

The second step in controlling congestion explicitly is taken by any intermediate node with a congested condition. (Typically, the congested node is one that has run out of software buffers.) In the headers of frames that the node sends, it sets an explicit congestion notification bit. The *forward explicit congestion notification, FECN* bit is set in frames sent to virtual circuit destinations while the *backward explicit congestion notification, BECN* bit is set in the headers of frames sent to the source. On receipt of frames with these bits set, the end-points voluntarily reduce their traffic, until such time as several consecutive frames have been received with the bits reset. Of course, the operative word here is "voluntary;" while the network explicitly notifies users of congestion, the success in reducing it may depend on the users' cooperation in implementing back-off policies. This is the case if the FRAD equipment is customer owned.

While X.25 speeds are typically less than 64 kbit/s, Frame Relay is at T1 or T3 rates.

Much of the motivation for Frame Relay comes from private industry. An industry consortium founded the Frame Relay (Implementor's) Forum in 1970. Its founding members included Cisco Systems, DEC, 3Com, Northern Telecom and Stratacom.

Packet switching and Frame Relay illustrate approaches that are more efficient uses of resources than private, leased line circuits. The case against using a private, leased line circuit with its circuit-switching (as opposed to packet-switching) characteristics arises when the facilities dedicated are likely to be idle for part of the time. Applications involving data, such as file transfers, inquiry/response, etc., are intrinsically "bursty," with idleness occurring between the bursts. Circuit switching here results in the waste of otherwise sharable facilities. This argues for more efficient systems, like packet switching, where resources are deployed dynamically, and only as needed.

Packet switched and Frame Relay switching systems are the logical choices. Since the intermediate nodes are intelligent, they accept packets or frames into their buffers, forwarding them to the next node in the virtual circuit only as the link to it becomes free. This implies no wasting of resources; but there is unpredictability as to when messages are forwarded. Some packets or frames may be delayed at the node while waiting for resources to become free.

Frame Relay is a higher speed, lower delay alternative to X.25. It is an interface to a network, and a switching methodology.

## ASYNCHRONOUS TRANSFER MODE (ATM)

The word "asynchronous" in ATM's name relates to the fact that the wide area network is not using "synchronous" circuit switching. (While SONET networks are synchronous and circuit switching, they nevertheless could be used, and are used, to transport ATM cells that are submitted to SONET *asynchronously*.)

Whereas Frame Relay is a software based switching technology enabling the network to multiplex the virtual circuits of different users on the same facilities, Asynchronous Transfer Mode is a hardware based switching technology. It, too, is connection-oriented, and offers the same multiplexing capability as does Frame Relay. But, by using fixed sized cells, the ATM approach minimizes the processing overhead that frame relay incurs in accommodating different sized frames. This enables ATM to handle more or speedier communications traffic.

The reader may observe that this approach is already taken by packet switched networks such as X.25. While this is correct to a degree, in contrast with X.25 (which, while it does limit packet size, uses software in analyzing the contents of packet headers), ATM's cells are smaller, and ATM uses hardware to perform rapid and predictable switching.

For conventional data processing applications, the delay incurred at intermediate packet or frame switches is unnoticeable or unnoticed. But for *isochronous* applications, unless the delay were held trivial, and constant, its effects would be unacceptable.

By definition, isochronous applications such as voice and video are delay sensitive. It would seem, therefore, that these applications are unsuitable candidates for packet or frame (or cell) handling in the first place. If an unpredictable delay is introduced every time a voice message is switched, the cumulative delay as the voice or video message passes from switch to switch is variable. By the time the message reaches its final destination, this cumulative variability could result in unacceptable jitter or hiatus to a conversation.

However, the problem could be averted if maximum delay could be guaranteed acceptably small and constant. ATM, by using hardware switches and *fixed length (53-octet) cells* is able to assure a 6 millisecond latency. Thus, with ATM, not only may data applications but isochronous applications may be switched with acceptable delay characteristics.

The key to the speed in switching is in the fixed length cell. The standard ATM cell size is 53 octets (identical with SMDS, surprise!), of which 5 octets are the header. As with Frame Relay, ATM's policy vis–à–vis error control is, on detecting an error, to drop the cell, without notification. Like Frame Relay, ATM assumes that the circuits are highly reliable. This is a reasonable assumption when using digital circuits and optical fiber transports such as STS-1. Any error validation is done by the end-points.

The ATM cell header, shown in Figure 9.1 identifies the virtual circuit by a 24-bit or 28-bit number. This consists of a 16-bit Virtual Channel Identifier (VCI) and an 8- or 12-bit Virtual Path Identifier (VPI). The VPI/VCI pair associates an individual cell with a particular virtual circuit. Using the VPI/VCI identifier, hardware is able to swiftly dispatch a cell arriving at the node, switching it to the appropriate outbound link. As with Frame Relay, there is a *Cell Loss Priority, CLP* bit in the header, the equivalent of Frame Relay's "Discard Eligible" flag. In the event of congestion, cells marked as lower priority are dropped. The *Generic Flow Control* group of 4 bits in the header is designed to alleviate short-term congestion. The 3-bit *Payload Type Identifier* enables the network to distinguish user data from network management cells. Finally, the header is protected by an 8-bit CRC called Header Error Control. In the event of any errors to its header, the cell is dropped.

| | 8 | 7 | 6 | 5 | 4 | 3 | 2 | 1 |
|---|---|---|---|---|---|---|---|---|
| 1 | Generic Flow Control* | | | | Virtual Path Identifier | | | |
| 2 | Virtual Path Id (cont.) | | | | Virtual Channel Identifier | | | |
| 3 | Virtual Channel Identifier (cont.) | | | | | | | |
| 4 | Virtual Channel Id (cont.) | | | | Payload Type Id | | | CLP |
| 5 | Header Error Control (CRC) | | | | | | | |

*Figure 9.1. ATM cell header.*

*Generic Flow Control* is only used at the User Network Interface i.e., in cells at the edge of the network. Alternatively, once the cell is *within* the network, the four bits may be used to extend the VPI.

The overall ATM network, thus, consists of end-points with intermediate nodes that link them together in a non-dedicated, statistically multiplexed fashion. For data connections, the end-points may include any type of customer premise equipment, but are most likely to be routers that, in turn, are connected to customer host systems or LANs. For voice, the end-points are PBXs or codecs. The intermediate nodes are ATM switches.

Viewed in the context of the OSI Reference Model, ATM occupies the Link Layer 2. Its lower sub-layer (closest to the Physical Layer 1) handles the node-to-node links by means of 53-octet cells. It is known as the *ATM Layer*. Above this resides the *ATM Adaptation Layer*. Here, different ATM Adaptation Layer types perform certain functions, for four different classes of service. We describe these classes first:

Applications are classified as belonging to *Classes A, B, C, and D* depending on the timing relationship, nature of bit rate submission and connection-mode between the communicating partners.

The first criterion, timing relationship, refers to the timing between source and destination. It differentiates applications that are tolerant of delay variations from those that are not. Applications that are *not* tolerant of delay variations fall into Class A or Class B.

The second criterion distinguishes applications that must submit data at constant rate—versus those able to use a variable bit rate. The latter will soon include commercially available video codecs that, recognizing when a pair of moving picture frames has less (or more) differences than the preceding pair, takes advantage of the situation, submitting correspondingly variable bit rates. Applications that must submit data at constant rates fall into Class A.

Finally, the mode of connection is connection-oriented or connectionless. If the application is connectionless, such as SMDS, it falls in Class D.

The protocol layers supporting applications with different combinations of classes reside above the ATM Layer. *ATM Adaptation Layer Type 1* provides services for Class A. Type 2 services Class B. Types 3 and 4 were recently combined as Type 3/4. Together with Type 5, Type 3/4 services Class C. Class D is serviced by Type 4. The major functions of these AALs are segmentation of the data units of the higher layer protocols into cells, and the converse reassembly. Also the AAL provides a *convergence sub-layer* which delivers functions expected by higher layers and not performed by the ATM (lowest) layer. For example, Type 1 performs a sequence numbering check to detect lost, or mis-inserted data units. One of the octets in the 48-octet payload is set aside for sequence checking by AAL Type 1.

Just as in SMDS (in fact, SMDS may be thought of as an ATM-like service) and in Frame Relay, the Achilles heel of ATM would be congestion. To avert or ease congestion, the end-nodes of the virtual circuit perform a policing function. Embedded in ATM technology are methods for managing congestion. These include congestion notification and *traffic shaping* in which an ATM node negotiates with the network service provider for pre-approval of the burst rate and throughput of a virtual circuit. The ATM Layer refuses requests for virtual circuits when it determines that it cannot maintain the agreed quality of service.

While ATM will always have the ability to transport voice, in the near term we can expect to see ATM used to transport both Frame Relay and SMDS traffic. Whether ATM will be adequate for all traffic that any future service may bring, is yet to be seen. It appears likely that, in the future, new adaptation layer types may become necessary. These would in all likelihood use the same ATM layer technology, however.

# 10

# IBM and SNA

The direction taken by commercial communications networks in the 1980s and 1990s has been shaped perhaps more by IBM than any other single vendor. IBM's influence has been felt through the extension of its communications practices to standards now accepted worldwide. These are implemented not only by IBM in its own products but by the communications industry as a whole. In this chapter, we discuss SNA, IBM's premier communications network architecture and its protocols. Our goal is to understand its structure and the issues for inter-operability of local, metropolitan and wide area networks involving its protocols.

IBM introduced *Systems Network Architecture, SNA* in 1975. At the time, most computer systems and networks were host-centric. Today, SNA embraces host-centric as well as peer-to-peer characteristics, in response to an environment when data processing is distributed and managed across wider geographies.

## SNA AND OSI REFERENCE MODEL COMPARISON

The introduction of SNA was motivated by IBM's desire to rationalize the diverse communications protocols developed for its many data communications products. While parallels may be drawn between the architecture of SNA and that of OSI's Reference Model, the OSI goal was for openness, that is, for inter-operability between products and services of *different* vendors, administrations and users. Despite this, there is a strong similarity between the Open Systems Interconnection model and SNA—particularly in the layering of their structures. The similarity is not a coincidence. On the contrary, it is evidence of SNA's influence on the development of the OSI model.

An illustration of the influence can be seen at the Data Link Layer. In the design of its own High Level Data Link Control (HDLC), OSI inherited and adopted in large measure the features of IBM's *Synchronous Data Link Control, SDLC.*

In Chapter 3, the principles and procedures for communicating between layers were described for the OSI Reference Model. These principles and procedures apply in a similar fashion to SNA. The layers of functions in an SNA network are shown in Figure 10.1. Each layer successively encapsulates or decapsulates the user's original message using headers and trailers.

SNA is an architecture, not a product. Over the years, all the newer data communications products released by IBM have been compliant with SNA.

| Number | Layer Name | Description |
|--------|------------|-------------|
| 7 | Transaction | network access for applications; Document Interchange Architecture; Document Content Architecture; SNADS "asynchronous distribution service" |
| 6 | Presentation | data formats; coordination of resource sharing |
| 5 | Data Flow Control | synchronization of data flow; full-/half-duplex; checkpoint restart; group data into units chaining long messages |
| 4 | Transmission Control | message pacing; encryption; message sequencing |
| 3 | Path Control | routing and network traffic control |
| 2 | Data Link Control | node-node integrity; SDLC |
| 1 | Physical | electrical and mechanical e.g., modems and DSUs |

*Figure 10.1. Layers of function in SNA.*

## PUs and LUs—What They Mean

Among the components that constitute a network, SNA distinguishes between those responsible for managing network resources such as lines, memory, terminals, controllers etc., and those that are applications such as user computer programs. The resource managers are called *Physical Units (PUs)*, the user programs *Logical Units (LUs)*. Specialized service program products offered by IBM, such as *Customer Information Control System (CICS)* and *Information Management System (IMS)*, are regarded as Logical Units.

Communication sessions may be defined as the facilities between two stations that enable them to exchange data. IBM permits users to establish sessions and then use and re-use the same session for successive "conversations." Session creation establishes and commits resources (the pipe); conversations are traffic through it.

By making a distinction between Physical and Logical Units, SNA may categorize communication sessions. The same software subroutines are used when the participating components have similar characteristics. Different communications software is needed for sessions that allocate resources from that which controls the exchange of data between two user programs. Further classification of Physical Unit or Logical Unit into *type* is done to highlight the significant distinctions of functionality found in each. (Figure 10.2 describes the various Logical Unit types.)

| **Type** | **Logical Unit Description** | **Comments** |
|---|---|---|
| 0 | Non-SNA | TCAM, IMS, CICS, JES/2 3270 BSC |
| 1 | Session with one, or more workstations; interactive or batch or DDP with SNA character stream | (Obsolete) card readers; 3770 IMS/VS IBM 8100 |
| 2 | Session with workstation/s; uses SNA 3270 data stream | 3270 display stations; IMS/VS 3179 |
| 3 | Session to line printer; uses SNA 3270 data stream | CICS/VS; 3287 printer via 3274 |
| 4 | Session with one or more workstations in interactive, batch, or DDP environment; using SNA character stream | CICS/VS to 6670; 6670s to other 6670s. |
| 6.1 | Application subsystem sessions with another subsystem in DDP | CICS/VS; IMS/VS |
| 6.2 | Sessions between applications in DDP; uses SNA Generalized data stream or user defined data stream | APPC VTAM S/36 S/38 AS/400 CICS/VS |
| 7 | Sessions between host and mid-range processors, e.g., S/3x | 3090 with S/38 |

*Figure 10.2. Logical Unit (LU) types.*

## HOST-CENTRIC SNA

Within the host-centric SNA, a single *Systems Services Control Point (SSCP)* controls all the resource managers in the network. The SSCP is the PU for the entire network. Its span of control is hierarchical. It covers, in SNA terms, a sub-area, or domain that includes all the equipment under control of the host and its front-end processors. The various resource manager PUs are subordinate to the SSCP.

## APPN—THE NEW SNA

Sometimes the hierarchical topology, described previously, lacked the flexibility to address varying network geographies, workgroup relationships and sizes. Local area networks, notably *Token Ring*, became more popular as a consequence. And, IBM introduced *Advanced Peer-to-Peer Networking*, *(APPN)*, to meet peer-to-peer network needs for the AS/400 (and other computers) in SNA networks *independent* of the SSCP. APPN grew in acceptance. APPN is described in more detail in Chapter 11, which is the chapter focused on routing.

In support of these non-hierarchical network structures, the new capabilities themselves raised new (variations of the same) problems. The problems confronting LAN users are found in small standalone networks, and on LANs interconnected with other networks. Foremost among these problems are *addressing* and *routing*: how to address messages knowing only network partner names but not their (adapter card IEEE MAC layer) hardware addresses; how to set up virtual circuits for connection-oriented sessions, or to send datagrams in connectionless sessions. Two capabilities solved these problems, *NetBIOS*, and *Advanced Peer-to-Peer Communications (APPC)*. Both are described later in this Chapter. Software developers of applications accessed these capabilities via defined Applications Programming Interfaces (APIs) provided by IBM.

## VTAM

Returning to the architectural description of SNA, an SNA element such as a PU, LU or SSCP that can and does receive messages, is called a *Network Addressable Unit*. (In subsequent years, the term NAU has been equivalently interpreted as Network Accessible Unit.) The software that implements the SSCP resides in a host, an IBM System/370, 4300, ES/9000, 308x, or 3090. The SSCP functions are implemented in a computer-memory-resident software module called *Virtual Telecommunications Access Method*, *VTAM*, (or

ACF/VTAM where ACF is "Advanced Communication Function"). As pictured in Figures 1.4 and 1.9, VTAM resides in the host. Regardless of the number of applications (LUs) that are run at the host, there is but a single copy of VTAM resident. This contrasts with earlier, pre-SNA, environments where multiple copies of BTAM (an older resource manager and control point) needed to be resident, one per application.

## NCP and Other Important PUs

Referring to the table in Figure 10.3 that describes Physical Unit types, SSCP is denoted as a PU Type 5. Closely linked with SSCP and responsible jointly with the remaining PUs for implementing SNA's hierarchical functions is the *Network Control Program, (NCP)*, software. It operates within the communications front-end equipment—in IBM's Models 3745, 3720, 3725 or 3705—as a PU type 4. Together with the SSCP, the PU Type 4 manages all path control, routing, data links and physical connections. In "sub-area" (i.e., hierarchical, non peer-to-peer) networks, users provide the detailed information about the network's configuration prior to its use. Tables, generated by a "net gen" procedure, must be updated every time the network's configuration changes. These repetitive manual network definitions are chores often associated with traditional SNA.

| PU Type | Physical Unit Description |
|---|---|
| 1 | (Obsolete) more-or-less intelligent terminal |
| 2.0 and 2.1 | Cluster controller. Type 2.1 is a cluster controller containing its own control point, enabling session establishment without requiring host participation. Type 2.1 also defines a Low Entry Networking (LEN) station that was an introductory product of APPN (see Chapter 11). Type 2.1 is found on the following platforms: AS/400 System/36, System/38 and PS/2. Type 2.0 does not have its own control point. Both Types 2.0 and 2.1 provide end-user access to the network; both support LU2, LU3 and LU6.2. |
| 3 | (Not used) intelligent controller, e.g., 3174, 3274, 3276, also PC, 3770 and AS/400. |
| 4 | (Front-end) Communications Controller, e.g., 3720, 3745, 3725, 3705. |
| 5 | Host node that contains the Systems Services Control Point (SSCP) such as ACF VTAM in the 308x, 9370, 3090, 4300. |

*Figure 10.3. Five Physical Unit (PU) types that control resources and sessions.*

Of the remaining PUs that we have not yet described, PU Type 2 is the resource manager within a cluster controller, minicomputer, or free-standing PC. It controls the resources of devices attached to it, such as "dumb terminals." Two sub-types of PU 2 exist: Type 2.0 and Type 2.1. PU Type 2.0 needs the services of PU Type 5, the SSCP, to jointly help manage the resources under its control. Type 2.1, on the other hand, may use the SSCP for certain applications, but for others it manages the attached devices from its own control point without involving or needing the SSCP. The AS/400, System/36, and /38 as well as the PS/2 have this capability.

Note that PU Types 1 and 3 are obsolete.

## LOW ENTRY NETWORKING

Since the early 1980s, IBM has offered a capability enabling two nodes to communicate with each other as peers. *Low Entry Networking (LEN)* nodes are Type 2.1 nodes that do not need the services of an SSCP. LEN is an element of the Advanced Peer-to-Peer Network. The RISC System/6000 is an example of a product that implements LEN functionality. The non-IBM vendors that manufacture equipment emulating the PU 2.1 include DEC, Apple, Hewlett-Packard, Sun and others.

## LU6.2 OR APPC/LU6.2

Different types of SNA Logical Units are listed in the table of Figure 10.2. The most significant LU is LU6.2, since this type figures prominently in program-to-program sessions. *Advanced Program-to-Program Communication* is the formal name for LU6.2, abbreviated to APPC or APPC/LU6.2. As an Application Program Interface, it is platform independent, running equivalently on PS/2s, mid-size minicomputers and mainframe computers. Like NetBIOS, APPC/LU6.2 provides name services and establishes sessions linking two applications.

Among the remaining LUs in the table of Figure 10.2, LU 2 is used for host communication sessions with workstations such as 3270s. LU 3 is defined for host sessions driving line printers.

## ESTABLISHMENT OF SNA SESSIONS

In what follows, we describe the general tasks undertaken by SNA in the processing of a session. Where appropriate, the functions of NetBIOS and APPC/LU62 are compared.

When two NAUs communicate, different types of session demand different software. For example, communication between two multi-domain SNA networks involves an SSCP-SSCP session between the VTAM on one host and VTAM on another. This uses IBM's "SNI" product. More often, however, are SSCP-PU sessions within a single domain. These occur between VTAM and PUs like 3174 controllers. Also common are SSCP-LU sessions such as VTAM exchanges with the CICS/VS service program. Peer-to-peer communications require LU-LU sessions.

The different types of sessions use the Path Control and other components of SNA. In initiating an SNA session, an application LU follows this procedure:

The LU sends a request for session initialization to the SSCP or to a PU 2.1 Control Point. The request is a message that contains parameters prescribing the intended behavior of the parties for the ensuing communication. Some parameters may be negotiable, others not. For example, an APPC LU6.2 parameter may be one that requires the sender to wait for responses prior to sending its next message. This is an example of a non-negotiable parameter that is called *Definite Response*. Another non-negotiable parameter regards the use of a *Bracket* protocol allowing for more data than can fit into a single frame by a process of chaining.

The control point checks if the target LU is in its domain. If not, cross-domain protocols are initiated to locate and link up with the target LU. If it is in the domain, the control point determines the path. It also confirms whether it is legal for these LUs to communicate. (Do they share the same protocol?)

Finally, with everything in order, the SSCP sends a (CONTROL) *INITIATE* message to the LU; the LU in turn sends a *BIND* message to its target, and the session is thereby inaugurated.

The software, by this time, has validated that the session could be established; it will maintain and eventually release it on its termination. For routing, it has determined whether a connection-oriented sequence of traffic is about to occur, or if the requirement was to process datagrams. At higher levels within the architecture, security has been invoked, and passwords and user's identifications have been validated.

### Bi-direction, Acknowledgment, Conversational Behavior

Three attributes define the protocol of the conversations that may take place within the session itself: bi-direction, acknowledgment and conversational behavior.

Bi-direction determines if both parties may transmit simultaneously (full-duplex), or whether they alternate transmitting and receiving (half-duplex). If only one-way datagrams are to be sent, simplex is called for.

Acknowledgment establishes whether "definite response" ACKs or NAKs are required for every message, or only in the event of exceptions. "No response at all" is the third possibility.

Conversational behavior concerns sequence and initiation. Which party transmits first? Must each party wait for the other to signal (via poll/final bits or the equivalent) when, or if it may transmit? Do they alternate in half-duplex fashion with station A sending multiple frames to station B; station B remaining the receiver until station A yields the right to send? May station B send "error" or "change direction" requests or "abends?"

The above session services are extensive and are representative of the sophistication in SNA. By comparison, the services provided by *Network Basic Input/Output System* (*NetBIOS*), are relatively simple.

## NETBIOS—Name, Session and Datagram Service

NETBIOS was introduced by IBM in 1984, for use with LANs. It was first implemented on the PC Network, an early IBM Ethernet LAN. Originally, the NETBIOS functions were implemented in Read-Only-Memory on adapter cards that connected the workstations (PCs) to the LAN bus or cable. Later, when IBM introduced Token Ring, NETBIOS functions were implemented in software (memory in the workstation). Today's equivalent functionality is included in the OS/2 Extended Edition Communications Manager. As can be seen by the following table, NETBIOS provides OSI Layer 5 session-oriented services for DOS, UNIX or OS/2.

| DOS | UNIX | OS/2 | DOS | UNIX | OS/2 | DOS | UNIX | OS/2 |
|---|---|---|---|---|---|---|---|---|
| NETBIOS | | | NETBIOS | | | NETBIOS | | |
| OSI | | | TCP/IP | | | Proprietary | | |
| 802.3 | 802.4 | 802.5 | 802.3 | 802.4 | 802.5 | 802.3 | 802.4 | 802.5 |

*Table 10.1.*

NETBIOS supports three services: Name, Session, and Datagram.

With *Name Service*, users assign convenient names for different entities (equivalent to LUs) within an individual station. Each hardware network adapter responds to a unique hardware address, the six byte IEEE-assigned address. The latter is a Media Access Control address (MAC Destination Address or Source Address). NETBIOS's Name Service equates a convenient user given local name to a hardware address. Each station maintains a table of registered names, including directories, and sub-directories. Name Service provides the user with a set of commands. These let the user add names, or group-names to the station's table of names; delete names and, significantly, find names, not only determining the locations of specified names, but returning with stations' MAC addresses and routing information. When adding new names, Name Service validates that there are no duplicates.

NETBIOS uses *Source Routing*. This mechanism provides routing information for messages that bridge multiple token ring segments. More will be said about Source Routing in *Chapter 11—Bridges and Routers*. A different concept has been adopted by APPN, which also is described in the next chapter.

NETBIOS's *Session service* is concerned with establishing a reliable data interchange via sessions between two names. Connection-oriented communications, so-called Type 2, are supported, providing reliable data transfer based on the establishment of a virtual circuit between two names. End-points may establish connections for the two-way exchange of data, and later may terminate these connections. The Session service provides the user with a set of commands: the *call* command starts a session with someone; *listen* lets the station be receptive for a call from the session partner; *hangup* closes the session; *send* sends data to the session partner; *send, no-ack* sends data requiring no acknowledgment to the session partner; *receive* receives data from partner (or from "any"); and *status* displays the station's hardware/session/name table.

Any one name (LU, in SNA terms) may have multiple sessions with other names—multiple links per station and multiple links per LU. However, the LU is not permitted more than one link with any other LU. Originally, the maximum number of sessions supported was 32. Now, 254 peer-to-peer sessions is the upper limit.

With the Source Routing procedure, described in the next chapter, the source station discovers the location of (and route via bridges to) any destination station that is not on its ring. In the same discovery process, the station determines, for each route, the maximum frame size supported by the bridges between them. This allows the station the flexibility of choosing an appropriate route, recognizing any frame size limitations of certain applications.

Finally, *Datagram* service supports the transfer of Type 1 (connectionless) unacknowledged messages to individual stations or broadcast widely through the LAN. The maximum message size is 512 bytes. The advantage of using Datagram Service is that messages may be sent or received without first establishing a connection. Like commands in the Name and Session Services, Datagram Service commands are straight-forward: Send a datagram; Send a Broadcast datagram; Receive a datagram; Receive a Broadcast datagram.

## Important Role of APPC/LU6.2

More versatile than NETBIOS, APPC/LU6.2 also serves the name and session needs of user applications. With APPC/LU6.2, an application program advises the network of its wish for a conversation with another application program. It may identify the partner by name and not know its location. LU6.2 was created by IBM in answer to the demand for peer-to-peer connectivity. Whereas other LUs in hierarchical networks must use the services of VTAM's SSCP, APPC/LU6.2 LUs have choices: either the Control Point in a PU Type 2.1 or that in the SSCP. The Control Point establishes sessions enabling conversations (the exchange of data) between applications, and provides a way for the conversations and sessions to end.

When an application wants to start communicating with another program, it issues an *Allocate* call to the APPC programming interface. APPC in turn sets up a *session* with the named partner. In requesting the sessions, an LU specifies the destination partner's *Logical Unit* name and *mode* name. The latter determines the network class of service and takes into account propagation delay, cost per byte, cost for connect time, effective capacity and security. (Requests for batch sessions will cause the network to try to find paths with higher capacity, yet lower cost. On the other hand, requests for interactive sessions will ask the network to find paths minimizing propagation delay.)

With LU6.2 parallel sessions are possible; an LU can have more than one session with a partner LU, and it may concurrently have sessions with other LUs.

Since the overall performance of the network may degrade in trying to support too many LU to LU sessions simultaneously, the control operator (human administrator) defines a maximum number of LU-LU sessions. Note that any session, once established, remains active until torn down; individual "conversations" occupy the session sequentially.

One of the LUs is designated primary, the other secondary. Under LU6.2, the LU that issued the BIND command is the primary. This establishes responsibility for error control, in the event that there are problems on the link, such as if the link is severed.

LU6.2 sessions operate in "definite response" mode. Each receipt of a frame requires a positive or negative acknowledgment.

LU6.2 enables *Distributed Transaction* processing. If LU A is conversing with B while B is conversing with C, and C with D, then all four LUs share in the same distributed transaction. This concept is useful for "syncpoint" and Commitment processing, which is important for transaction tracking.

A large IBM Token Ring network may be split into a number of smaller networks interconnected by one or more bridges. In the next chapter, we discuss bridges, routers and gateways in general, and talk about Source Routing, the bridging approach that IBM uses for interconnecting multiple Token Rings.

# 11

# Bridges and Routers

In this Chapter, we discuss the building of networks consisting of computers communicating across wide geographies and diverse functional areas. We describe bridges, routers and gateways, take a close look at Source Routing and examine two major networking technologies, TCP/IP and IBM's APPN used for enterprise-wide networking.

The growth in the use, size and number of LANs has stimulated a demand for devices that can interconnect them. The demand arises firstly from a need to improve the performance of individual LANs as the volume of data traffic on them increases. Secondly, bridges and routers provide the connectivity enabling access to data resources within an organization, as well as network access to all the participants linked to it in an *enterprise*. These are business partners, vendors or customers external to the company.

LAN traffic increases with the normal growth of the business and also when new applications and users are added. Organizationally, it is the users themselves (at departmental level) who are doing the latter. Their experience is that the installing and attaching of new equipment to LANs are relatively straight-forward operations, with the result that any requests for new applications (or new workstations and servers) are readily accommodated. Departmental decisions of this type tend to be immune from the administrative red-tape that would otherwise apply (as when acquiring centrally managed data processing equipment).

Growth of traffic on a LAN may cause degradation in its performance, how-ever. More users sharing the same medium may mean less LAN capacity is available per station. At some level of traffic intensity, a LAN may need to be split into smaller LANs in order to improve, or at least maintain, its prior level of performance or responsiveness. If the LAN had been serving more than one department, the recommended division may be departmental. In particular, when the bulk of a department's data traffic is destined to users in the same department, a separate departmental LAN is frequently justified. Mutually uncongested by the internal data traffic of other departments, departmental LANs will operate more efficiently. Transmissions destined for users outside the department are accommodated by bridging or routing devices. In well designed systems, the incidence of these inter-LAN transmissions are relatively few when measured against intra-LAN traffic.

There is a useful taxonomy of the tools for inter-networking. We may view the interconnection of networks as occurring at a level corresponding to a layer of functionality in the OSI Reference Model. Connectivity occurs at four conceptual levels: physical, data link, network, or some combination of the remaining higher layers.

## REPEATERS AND BRIDGES

At the physical layer, a *repeater* is a device that effectively extends the length of a single segment of a medium by reshaping electrical or optical pulses bit-by-bit or by amplification of the input signal. Two segments are physically connected by the repeater and function as one longer segment. The repeater is not aware of the information content of any frame, nor of its destination.

*Bridges* are devices that connect networks at the data link layer. Bridges provide for the seaming of two or more networks. The joined networks create the illusion of a single network. Each bridge is usually a computer dedicated for the bridging function. Bridges are required when networks are split into two or more smaller (though not necessarily similar) networks. Bridges commonly link Ethernet LANs together, or Token Ring LANs together, but they may also link different LANs such as Ethernet with Token Ring.

Two independent networks may have different timing characteristics, including transmission rate and frame start times. The bridges linking them must maintain buffers to allow for the differences. For example, when a second network is busy or unavailable, the bridge must store any frame received from the first network in a buffer, forwarding it to the second network when it becomes free. With the use of buffers, the bridge also accommodates any differences in the transmission speeds of the two networks.

## ROUTERS

A *router* is an intelligent device (computer) that performs its functions at the network level of the OSI Reference Model. Whereas the scope of a bridge is to forward (or filter) frames originating on one segment in a network to another segment under the control of the bridge (based on the bridge examining MAC addresses and associating them with segments), the scope of the router allows for frames to be transmitted between stations on totally different networks. Routers successively forward a message through any number of other routers *en route* to the router that "owns" the destination station (that is, the one that supports that station's LAN). That router, in turn, forwards the message to the station using a data link specifying its MAC address.

The messages processed by the networks themselves are not restricted to conform to only one protocol. Routers that process packets between totally different networks such as X.25, IPX (Novell), and IP (from TCP/IP) are called *multi-protocol routers*.

## GATEWAYS

*Gateways* are devices that reconcile communication differences between stations with different functionality at OSI layers 4, 5, 6 or 7. Gateways usually include subordinate router or bridge capabilities as well. Gateways map the functions of one operating system conforming to IBM's SNA or DEC's DNA, for example, to another, resolving all incompatibilities that occur above the *OSI Network* layer. They interconnect mixed networks that use different protocol suites.

Gateways are the most complex of the connectivity components, and this is reflected in their higher costs. (We note that the word "gateway" used in a TCP/Internet context denotes a router.)

## MORE ABOUT BRIDGES

Typical bridge equipment includes at least two adapter cards, or interfaces, one for each attached network. The bridge monitors the traffic occurring on each adapter it possesses. In the normal course of operation, stations on a network are transmitting messages to addressed destinations. Bridges on the sending station's network behave as do other stations, except that they do not (usually) create user messages, while they do perform a special monitoring and copying function.

When the bridge monitors messages, it examines the MAC destination address in the message header. The bridge ignores a message (i.e., takes no steps) if it determines that the destination is a station on the same LAN. But if the destination station is not on the LAN, the bridge copies the message to every other LAN to which it is connected, using its other adapter port or ports, and applying the appropriate protocol (CSMA/CD, Token Ring, or as the case may be).

## Broadcast Storms

A problem with this approach occurs when multiple bridges are connected to the same LANs. When two or more bridges operate in parallel between two LANs, undesirable message looping is possible. Unless techniques such as Source Routing or the Spanning Tree Algorithm (see below) are in place, a bridge may receive messages previously sent by it. The bridge may forward the message from one LAN to a second LAN only to receive it back via a parallel bridge's connection to the first LAN. The bridge then sees these same messages for a second time, resends them, and the messages recirculate endlessly. This can create a "broadcast storm" that can incapacitate a network if unchecked.

## Source Routing at the Data Link Layer

Source Routing is a *bridging* approach for routing messages addressed to stations on other networks that are linked together by means of bridges. We see this approach implemented on IBM Token Rings. Stations reach each other, regardless of the ring either belongs to, by arranging that the messages embed Source Routing information. That information instructs the bridge receiving it as to which output port the bridge should select for forwarding the message.

Let us examine the format of the Routing Information contained in each message. Later, we will see how the information is interpreted and processed.

In the IEEE 802.5 MAC layer protocol data unit (see Figure 7.5), the most significant bit of the Source Address field indicates whether routing information is included in the message frame. If the bit is set, a *Routing Information* field exists. It appears just prior to the LLC, ahead of the Destination Service Access Point field. The Routing Information is a variable length field consisting of a header plus at most 14 entries. Figure 11.1 is the format of the Routing Information field—each entry is two bytes long:

| | |
|---|---|
| Routing | Control |
| Route | Designator #1 |
| Route | Designator #2 |
| | |
| Route | Designator #13 |
| Route | Designator #14 |

*Figure 11.1. Format of Routing Information field.*

The *Routing Control* bytes indicate to bridges that receive the message that routing for the message exists. Alternatively, they indicate that the message is a "discovery" type frame that the bridge should simply broadcast on all its output ports. These indications are found within the first byte of Routing Control whose format is *bbbrrrrr*. The rrrrr field refers to the number of Route Designator entries.

The maximum length of any message (or fragment of message) must be no larger than the smallest bridge buffer throughout the route that will accommodate it. The second Routing Control byte (whose format is dfff0000), contains a code (*fff*) for the largest message size or "frame-size" that may be forwarded. This field advises the parties at the end-points of the largest buffer size available to messages on this route. When a bridge forwards a "discovery" type frame, it examines the *fff* code. If the size of its buffer for accepting messages is smaller, it amends the code.

Finally, also found in the second byte of Routing Control is the "message direction." This defines whether the Route Designators are being processed top-down or bottom-up. The *d* bit in the second Routing Control byte indicates message direction.

Up to 14 *Route Designators* follow Routing Control. (However, in IBM Token Rings, the maximum number of Route Designators is 7.) Each 2–byte entry contains Ring Number (3 hex digits) followed by Bridge Number (1 hex digit).

Now that we have described the format of Routing Information, let us see how it is interpreted and processed. Firstly, a source station sends the destination station a special message (a Test or Exchange Id command). This determines whether or not Source Routing is required. If the destination station is on the same Token Ring, the source station will get a positive response. Otherwise, it "broadcasts" a message to the destination, setting broadcast (*bbb*) bits in Routing Control. When a bridge receives one of these messages, it inserts a new Route Designator entry into the message and then copies it on all its output ports. (Each of the bridge's output ports connects to a different network.)

The Route Designator includes the network's 3 hex digit number and the number by which the connecting bridge is known to the new ring. (Each ring identifies any one of sixteen different bridges by means of a hex digit.)

As the message proceeds from ring to ring, the number of Route Designators entries increments and so a longer Routing Information field builds up. Descendant copies of the message thread through different rings, each building up different Routing Information. A bridge will discard frames that have looped back to it without having reached the destination.

Eventually, the messages arrive at the destination station. It responds by returning every frame, changing the direction bit and the broadcast bits in the header. The frames return on the same paths they took, now moving towards the source station. Whereas in the outbound direction, any multi-port bridge makes (clones or) descendants of the message received, messages traveling in this direction do not generate clones, and only a single message exits from each bridge on the port identified by a Route Designator.

After the source station has received all the response messages, it selects a route based on application needs. The criteria for selection are usually shortest delay, minimum number of bridges traversed or greatest maximum frame length allowable in the route. The chosen route's Routing Information field is then copied from the response used, and retained in the station. Later, it will be embedded in every message sent to the destination.

An advantage of Source Routing is that redundant configurations of links and bridges can be used in a way that balances the traffic. This is particularly the case when there is more than one path between two LANs. Using Source Routing, parallel bridges may be selected by different applications to spread the traffic more evenly.

Another advantage of Source Routing is that bridges, which are simpler devices than routers, forward the messages. Bridges do not incur the processing overhead of routers, and so are able to offer higher performance at a lower cost. Also, by establishing a connection-oriented virtual circuit prior to transmission, the benefit gained is that the application knows beforehand what network elements will be used in the message's path.

Source Routing has some disadvantages. First is the operational consequences of the discovery process. Target stations must not only be physically attached to the network, but they need to be powered on and operating. In other words, stations need to actively participate in the discovery process. Likewise, if stations change locations or adapter cards for whatever reason, procedures must be in place to implement new route discovery.

Second, multi-cast performance may put the performance of the network at risk. Discovery frames cause descendants to appear at all paths out of every bridge. These route discovery descendant frames can proliferate, swamp the network and cause frames to be lost. Lost frames in turn exacerbate the problem by triggering re-transmissions in an already congested environment. Some of these may be redundant, and will be discarded on their looped return to the bridge. But the extra processing is a penalty on the bridge's performance, and thus the network's performance.

Third, the presence of routing information in every frame adds to the stations' buffer sizes and lowers the network's throughput rate since more bytes are being transmitted.

The fourth disadvantage of Source Routing is inflexibility. Bridges en route *have* to select the pre-assigned path. In the event a port is closed at a particular bridge specified in the routing, the bridge has no freedom to select an alternate route. Additionally, the responsibility and processing to discover and select the route is assumed by the communicating stations.

## Transparent Bridges

The *transparent* bridge is a "Learning Bridge." It maintains a dynamic software record of the station identifications that are on each network that the bridge directly supports. It monitors every frame's source address and notes the network (i.e., the adapter card port) the frame was received on. The IEEE 802.1 has standardized a protocol and algorithm called the *Spanning Tree* that operates on transparent bridges and provides a solution to the "broadcast storm" problem. The algorithm is an alternative to the *Source Routing* bridge's procedure described above. (Recall that Source Routing bridges maintain no records, using each frame's Routing Information field instead.)

## Source Routing Transparent Bridges

*Source Routing Transparent bridges* are able to handle both source routed and transparent frames. These are bridges that will use the frame's source routing information if it is present, and perform transparent routing if not. Many Source Routing Transparent bridges are able to achieve forwarding rates close to 15,000 frames per second.

To perform their functions, Source Routing Transparent bridges scan for a *Routing Information Indicator* in the frame (most significant bit of Source Address). The bit's value dictates whether the bridge will forward the message according to the Source Routing protocol or by means of Transparent procedures.

## Spanning Tree Algorithm

To avert broadcast storms, a non-looping path needs to be determined for every pair of stations in configurations of interconnected networks. The Spanning Tree algorithm provides a mechanism of finding such paths. Executing the algorithm results in a tree topology where the individual LANs are "limbs" and a particular bridge is at the tree's root. The tree assures that there is only one path between any two LANs.

Figure 11.2 shows a configuration of eight LANs and seven bridges. In the figure, the notation b1, b2, etc. indicates numbered bridges. One of the bridges is selected as a "root bridge." (In Figure 11.2, this is b4). We define the term "root bridge" and the notations "DP" and "RP" below.

In an inter-network, when a LAN is connected by two or more bridges to a second LAN, the Spanning Tree algorithm selects only one bridge as the path for routing messages to a LAN. For example, in Figure 11.2, bridge b1 has been chosen for connecting LAN1 with the *root*. (Bridge b3 could have been selected instead, but wasn't.) Bridge b1 in the figure is also the *designated bridge* to LAN2 and LAN3. Of bridge b1's ports, the one attached to LAN1, LAN2 or LAN3 is called the *designated port* (DP in Figure 11.2) to that LAN.

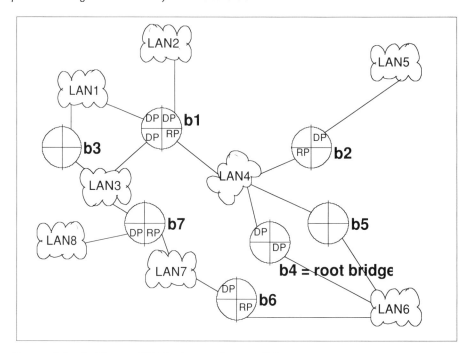

Legend: b*n* bridge *n*; DP designated port; RP root port.

*Figure 11.2. Spanning Tree. In configurations where more than one bridge connects to a LAN, a single path is selected between one LAN (a "leaf" of the tree) and any other. Only one bridge is the base of the tree or root.*

A bridge's port that is used to *connect* with a LAN that is closer to the "root bridge" is known as its *root port* (RP). In Figure 11.2, the root port of bridge b1 is connected to LAN4.

The *root bridge* is an exception in that it is the only bridge in the network that has no root ports. By definition, it has designated ports only. (It has no root ports, because it is at the root.) The root bridge gets chosen by the algorithm to carry the bulk of traffic since it connects the two halves of the network.

The process of finding the designated port and root port is similar to the discovery process used for Source Routing in determining a route between source and destination. Special messages called *bridge protocol data units* are used whose discovery goal is the "reachability" of different LANs from each bridge.

Token Ring bridges may use the Spanning Tree algorithm but do not have to, particularly if Source Routing is an alternative. Ethernet relies on the Spanning Tree algorithm. The reconstruction of the Spanning Tree table after network changes or failures is a lengthy process and could delay users undesirably. This disadvantage, coupled with the exclusion of certain paths to avoid loops, may make its use for bridged networks unattractive.

# ROUTING

*Routing* is the process of first of all determining the path (though not necessarily commandeering resources for it) that a message may take between two endpoints across intermediate nodes. Alternatively, and additionally, it is the process of actually forwarding the message based on such route knowledge. Two different philosophies are propounded as regards routing.

## Source Routing

The first philosophy is called *Source Routing*. It asserts that the sender knows exactly how the message should be routed and is able to incorporate such knowledge within a header of the message itself. The approach is similar to Source Routing at the bridge level, (which should have been named Source Bridging instead!) All information about how to forward the message from the source to its final destination is included as part of the message. That includes the node or router number that is selected to be the next processor of the message. As a matter of interest, TCP/IP supports Source Routing as an option. In this case, the path is obtained using "routing algorithms" rather than by using the discovery mechanism described earlier.

## Node-routing

The second philosophy is called *node-routing*, or "*hop-by-hop*." The assertion is that the network nodes know best how the message should be routed. The network nodes, in turn, are empowered to make the routing decisions autonomously. All information about how to forward any received message is maintained in tables at the nodes. In operation, sending stations simply submit messages to a network. The network nodes have knowledge about other network nodes and so will select one exit port that gets the message closer to its destination. The node makes its selection based on a number of criteria defining a route's "cost." These include propagation delay, transmission speed, processing delay, etc. No routing information is included within the message from the sender, other than the name of the final destination.

Node-routing is a feature both of TCP/IP and of IBM's APPN.

# TCP/IP ROUTERS

Among the more popular routers are those that support traffic between *Transmission Control Protocol/Internet Protocol* (*TCP/IP*) stations. Originally designed for military network research, the Transmission Control

Protocol/Internet Protocol has gained corporate acceptance as the protocol of choice for UNIX environments. TCP/IP is attractive for its higher layer services including *File Transfer Protocol*, *FTP*, *Simple Mail Transfer Protocol*, *SMTP*, as well as the terminal emulation application *Telnet*.

TCP/IP is available on a wide range of platforms (primarily, but not exclusively UNIX-based) and is available from many vendors. The protocol operates above the data link layer and physical layer, and so is independent of local area networks such as Ethernet and Token Ring, and wide area links such as asynchronous communications, SDLC, Frame Relay and so on.

## ROUTING ISSUES

In examining the architecture of any routing capability, questions of its efficiency and maintainability need to be kept in mind. How does the network handle congestion? What procedures are followed for detecting errors and correcting them? Does the network allow for different classes of service? What is the procedure for making sure that the routing information base is up to date?

In the TCP/IP environment, all computer and communications equipment is organized into *hosts* that are part of some *network*. The word "host" is used by the TCP/IP community of users to mean a computer—not necessarily a large one. It may refer to a mainframe, or to a minicomputer, or to a workstation. Each host usually operates UNIX and contains some inter-networking software.

## INTERNET VS. iNTERNET

The term *Internet*, with a capital I, is the name given to a global interconnection of networks operating the TCP/IP protocol and, possibly some networks with OSI protocols. In scope, these networks are local, metropolitan, national or international. The network, originally called ARPANET (Advanced Research Projects Agency Network, funded by the Department of Defense) was later split into MILNET for military use only, and Internet. The latter consisted originally of a number of connected universities and research establishments. By the end of 1994, Internet had over 4 million hosts in about 60,000 networks that connect using TCP/IP. The Internet's sponsors include the National Science Foundation, the Department of Energy, NASA and DARPA.

Users of the protocols in TCP/IP do not have to subscribe to the Internet (capitalized I). TCP/IP is then applied by these users for their own private networks. Users that elect to build and use their own networks and not use Internet may establish any set of network and host names. However, if there is a chance that the user may subscribe to the Internet, users would be well advised to choose network and host numbers that would be compatible.

In what follows, we describe the approach taken for defining network and host names.

## TCP Routing Approach

In a TCP/IP network, some hosts are designated as *gateways* or *IP Routers*. (As an aside on terminology, we note that the device Internet calls a *gateway* is a router.) Each IP router maintains routing tables to inform it where adjacent routers and hosts are. In a TCP/IP internet, computers connect to different networks. The routers route messages to destination networks. The final router reached in a routing sequence routes the message to an individual host on that network. Only this final router knows the MAC address of the host.

Routing provides for addressing flexibility. Routers on all other networks do not need to know the specific MAC address of any host on a destination network. A user may move his or her host from one network and simply connect to another without severe administrative hardship. If a host had earlier changed its adapter card, it could still be addressed (by the same software at the source) despite the new hardware address. For moves within the same network, the hardware address change does not need to be advertised to all routers everywhere. Clearly, this is a practical way to implement today's networks that are characterized by constant change.

Internet identifies users at a logical (layer 3) level. It differentiates three different sizes or Classes of network. Class A networks are large, each possessing up to

$2^{24} = 16,777,216$ hosts.

Class B networks are medium to large, having

$2^{16} = 65,536$ hosts.

Class C networks are small with less than 256 hosts each.

## Internet Addressing

The *Internet address* is always a 32-bit number consisting of a network identifier and a host identifier. For Class A networks, the network identifier is a 7-bit number prefixed by a 0 bit. This allows the range of network numbers from 0 through 127. The specific network numbers 0 and 127 are reserved for "this network" and "all networks," respectively. The seven network bits plus the prefix 0 bit plus 24 host bits comprise the Internet address format used to identify a single host in a Class A network.

For Class B networks, the network identifier is a 14-bit number prefixed by the bits 1 and 0. This allows the range of network numbers from 32,768 through 49,151. The two prefix bits plus fourteen network bits plus 16 host bits comprise the Internet address format in Class B networks.

For Class C networks, the network identifier is 21 bits long, prefixed by the bits 1, 1 and 0. This allows for approximately two million network numbers numbered from 12,582,912 through 14,680,063. The three prefix bits plus 21 network bits plus 8 host bits constitute the 32-bit Class C Internet address format.

### Dotted Decimal Notation—a Convenience

TCP/IP users prefer, however, to quote the network numbers (and host numbers) in ways that make them readily written in binary. The convention used is called *dotted decimal*. The binary value of any byte is a decimal value between 0 and 255. The number 49,151 in binary, for example, is 10111111 11111111. Since the left byte is binary for 191, and the right byte is binary for 255, the number 49,151 when written in dotted decimal notation is 191.255. Likewise, the number 12,582,912 written in binary is a 3-byte number 11000000 00000000 00000000 which is written as 192.0.0 in dotted decimal.

The dotted decimal notation is also used on the host fields.

When messages arrive at an IP Router, it examines their destination IP network addresses. The IP Router maintains *Routing Tables* that consist of pairs of entries of network number with its associated "next" IP Router number. On recognizing a network in the IP address of the message, the IP Router forwards the message to the "next" IP Router. If its destination LAN is one that is directly connected to the IP Router, IP Router sends the datagram in a frame to the "host" on the LAN, using an appropriate data link Medium Access Control (MAC) address.

### ARP Maps MAC to IP Name

The *Address Resolution Protocol*, *ARP*, is used to obtain MAC addresses for each 32-bit IP address. When a Router receives a message addressed to an unknown host on a directly connected network, it broadcasts on the LAN e.g., "who is host 123?" The target station then responds to the router with its MAC 6-byte identifier.

IP Routers send complete routing tables to each other during routine updates. This process is part of the *Routing Information Protocol (RIP)*. To relieve the onerousness of this process, the *Open Shortest Path First*, *OSPF* router-to-router protocol has been devised. This only sends updates when the topology of the routers changes.

TCP/IP inter-network architecture combines the *Internet Protocol* which uses datagrams (connectionless messages) at OSI level 3 and the end-to-end integrity transport TCP at layer 4. The IP part of the TCP/IP name refers to the Internet Protocol. This takes user messages, segments them if necessary into smaller fragments, appends a header and transmits the datagram.

Receiving IP routers reciprocally receive the datagram, and examine the IP destination field (see Table 11.1). At the eventual destination, IP strips off the header and reassembles the datagram. If any errors occur in this process, IP simply discards the message, leaving the responsibility of error control to the Layer 4 Transmission Control Protocol in the end nodes.

### The IP Packet Explained

The following table shows the format of the IP datagram. Each row is 32 bits long.

| Ver 4 bits | Hdr 4 bits | Service Type 8 bits | Total Length 16 bits | |
|---|---|---|---|---|
| Identification 16 bits | | | Flags 4 bits | Fragment Offset 12 bits |
| Time to Live 8 bits | | Protocol 8 bits | Header Checksum 16 bits | |
| Source IP Address 32 bits | | | | |
| Destination IP Address 32 bits | | | | |
| IP protocol options 24 bits | | | | Pad 8 bits |
| 1st hop IP Address      32 bits (option) | | | | |
| 2nd hop IP Address      32 bits (option) | | | | |
| | | | | |
| Last hop IP Address      32 bits (option) | | | | |
| data | | | | |
| data | | | | |

*Table 11.1. Format of IP datagram.*

In this format, Header length is a number of 32-bit words, typically 5. The Total Length field, measured in bytes, includes header and data and is no larger than 65,535. IP, through the use of the Service Type field in the header, does have the potential for supporting different classes of service. Although many devices ignore them, these flags could be used to select services such as route security, reliability, bandwidth, cost and propagation delay.

Among the other fields, "Identification" is a number that is shared by fragments of the datagram. Fragmentation is done to accommodate the smallness of the frame buffers in any of the routers in the path of the transmission. The datagram's fragments are reassembled through the use of the "Fragment Offset" contents. When multiplied by 8, Fragment Offset points to a byte number in the datagram's 65,536-byte buffer. The Flags field is used to manage fragmentation. The Flags indicate if a message is a fragment, and, if so, whether more fragments follow. They also indicate when a datagram may not be fragmented. Finally, the "Time to Live" field is decremented on each hop of the message. If the count reaches zero, the message is dropped. Its *raison d'etre* is to prevent erroneously addressed datagrams from endlessly recirculating in the network.

## IBM'S APPN

A major node-routing capability is *Advanced Peer-to-Peer Networking*, *APPN*. As mentioned in Chapter 10, APPN is IBM's networking architecture that enables large and small computers to communicate as peers across both local and wide area networks. APPN use does not require SNA's VTAM, the kernel of IBM's traditional sub-area networks. But, both APPN can SNA can coexist on the same network, using sub-area SNA for terminal to host connectivity, and APPN for peer-to-peer connections between workstations, PCs and hosts.

Within APPN, three different types of node exist. The first is called a *Low Entry Networking*, or *LEN* node. The second and third types are *End nodes* and *Network nodes*.

### LENs and End Nodes

*LEN nodes* were introduced in the 1980s as forerunners to full peer-to-peer networking. LEN nodes have limited capabilities. Their functions do not change dynamically with changes to the network configuration or topology as do the other two types. When LEN nodes communicate with other LEN nodes, they have full details of each other's specifications. These definitions are pre-set, and must be maintained by (human) operators to reflect the network configuration or topology. Thus, any changes to the LEN network need to be manually recorded by operators.

*End nodes* are able to take advantage of the services of APPN networks. When an End node connects to an APPN network, it identifies itself and the various applications (LUs) that it supports. When an LU wishes to connect to another LU, the End node can request APPN to help find the other LU anywhere on the network. End nodes do no routing.

### Network Nodes are Really Routers

A *Network node* is capable of performing all the functions of an end node, plus it provides two additional services. The first is routing. All Network nodes collaborate to jointly route traffic from one node to another, and then finally to the destination station. Second, Network nodes help End nodes locate partner LUs.

As mentioned earlier, when LEN nodes communicate with other LEN nodes, they need full details of each other's specifications. These definitions are maintained by (human) operators as the network configuration or topology changes. By contrast, Network nodes perform these functions automatically. An End node simply asks the Network node to locate the destination LU; it does not concern itself with the possibility of changes that have taken place since the last time.

Network nodes know the identities of all the End nodes directly attached to it, plus the identity of all the Network nodes that are directly reachable by the (Network) node. The Network node registers in its memory all the LUs for each directly attached End node. APPN Network nodes (routers) do not know all the End nodes and LUs in the network. Each Network node maintains information about other Network nodes in a *topology database* similar to the routing tables maintained by TCP/IP.

End nodes do not link with other End nodes without the use of at least one intermediate Network node. An End node may have one or more links with the network. Whenever an End node first establishes a link to a new Network node, the latter offers itself as a *network server*. Any Network node may be a network server. However, only one of the Network nodes to which an End node connects may act as its *network server*.

### Tie in the APPC API with APPN

Let us revert, for a moment, back to the use of the APPC LU6.2 Application Programming Interface. When an APPC application (LU) intends to start a conversation with another LU—named, for illustration, FARAWAY—it requests its network server to locate the LU FARAWAY. The Network node scans its tables for any locally registered entry with that name. If it finds one, it establishes a link (a session) between it and the requesting LU. If it does not, it broadcasts a request to the Network nodes to which it is connected. Each of these Network nodes in turn scans among its registered names for FARAWAY. If one of them finds an entry, it passes the information back to the requesting Network node. The latter in turn establishes the session as before. However, the Network node also remembers the routing to FARAWAY for any subsequent request that may be made.

## When to Update Routing Tables

Note that APPN does not go through a process of regularly submitting updates between its member routers (Network nodes). Instead, only routing changes are communicated on the network. In this respect, there may be an advantage to using APPN as compared to TCP/IP, particularly when the latter has not implemented OSPF.

A potential drawback to APPN's routing is its static nature. All APPN packets for a session follow the same route through the network. If a route fails, the session fails. However, with an APPN enhancement called *High Performance Routing* dynamic rerouting may take place. This compares with the connectionless approach of TCP/IP where IP shields the application from link failure. IP and HPR merely select the next best available route.

We mentioned earlier that IP routers have the potential for "Class of Service" routing. APPN offers the equivalent capability. In establishing the session between two LUs, parameters may be chosen specifying delay, security, cost or bandwidth capacities.

Finally, APPN nodes have adopted *adaptive pacing*. This is the process whereby end nodes voluntarily reduce their submission of messages based on conditions of network congestion. The nodes either deduce implicitly that congestion is occurring, (from the number of errors), or are themselves explicitly notified by means of congestion indications (flagged in the headers of messages received from the network).

---

Bridges and routers help create networks that span wide geographies. Businesses may link branches with headquarters, for example.

Apart from applications concerns, a number of issues exist when constructing networks. Foremost among the issues to consider are standards compliance, performance, and network management.

Some networks employ both proprietary and standard interfaces. While the ownership of LANs may be proprietary, if metropolitan MANs are to link bridges or routers over a county, city or metropolitan area, compliance with non-proprietary (standard) interfaces is mandatory. This applies even more strongly when wide area networks join the bridges and routers together. Using the services of national and international entities (such as the PTTs) may place demands on the user for compliance with standards in interfacing to, and inter-operating with, public wide area and metropolitan area networks. This requirement will apply particularly when linking equipment in one network (via bridges or routers) to like equipment in some other country.

Regarding performance, the majority of MAN/WAN networks today operate at 56 kbit/s or 1.5 Mbit/s. One long range objective is a single communications capability that can support LANs operating at or beyond 10 Mbit/s, via MANs and WANs operating at and beyond 100 Mbit/s. The same single communications capability will service multiple applications, satisfying the full range of diverse communications needs.

A boding problem is that as the number, speed and functions of the networks increase, the proliferation of different bridges and routers will make network management unwieldy or untractable. Relief appears to be on the horizon in the shape of ATM. This versatile technology, described in Chapter 9, has stimulated a lot of industry interest. ATM has spurred sufficient industry momentum that profuse numbers of products and services are already forthcoming, many from the common carriers themselves. One vision of the future has network managers using ATM to integrate diverse (multi-application), high-speed communications services within a single network while, at the same time, delegating the concerns and issues of network management to a common carrier. Only time will tell whether and when the promised services, features, *and* manageability benefits will materialize. Nevertheless, as seen from the vantage of today, the prospects are good.

# Appendix A

# Bibliography

*An American National Standard IEEE Standards for Local Area Networks: Logical Link Control*; published 1984 by The Institute of Electrical and Electronic Engineers, Inc., 345 East 47th Street, New York, NY 10017.

*Broadband: Business Services, Technologies and Strategic Input*; David Wright 1993; Artech House, Inc., 685 Canton St, Norwood, MA 02062.

*A C Programmer's Guide to the IBM Token Ring*; William H. Roetzheim 1991; Prentice Hall, Inc., A Division of Simon & Schuster, Englewood Cliffs, NJ 07632.

*Computer Communications*; K.G. Beauchamp 1987; Van Nostrand Reinhold (UK) Co. Ltd., Molly Millars Lane, Wokingham, Berkshire, England.

*Data Communications and Networks 2*; edited by R.L. Brewster 1989; Peter Peregrinus Ltd on behalf of the Institution of Electrical Engineers, London, U.K.

*Data Communications, Facilities, Networks and Systems Design*; Dixon R. Doll 1978; John Wiley & Sons, 605 Third Avenue, New York, NY 10016.

*Data Network Design*; Darren L. Spohn with Jay Ranade, Series Advisor 1993; McGraw-Hill Inc., 1221 Avenue of the Americas, New York, NY 10020.

*Emerging Communications Technologies*; Uyless Black 1994; PTR Prentice Hall, Prentice Hall, Inc., A Paramount Communications Company, Englewood Cliffs, NJ 07632.

*Frame Relay Networks, Specifications & Implementation*; Uyless Black 1994; McGraw-Hill Inc., 1221 Avenue of the Americas, New York, NY 10020.

*The Handbook of International Connectivity Standards*; edited by Gary R. McClain Ph.D 1992; Van Nostrand Reinhold, 115 Fifth Avenue, New York, NY 10003.

*IBM's Token-Ring Networking Handbook*; George C. Sackett with Jay Ranade, Series Advisor 1993; McGraw-Hill Inc., 1221 Avenue of the Americas, New York, NY 10020.

*Internetworking LANs and WANs, Concepts Techniques and Methods*; Gilbert Held 1993; John Wiley & Sons Ltd., Baffins Lane, Chichester, West Sussex PO19 1UD, England.

*Internetworking with TCP/IP Volume I, Perinciples, Protocols and Architectures*; Douglas E. Comer 1991; Prentice Hall, Inc., A Division of Simon & Schuster, Englewood Cliffs, NJ 07632.

*ISDN Second Editiion—ATM, B-ISDN, Frame Relay*; Gary C. Kessler with Jay Ranade, Series Advisor 1993, 1990; McGraw-Hill Inc., 1221 Avenue of the Americas, New York, NY 10020.

*Local Area Networks and their applications*; Brendan Tangney, Donal O'Mahony 1988; Prentice Hall International (UK) Ltd., 66 Wood Lane End, Hemel Hempstead, Hertfordshire HP2 4RG, England.

*Local Area Networks Architectures and Implementations*; James Martin with Kathleen Kavanaugh Chapman 1989; Prentice Hall, Inc., Englewood Cliffs, NJ 07632.

*Local Area Networks The Next Generation*; Thomas W. Madron 1990; John Wiley & Sons, 605 Third Avenue, New York, NY 10158-0012.

*Network Protocol Handbook*; Matthew Naugle with Uyless Black Series Advisor 1994; McGraw-Hill Inc., 1221 Avenue of the Americas, New York, NY 10020.

*Networks for the 1990s*; edited by Ray Reardon 1988; Online Publications, Pinner Green House, Ash Hill Drive, Pinner, Middlesex HA5 2AE, England (distributed in the USA by John Wiley & Sons, 605 Third Avenue, New York, NY 10158-0012).

*Open Systems LANs and their global interconnection*; Jack Houldsworth, Mark Taylor, Keith Caves, Alan Flatman and Keith Crook 1991; Butterworth-Heinemann Ltd., Linacre House, Jordan Hill, Oxford OX2 8DP England.

*Open Systems Networking, TCP/IP and ISO*; David M. Piscitello, A. Lyman Chapin 1993; Addison-Wesley Publishing Company, One Jacob Way, Reading, MA 01867.

*Satellite Technology—An Introduction*; Andrew F. Inglis 1991; Butterworth Heinemann, a division of Reed Publishing (USA) Inc., 80 Montvale Avenue, Stoneham, MA 02180.

*SNA: Architecture, Protocols, and Implementation*; Atul Kapoor 1992; McGraw-Hill Inc., 1221 Avenue of the Americas, New York, NY 10020.

*System Integration for the IBM PS/2 and PC*; Larry Jordan 1990; Simon & Schuster, 15 Columbus Circle, New York, NY 10023.

*Token Ring Networks*; Jesper Nilausen 1992; Prentice Hall International (UK) Ltd, Campus 400, Maylands Avenue, Hemel Hempstead, Hertfordshire HP2 7EZ, England.

*Token Ring Networks Design, Implementation and Management*; J.R. Abrahams 1991; NCC Blackwell Limited, 108 Cowley Road, Oxford OX4 1JF, England.

# Appendix B

## Glossary of Data Communications Acronyms

(courtesy BCR Enterprises, Inc.)

Entries marked * provided by author

| | |
|---|---|
| 1Base5 | IEEE 802.3 1-Mbit/s Baseband LAN using 500m (max.) unshielded twisted pair cable segments; also called StarLAN* |
| 10Base2 | IEEE 802.3 10-Mbit/s Baseband LAN using 185m (max.) cable segments (coaxial, thin); also called Cheapernet or Thinnet* |
| 10Base5 | IEEE 802.3 10-Mbit/s Baseband LAN using 500m (thick coaxial) cable segments; similar to Ethernet* |
| 10BaseT | IEEE 802.3 10-Mbit/s Baseband LAN using unshielded twisted pair cable segments* |
| 10Broad36 | IEEE 802.3 10-Mbit/s Broadband LAN using 3600m (max.) coaxial cable segments* |
| 4B/5B | Encoding scheme mapping 4-bit nibbles to/from 5-bit quintets* |
| μ-law | North American companding standard used by LECs and IXCs* |
| A-law | ITU-TS companding standard used by European PTTs* |
| AAL | ATM Adaptation Layer* |
| ACF | Advanced Communication Function* |
| ACK | Positive Acknowledgment |
| AM/PSK | Amplitude Modulation/Phase Shift Keying* |
| ANSI | American National Standards Institute |
| API | Applications Programming Interface |
| APPC/LU 6.2 | Advanced Program to Program Communication (IBM Protocol) |

| | |
|---|---|
| APPN | Advanced Peer-to-Peer Networking (IBM Protocol)* |
| ARP | Address Resolution Protocol (part of TCP/IP protocol suite) |
| ARPAnet | Advanced Research Projects Agency Network |
| ARQ | Automatic Request for Repeat or Automatic Request for Retransmission* |
| ASCII | American Standard Code for Information Interchange* |
| ASR | Automatic Send-Receive Teletypewriter Machine |
| ATM | Asynchronous Transfer Mode |
| AUI | Attachment Unit Interface (transceiver cable) |
| AWG | American Wire Gauge* |
| B8ZS | Binary 8-Zeros Substitution* |
| BCDIC | Binary Coded Decimal Interchange Code* |
| BECN | Backward Explicit Congestion Notification* |
| BERT | Bit Error Rate Test |
| B-ISDN | Broadband Integrated Services Digital Network |
| BNC | Standard connector used with IEEE 802.3 10Base2 coaxial cable* |
| BRI | Basic Rate Interface (ISDN) |
| BSC | Binary Synchronous Communications (IBM Protocol)* |
| BTAM | Basic Telecommunications Access Method |
| CATV | Community Antenna Television  (or Cable TV)* |
| CAU | Controlled Access Unit* |
| CCITT | *see ITU-T* |
| CIR | Committed Information Rate* |
| CLP | Cell Loss Priority* |
| CODEC | Coder-decoder transforming analog signals to/from digital signals* |
| Compand | Compress/Expand analog to and from digital* |
| CPE | Customer Premises Equipment |
| CPU | Central Processing Unit |
| CRC | Cyclic Redundancy Check |
| CRC | Cyclical Redundancy Characters* |
| CSMA/CA | Carrier Sense Multiple Access with Collision Avoidance* |
| CSMA/CD | Carrier Sense Multiple Access with Collision Detection |
| CSU | Channel Service Unit |
| dB | decibel* |

| | |
|---|---|
| DAA | Data Access Arrangement |
| DACS | Digital Access and Cross-connect System |
| DARPA | Defense Advanced Research Projects Agency* |
| DASD | Direct Access Storage Device* |
| DC1 | Device Control 1 |
| DC3 | Device Control 3 |
| DCCS | Digital Cross-Connect System |
| DCE | Data Communications Equipment |
| | Data Circuit Terminating Equipment * |
| DDCMP | Digital Data Communications Message Protocol (DEC)* |
| DDS | Dataphone Digital Service |
| DLCI | Data Link Connection Identifier* |
| DNA | Digital Network Architecture |
| DNS | Domain Name System |
| DS0 | Digital Service, Level 0 (64 kbit/s) |
| | Digital Signal, Level 0 (64 kbit/s)* |
| DS1 | Digital Service, Level 1 (1.544 Mbit/s) |
| | Digital Signal, Level 1 (1.544 Mbit/s)* |
| DS1C | Digital Signal, Level 1C (3.152 Mbit/s)* |
| DS2 | Digital Signal, Level 2 (6.312 Mbit/s)* |
| DS3 | Digital Service, Level 3 (44.736 Mbit/s) |
| | Digital Signal, Level 3 (44 .736 Mbit/s)* |
| DSAP | Destination Service Access Point* |
| DSL | Digital Subscriber Loop* |
| DSU | Digital Service Unit |
| | Data Service Unit* |
| DQDB | Distributed Queue Dual Bus |
| DSAP | Destination Service Access Point |
| DTE | Data Terminal Equipment |
| E1 | European standard digital transmission facility @ 2.048 Mbit/s* |
| E.164. | ITU-TS Recommendation for international telecommunication numbering in ISDN, B-ISDN, SMDS etc* |
| EAM | Electronic Accounting Machine* |
| EBCDIC | Extended Binary Coded Decimal Interchange Code |
| EDI | Electronic Data Interchange |

| | |
|---|---|
| EIA | Electronics Industries Association |
| EMI | Electro-Magnetic Interference* |
| EISA | Extended Industry Standard Architecture (32-bit bus in Intel-based PCs)* |
| EN | End Node* |
| ESS | Electronic Switching System |
| FC | Frame Control* |
| FCC | Federal Communications Commission |
| FCS | Frame Check Sequence* |
| FDDI | Fiber Distributed Data Interface |
| FDX | Full-Duplex |
| FDM | Frequency-Division Multiplexer |
| FECN | Forward Explicit Congestion Notification* |
| FEP | Front-End Processor |
| FRAD | Frame Assembler and Disassembler* |
| FS | Frame Status* |
| FSK | Frequency Shift Keying* |
| FTAM | File Transfer, Access and Management (OSI)* |
| FTP | File Transfer Protocol (part of TCP/IP protocol suite) |
| GOSIP | Government Open System Interconnect Profile |
| GUI | Graphical User Interface* |
| HDLC | High-Level Data Link Control |
| HDX | Half-Duplex |
| HPR | High Performance Routing* |
| I.123 | ITU-TS Recommendation for Frame Relay |
| I.233 | ITU-TS Recommendation for Frame Relay |
| IA5 | International Alphabet Number 5, essentially the same as ASCII* |
| ICL | International Computers Limited* |
| IEEE | Institute of Electrical and Electronics Engineers |
| IEC | *see IXC** |
| Internet | (with capital initial I) worldwide network of networks and "hosts" using TCP/IP protocols (DOD-originated)* |
| IP | Internet Protocol |
| IPX | Internetwork Packet Exchange (Novell protocol)* |
| IR | Infrared* |

| | |
|---|---|
| ISDN | Integrated Services Digital Network |
| ISA | Industry Standard Architecture (16-bit bus in Intel-based Personal Computers)* |
| ISO | International Organization for Standardization* |
| ISSI | Inter-Switching Systems Interface* |
| ITA2 | International Telegraph Alphabet Number 2* |
| ITU-T | International Telecommunications Union Telecommunications (formerly known as CCITT) |
| ITU-TS | (*also see ITU-T*) International Telecommunications Union—Telecommunications Standardization Sector* |
| IXC | Interexchange Carrier |
| LAN | Local Area Network |
| LAPB | Link Access Procedure - Balanced |
| LAPD | Link Access Procedure for the D Channel* |
| LAPF | Link Access Procedures to Frame-Mode Bearer Services* |
| LAPM | Link Access Procedure for Modems* |
| LATA | Local Access and Transport Area |
| LEC | Local Exchange Carrier |
| LED | Light Emitting Diode* |
| LEN | Low-Entry Networking node* |
| LLC | Logical Link Control* |
| LSB | Least Significant Bit* |
| LU | Logical Unit (IBM SNA)* |
| MAC | Medium Access Control |
| MAN | Metropolitan Area Network |
| MAU | Multistation Access Unit (Token Ring) |
| MHS | Message Handling Service (see X.400)* |
| MIS | Management Information System* |
| MSB | Most Significant Bit * |
| MTBF | Mean Time Between Failure |
| MTTR | Mean Time To Repair |
| NAK | Negative Acknowledgment |
| NAU | Network Addressable Unit* |
| NAUN | Nearest Active Upstream Neighbor (used in Token Ring)* |
| NCP | Network Control Program |

| | |
|---|---|
| NFS | Network File System |
| NOS | Network Operating System |
| NRZ | Non Return to Zero* |
| NRZI | Non Return to Zero, Inverted* |
| OC-1 | Optical Carrier, Level 1 (51.84 Mbit/s) |
| OC-3 | Optical Carrier, Level 3 (155.52 Mbit/s) |
| OSI | Open Systems Interconnection |
| OSPF | Open Shortest Path First* |
| PABX | Private Automatic Branch Exchange |
| PAD | Packet Assembler/Disassembler |
| PAM | Pulse Amplitude Modulation |
| PAM | Phase Amplitude Modulation* |
| PBX | Private Branch Exchange |
| PCM | Pulse Code Modulation |
| PDN | Public Data Network |
| POTS | Plain Old Telephone Service |
| PRI | Primary Rate Interface (ISDN) |
| PROFS | Professional Office System (IBM) |
| PTT | Postal, Telephone & Telegraph administration |
| PU | Physical Unit (IBM SNA)* |
| Q.922 | ITU-TS Recommendation for LAPF* |
| QAM | Quadrature Amplitude Modulation* |
| QPSX | Queued Packet and Synchronous Exchange* |
| RF | Radio Frequency* |
| RG | Radio Government* |
| RI | Ring In* |
| RIP | Routing Information Protocol |
| RJ-11 | 4-wire standard connector for telephone lines* |
| RJ-45 | 8-wire standard connector for 1Base5 (StarLAN)* |
| RO | Ring Out* |
| RZ | Return to Zero* |
| SABM | Set Asynchronous Balanced Mode* |
| SAP | Service Access Point* |
| SAP | Service Advertising Protocol* |

| | |
|---|---|
| SCSI | Small Computer System Interface* |
| SDLC | Synchronous Data Link Control |
| SDH | Synchronous Digital Hierarchy (known in Europe as SONET)* |
| SDH-n | Synchronous Digital Hierarchy, level n* |
| SFD | Start Frame Delimiter* |
| SMDS | Switched Multi-Megabit Data Service |
| SME | Society for Mechanical Engineering* |
| SMTP | Simple Mail Transfer Protocol |
| SNA | Systems Network Architecture (IBM) |
| SNADS | SNA Distribution Services (IBM)* |
| SNMP | Simple Network Management Protocol |
| SONET | Synchronous Optical Network |
| SPE | Synchronous Payload Envelope* |
| SPX | Sequenced Packet Exchange (Novell)* |
| SSAP | Source Service Access Point* |
| SSCP | Systems Services Control Point* |
| SSR | Spread Spectrum Radio* |
| STP | Shielded Twisted Pair |
| STS-n | Synchronous Transport Signal, level n* |
| SYN | Synchronizing Character (ASCII and EBCDIC abbr.)* |
| T1 | Digital transmission facility US standard @ 1.544 Mbit/s* |
| T1.606 | ANSI standard for Frame Relay* |
| T3 | Digital transmission facility US standard @ 44.736 Mbit/s* |
| TAT | Transatlantic Telecommunications Cable |
| TCAM | Telecommunications Access Method |
| TCP/IP | Transmission Control Protocol/Internet Protocol |
| TCU | Transmission Control Unit |
| TDM | Time Division Multiplexing |
| TIA | Telecommunications Industries Association |
| TP-PMD | Twisted Pair Physical Layer Medium Dependent* |
| TTRT | Target Token Rotation Time* |
| TTY | Teletypewriter Equipment |
| UDP | User Datagram Protocol (Internet option)* |
| UTP | Unshielded Twisted Pair |
| V.1 | ITU-TS Recommendation defining telegraphic states* |

| | |
|---|---|
| V.4 | ITU-TS Recommendation for International Alphabet #5 (ASCII)* |
| V.21 | ITU-TS Recommendation for 300-bit/s full-duplex FSK modem* |
| V.29 | ITU-TS Recommendation for 9,600-bit/s half-duplex QAM modem* |
| V.32 | ITU-TS Recommendation for 9,600-bit/s full-duplex QAM echo-cancellation modem * |
| V.35 | An ITU-TS defined high-speed DTE/DCE interface* |
| VAN | Value-Added Network |
| VCI | Virtual Channel Indicator* |
| VPI | Virtual Path Indicator* |
| VSAT | Very Small Aperture Terminal* |
| VT-n | Virtual Tributary, level n* |
| VTAM | Virtual Telecommunications Access Method |
| VTG | Virtual Tributary Group* |
| WAN | Wide Area Network |
| WATS | Wide Area Telecommunications Service |
| X.25 | ITU-TS Packet Switching Protocol* |
| X.200 | ITU-TS ISO OSI Reference Model* |
| X.400 | ITU-TS Message Handling Services* |
| XON | Transmit On* |
| XOFF | Transmit Off* |
| XOR | Exclusive OR* |

# Appendix C

# Cyclical Redundancy Checks (CRC)

## CRC IS A REMAINDER

In what follows, we describe the use, theory and implementation of CRC. The idea behind the CRC is to protect an entire block of characters to be transmitted by treating it as one long binary number and using a special mathematical procedure on the number together with "redundant" bits that are also submitted with it. Typically, the sender affixes two or four redundant bytes to the end of the block, in much the same way that a checksum character is appended. The value of the redundant bits is the result of a special mathematical operation on the binary number and has to be the same for both the sender and the receiver.

The process of calculating a CRC on a block of characters is similar to the process of long division in arithmetic that finds a quotient and remainder after dividing one number by another. The block of characters to be protected by the CRC is viewed as a long binary number. It becomes the *dividend*. A block containing 1,500 8-bit characters, for example, is a dividend 12,000 bits long for purposes of CRC calculations.

We make a note here about the string of bits that is the dividend. Recall that since the bits within a byte are transmitted right-to-left, the first bit of each group of eight bits that is transmitted derives from the right-most bit of a byte in the user's buffer, while every eighth bit transmitted comes from the left-most bit of a byte.

After the last bit of the dividend is transmitted, the string of bits representing the *remainder* (calculated by the process described below) is transmitted as the CRC. The receiver, in turn, uses an identical algorithm to calculate a CRC presumably on the same string of dividend bits. The receiver views the transmission as successful if its newly calculated CRC matches the redundant bits appended after the dividend.

229

Alternatively and equivalently, the receiver may calculate CRC on an *extended* string of bits consisting of the bits of the original block concatenated with the bits of the sender's CRC. The transmission is viewed as successful if the result of the CRC calculation on the extended string is zero (a remainder consisting entirely of 0 bits).

Although rare, errors in transmission may occur despite the block appearing to have passed the CRC comparison mechanism. One cannot assume that the transmission is error-free simply because the receiver's calculation matches. There could be more than one bit error in the transmission that mutually compensate to yield an apparently successful CRC calculation. However, an approach does exist to improve the confidence of detecting any errors: increase the size of the field used for the CRC. The greater the number of bits used for this field, the greater the probability that any errors in the transmission of the block will be detected by the receiver. The CRC may be any number of bits long, agreed on by the communicating partners prior to the transmission. In practice, CRCs are 16 or 32 bits long.

The length of the CRC is defined by a *generating polynomial*. The highest power among the X terms dictates the number of bits in the CRC. For example, CRC-CCITT's generating polynomial is $X^{16}+X^{12}+X^5+1$. CRC-CCITT is, therefore, 16 bits long.

To determine the divisor, substitute 2 for X in the generating polynomial. For the cited CRC-CCITT example, the divisor becomes $2^{16}+2^{12}+2^5+1$. In binary notation this is $1000100000100001$, a number that is seventeen bits long. Any remainder after division will not be more than sixteen bits long.

A pen and paper process of dividing one binary number by another to calculate the CRC follows:

Step 1:    write the dividend on the top line.

Step 2:    write the divisor on the next line, aligning it horizontally so that its left-most 1 bit is under the left-most 1 bit of the dividend.

Step 3:    "Subtract" each divisor bit from the corresponding dividend bit immediately above it using the following *Boolean logic exclusive or (XOR)* rules:

$$1 - 0 = 1$$
$$1 - 1 = 0$$
$$0 - 0 = 0$$
$$0 - 1 = 1$$

Step 3A:  Subtract 0 from each of the other dividend bits.

Step 4:    Write the result of the subtraction on the next line. For legibility, do not write leading 0s. If the left-most 1 of the result aligns to the right of the **original** dividend, the operation is complete: go to Step 6.

Step 5:   Repeat steps 2 through 4. However, for "dividend" use the most recent result from Step 4.

Step 6:   The final result now is the CRC (the remainder).

As an example, let us calculate CCITT-CRC on an arbitrary message, which appears in the user's sending buffer as hexadecimal 1 3 D B. (Note that because bits are transmitted from the right, the dividend's sequence looks like hexadecimal C 8 D B.)

```
       dividend 1100100011011011|
        divisor 100010000001000011
                                |
              10000001100101111
              1000100000010001011
                                |
                100110000111111
                10001000000|100001
                                |
                  100000111010001
                  10001000|000100001
                                |
                     1011|010101001
                     1000|1000000100001
                                |
                      1111101010110001
                      10|001000000100001
                                |
                       11111101011100101
                       1|0001000000100001
                                |
         remainder  |1110010111101011
```

The hardware and software that actually implements CRC uses a shift register. The number of bit positions needed in the register is defined by the number of bits in the CRC. For the CCITT-CRC generating polynomial this is 16. The bits at either ends of the register are numbered #0 and #15. When the register shifts once, each bit of the register shifts from position #n into position #(n+1), and 0 is moved into position #0.

A *Boolean logic XOR* operation (defined above in Step 3) is done on those bit positions n of the shift register where $X^n$ is a term in the generating polynomial. From the generating polynomial $X^{16}+X^{12}+X^5+1$ we see that the affected bits of the shift register are #12, #5 and #0.

The steps in hardware implementation follow:

A. Prior to the transmission, initialize the shift register to all zeros.

B. Arrange that as each bit of the message is transmitted, the register simultaneously shifts one position. In the diagram, the register shifts from right to left. Bit #0 is the right-most bit.

C. Perform an XOR on the value of the bit *transmitted* with the *prior* value of the bit in shift register position #15. The result of the XOR becomes "bit #16" (some temporary memory cell, such as a flipflop).

D. Replace each bit at position *n* if $X^n$ is a term in the generating polynomial. For $X^{16}+X^{12}+X^5+1$, this applies to bits #12, #5 and #0. ($1 = X^0$). The new value that replaces bit #n is the XOR result between itself and bit #16.

E. Repeat Steps B through D until no more message bits are transmitted. Then the contents of the shift register are the CRC.

In the following diagram, the left-most column identifies the step that gives the results shown on its right *after* it has been performed. The second column, headed "DATA," shows the message bit transmitted. We now perform steps A through E on the same data as before viz. the dividend string binary 1100100011011011.

Note that the contents of the shift register at step E will correspond to the remainder of division in Step 6.

| | DATA | 16 | 15 | 14 | 13 | 12 | 11 | 10 | 9 | 8 | 7 | 6 | 5 | 4 | 3 | 2 | 1 | 0 |
|---|---|---|---|---|---|---|---|---|---|---|---|---|---|---|---|---|---|---|
| A | | | 0 | 0 | 0 | 0 | 0 | 0 | 0 | 0 | 0 | 0 | 0 | 0 | 0 | 0 | 0 | 0 |
| B | **1** | **0** | 0 | 0 | 0 | 0 | 0 | 0 | 0 | 0 | 0 | 0 | 0 | 0 | 0 | 0 | 0 | 0 |
| C | | | 1 | | | | | | | | | | | | | | | |
| D | | | 0 | 0 | 0 | **1** | 0 | 0 | 0 | 0 | 0 | 0 | **1** | 0 | 0 | 0 | 0 | **1** |
| B | **1** | **0** | 0 | 0 | **1** | 0 | 0 | 0 | 0 | 0 | 0 | **1** | 0 | 0 | 0 | 0 | **1** | 0 |
| C | | | 1 | | | | | | | | | | | | | | | |
| D | | | 0 | 0 | **1** | **1** | 0 | 0 | 0 | 0 | 0 | **1** | **1** | 0 | 0 | 0 | **1** | **1** |
| B | **0** | **0** | 0 | **1** | **1** | 0 | 0 | 0 | 0 | 0 | **1** | **1** | 0 | 0 | 0 | **1** | **1** | 0 |
| C | | | 0 | | | | | | | | | | | | | | | |
| D | | | 0 | **1** | **1** | 0 | 0 | 0 | 0 | 0 | **1** | **1** | 0 | 0 | 0 | **1** | **1** | 0 |
| B | **0** | **0** | **1** | **1** | 0 | 0 | 0 | 0 | 0 | **1** | **1** | 0 | 0 | 0 | **1** | **1** | 0 | 0 |
| C | | | 0 | | | | | | | | | | | | | | | |
| D | | | **1** | **1** | 0 | 0 | 0 | 0 | 0 | **1** | **1** | 0 | 0 | 0 | **1** | **1** | 0 | 0 |
| B | **1** | **1** | **1** | 0 | 0 | 0 | 0 | 0 | **1** | **1** | 0 | 0 | 0 | **1** | **1** | 0 | 0 | 0 |
| C | | | 0 | | | | | | | | | | | | | | | |
| D | | | **1** | 0 | 0 | 0 | 0 | 0 | **1** | **1** | 0 | 0 | 0 | **1** | **1** | 0 | 0 | 0 |
| B | **0** | **1** | 0 | 0 | 0 | 0 | 0 | **1** | **1** | 0 | 0 | 0 | **1** | **1** | 0 | 0 | 0 | 0 |
| C | | | 1 | | | | | | | | | | | | | | | |
| D | | | 0 | 0 | 0 | **1** | 0 | **1** | **1** | 0 | 0 | 0 | 0 | **1** | 0 | 0 | 0 | **1** |
| B | **0** | **0** | 0 | 0 | **1** | 0 | **1** | **1** | 0 | 0 | 0 | 0 | **1** | 0 | 0 | 0 | **1** | 0 |
| C | | | 0 | | | | | | | | | | | | | | | |
| D | | | 0 | 0 | **1** | 0 | **1** | **1** | 0 | 0 | 0 | 0 | **1** | 0 | 0 | 0 | **1** | 0 |
| B | **0** | **0** | 0 | **1** | 0 | **1** | **1** | 0 | 0 | 0 | 0 | **1** | 0 | 0 | 0 | **1** | 0 | 0 |
| C | | | 0 | | | | | | | | | | | | | | | |
| D | | | 0 | **1** | 0 | **1** | **1** | 0 | 0 | 0 | 0 | **1** | 0 | 0 | 0 | **1** | 0 | 0 |
| B | **1** | **0** | **1** | 0 | **1** | **1** | 0 | 0 | 0 | 0 | **1** | 0 | 0 | 0 | **1** | 0 | 0 | 0 |

| | DATA | 16 | 15 | 14 | 13 | 12 | 11 | 10 | 9 | 8 | 7 | 6 | 5 | 4 | 3 | 2 | 1 | 0 |
|---|---|---|---|---|---|---|---|---|---|---|---|---|---|---|---|---|---|---|
| C | | 1 | | | | | | | | | | | | | | | | |
| D | | | 1 | 0 | 1 | 0 | 0 | 0 | 0 | 0 | 1 | 0 | 1 | 0 | 1 | 0 | 0 | 1 |
| B | 1 | 1 | 0 | 1 | 0 | 0 | 0 | 0 | 0 | 1 | 0 | 1 | 0 | 1 | 0 | 0 | 1 | 0 |
| C | | 0 | | | | | | | | | | | | | | | | |
| D | | | 0 | 1 | 0 | 0 | 0 | 0 | 0 | 1 | 0 | 1 | 0 | 1 | 0 | 0 | 1 | 0 |
| B | 0 | 0 | 1 | 0 | 0 | 0 | 0 | 0 | 1 | 0 | 1 | 0 | 1 | 0 | 0 | 1 | 0 | 0 |
| C | | 0 | | | | | | | | | | | | | | | | |
| D | | | 1 | 0 | 0 | 0 | 0 | 0 | 1 | 0 | 1 | 0 | 1 | 0 | 0 | 1 | 0 | 0 |
| B | 1 | 1 | 0 | 0 | 0 | 0 | 0 | 1 | 0 | 1 | 0 | 1 | 0 | 0 | 1 | 0 | 0 | 0 |
| C | | 0 | | | | | | | | | | | | | | | | |
| D | | | 0 | 0 | 0 | 0 | 0 | 1 | 0 | 1 | 0 | 1 | 0 | 0 | 1 | 0 | 0 | 0 |
| B | 1 | 0 | 0 | 0 | 0 | 0 | 1 | 0 | 1 | 0 | 1 | 0 | 0 | 1 | 0 | 0 | 0 | 0 |
| C | | 1 | | | | | | | | | | | | | | | | |
| D | | | 0 | 0 | 0 | 1 | 1 | 0 | 1 | 0 | 1 | 0 | 1 | 1 | 0 | 0 | 0 | 1 |
| B | 0 | 0 | 0 | 0 | 1 | 1 | 0 | 1 | 0 | 1 | 0 | 1 | 1 | 0 | 0 | 0 | 1 | 0 |
| C | | 0 | | | | | | | | | | | | | | | | |
| D | | | 0 | 0 | 1 | 1 | 0 | 1 | 0 | 1 | 0 | 1 | 1 | 0 | 0 | 0 | 1 | 0 |
| B | 1 | 0 | 0 | 1 | 1 | 0 | 1 | 0 | 1 | 0 | 1 | 1 | 0 | 0 | 0 | 1 | 0 | 0 |
| C | | 1 | | | | | | | | | | | | | | | | |
| D | | | 0 | 1 | 1 | 1 | 1 | 0 | 1 | 0 | 1 | 1 | 1 | 0 | 0 | 1 | 0 | 1 |
| B | 1 | 0 | 1 | 1 | 1 | 1 | 0 | 1 | 0 | 1 | 1 | 1 | 0 | 0 | 1 | 0 | 1 | 0 |
| C | | 1 | | | | | | | | | | | | | | | | |
| D | | | 1 | 1 | 1 | 0 | 0 | 1 | 0 | 1 | 1 | 1 | 1 | 0 | 1 | 0 | 1 | 1 |
| E | | | 1 | 1 | 1 | 0 | 0 | 1 | 0 | 1 | 1 | 1 | 1 | 0 | 1 | 0 | 1 | 1 |

# Appendix D

# LLC Structure and Protocol

This Appendix contains more detail on Logical Link Control's format and procedures.

## LOGICAL LINK CONTROL (LLC) HEADER

The LLC header normally consists of three bytes making up the three fields illustrated in Figure D.1. The Destination Service Access Point (DSAP) and Source Service Access Point (SSAP) comprise the first two fields of the header. The control field is third. The control field is a one-byte or two-byte field. When it is two bytes long, the LLC header consists of four bytes.

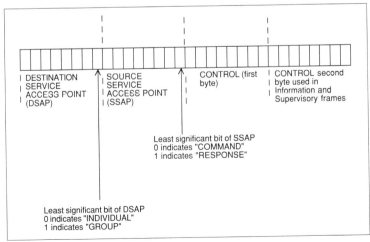

*Figure D.1 Format of the three fields comprising Logical Link Control (LLC).*

## DESTINATION AND SOURCE SERVICE ACCESS POINTS

The destination service access point identifies the software element or application that is the intended recipient of the data that follows the LLC header in the message frame. The DSAP identified by the first field is a number whose value ranges between 0 to 127. In binary, this only occupies at most seven bits of the field, however. The eighth bit is set to 1 if the message itself is targeted to a *group* of SAPs within the same station. Here, DSAPs that belong to the same group number all receive the message. An all 1s DSAP pattern tells the destination station to broadcast the message to all the service access points at that station.

The source service access point, SSAP, identifies the message generating software element or application and is recorded in the second field of the LLC header. Once again, this number has a value ranging between 0 to 127 thereby defining a SAP number. (It never a defines a group since a 1 in the least significant bit here indicates a response packet; 0 a command).

There are three different control field formats, the *information*, *supervisory* and *unnumbered*. The *information* and *supervisory* formats are each two bytes long. These formats contain sequence numbers to assure the integrity of the communication. The third format, *unnumbered*, is one byte long.

## INFORMATION FORMAT

The three control fields may be differentiated from each other by the value of their first two bits transmitted. The *information* format is distinguished from both the others in that its least significant bit in the first byte is 0. Recall that this bit is transmitted first.

| ←← | | | N | (S) | | → | 0 |
|----|---|---|---|-----|---|---|---|
| ←← | | | N | (R) | | → | P/F |

### Sequence Numbers

As introduced in Chapter 2, appearing in the control field of each frame or packet are two *sequence* numbers. One advises the recipient what number the packet has, leaving the sender. The other specifies what number the sender *expects* to see in its partner's next *incoming* packet, (that is when roles of sender and receiver will be reversed). The two 7-bit send and receive sequence number fields are labelled N(S) and N(R). N(S) identifies the sender's sequence number for the current frame. N(R) advises the recipient what number the sender expects to find in the N(S) field of the frame it next gets.

The N(R) and N(S) numbers are expressed modulo 128. The modulo 128 value of any positive number is its remainder after division by 128. The modulo 128 expression of a negative number is obtained by first multiplying it by -1, to get a positive number, dividing this positive result by 128 and finally subtracting the remainder from 128.

Although no explicit ACK/NAK transmission is done, each end-point confirms the frame check sequence (the FCS is a CRC) of a received packet, and that the packet's send sequence number N(S) equalled the expected number. This is communicated to the partner: the next time a partner sends a packet, the number it places in its N(R) field is the value that appeared in the N(S) field of the last packet it received successfully, duly incremented (by 1 modulo 128). The end-point expects this number in the N(S) field of the next packet it receives.

## Windows and Flow Control

N(R) and N(S) numbers allow simultaneous full-duplex transmission of more than one packet between two end points. As many as the maximum window size, 127 packets, may be transmitted by a sender without seeing any packet from its partner. As far as the sender is aware, the difference N(S)-N(R), expressed modulo 128, is the number of packets it has sent that have not yet been acknowledged by the recipient. (Note that the N(R) is taken from the packet last received from the partner.) The sender may not transmit another packet while this difference is at the window maximum, 127. Disregarding this rule, an N(S) number would duplicate that of an unacknowledged packet. The parties could not then discern whether an acknowledged packet had true sequence number *n* or *n-128*. 128 packets could be lost without detection! Only while the sender sees a difference N(S)-N(R) of less than 127, may it proceed and send new packets.

## Poll/Final

The Poll/Final P/F bit is used to communicate a station's wish to continue transmitting packets after this one, or to solicit the other station to transmit. A P/F bit that is 0 indicates that the sender has more packets to send after this one. When a receiver gets a packet with P/F set to 1, it responds by sending any packet ready for transmission. If it has none, the receiver sends a *supervisory* formatted response.

## SUPERVISORY FORMAT

The supervisory format control field, like that of the information format, also contains a sequence number and so is two bytes long. It differs from the other two formats in that its least significant bit is 1, while its next to least significant bit is a 0. Its format follows:

| Supervisory format | 0 | 0 | 0 | 0 | X | X | 0 | 1 |
|---|---|---|---|---|---|---|---|---|
| (2 bytes long) | N(R) | | | | | | | P/F |

As mentioned above, the supervisory format is used in packets to acknowledge receipt when the receiver has been solicited to send (with P/F bit 1 in the last packet it received) but it has no information packet to send. It is also used to notify the ability of the receiver to receive packets. And it may be used to request retransmission of rejected packets. The two bits marked XX are interpreted as follows:

XX 00 Receive Ready (RR)

01 Receive Not Ready (RNR)

10 Reject (REJ); (means "please retransmit packets whose N(S) numbers are N(R) and higher")

11 Selective Reject (SREJ); (means "please retransmit packet whose N(S) number is N(R)")

## UNNUMBERED FORMAT

The one-byte *unnumbered* format control field is identified by ones only in its two least significant bit positions:

| Unnumbered format | M | M | M | P/F | M | M | 1 | 1 |
|---|---|---|---|---|---|---|---|---|

This type of control field is used when sending unnumbered packets and datagrams. It is also used to acknowledge receipt of unnumbered packets, and to manage the connection. The five M bits are interpreted as follows:

MMMMM 11101 Acknowledge connectionless Information Sequence 1. This response alternates with Acknowledge connectionless Information Seq 0 in an acknowledgement procedure similar to that used in IBM's Binary Synchronous protocol. The alternate use of *ACK* 0 and *ACK 1* guards against the possibility of losing both a packet and its acknowledgement.

01101    Acknowledge connectionless Information Sequence 0.

01111    Set Asynchronous Balanced Mode Extended. This command is used in networks capable of supporting multiple modes. The word *balanced* indicates that the communicating stations are equal in status, each able to operate as a combined primary and secondary. The word *extended* indicates that 7-bit N(S) and N(R) sequence numbers are being used.

10111    Exchange Identification. This command, and response, is used optionally by implementers to determine details of the services supported in a connection-oriented network.

10001    Frame Reject. This response is sent when retransmission will not correct the error condition. The receiver of this packet may either disconnect or establish a new connection.

00011    Disconnected Mode (Response).

01000    Disconnect (Command).

11100    Test (Response and Command).

01100    Unnumbered Acknowledgement (Response).

00000    Unnumbered Information (Command).

# Appendix E

# How Optical Fibers Work

By observing the properties of a ray of light leaving one medium, and entering another, we can draw some helpful conclusions about light and how optical fibers may be designed to contain or "guide" light. In Figure E.1, light from a source (such as a flashlight) in air bends towards the "normal" as it penetrates another medium, in this case, water. The "normal" is an imagined line at right angles to the air/water surface. Since the air/water surface is horizontal, the "normal" is vertical. The ray's plane is defined by three points: the flashlight itself, the ray's point of entry into the water and a point on the water vertically below the flashlight. We observe an equivalent phenomenon when we immerse a stick in water. In this case, reflected light gives the impression of the stick bending.

In the water, the angle of the ray in relation to the "normal" is known as the *angle of refraction, r*. It is smaller than the *angle of incidence i*, also measured from the "normal," at which the ray in air struck the water. (However, we note that when the angle of incidence is zero, the angle of refraction is also zero; rays striking the water vertically are unbent.)

When the incident ray of light is almost parallel to the surface, its angle of incidence is almost 90°. At a 90° angle of incidence, there is no incidence!

The following table shows the different angles that the ray will refract in water for some angles of incidence in air:

| Angle of incidence i | 0° | 15° | 30° | 45° | 60° | 75° | < 90° |
|---|---|---|---|---|---|---|---|
| Angle of refraction r | 0° | 11.2° | 22.1° | 32.1° | 40.6° | 46.6° | < 48.8° |

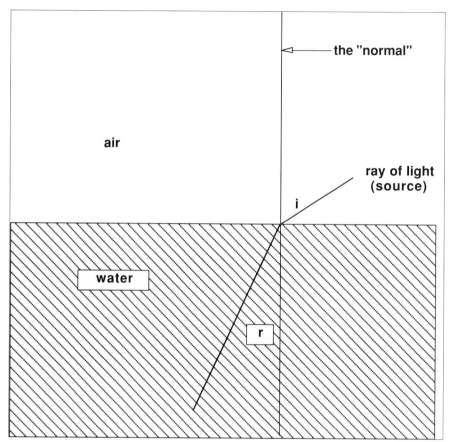

*Figure E.1. Refraction of light in water. Maximum angle of incidence i is less than 90°. Maximum angle of refraction r is less than 48.8°.*

In different media, the size of the *refracted angle* will be different. In optics, the Snell-Descartes law gives us a way to calculate the angle. The result depends on the *refractive indexes* of each of the two media. In what follows, we write $n_i$ to represent the refractive index of the source medium, (where the ray is incident), and $n_r$ as the refractive index of the destination medium. The calculation is $n_i \sin i = n_r \sin r$. The refractive index for air is taken as 1. For water, it is 1.33. For glass, different indices may be obtained ranging between 2 and 1.5.

Light moving in the other direction, i.e. from water to air behaves equivalently. Figure E.2 illustrates that when an underwater diver's lamp emits a ray of light towards the surface, the ray exits at an angle bending away from the "normal", i.e., more towards the surface. Once again, only if the angle of incidence is 0° does the light emerge unbent. The angle of incidence *i* at the boundary of the dark-shaded part of the figure is the *critical angle*. If the diver positions the lamp within but just shy of the critical angle (i.e., closer to the "normal"), the emerging ray would skim above the surface. But if the diver moves the lamp outside the critical angle—illustrated by the darker shading in the example—the ray would not exit. Rather it *reflects* at the surface.

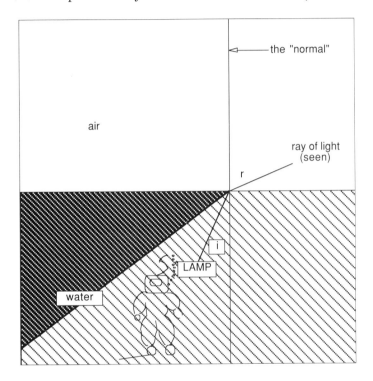

maximum angle of incidence i is less than 48.8°
maximum angle of refraction r is less than 90°

*Figure E.2. Refraction of light from water to air.*

Reflection is illustrated in Figure E.3. Here we see a longitudinal section of the fiber optic core (unshaded region) with refractive index 2, surrounded by cladding with index 1.5 (shaded region). Notice that the surfaces that separate core and cladding appear as two parallel straight lines (shown horizontally in the figure). Since the core is a cylinder, and the cladding is a tube or hollow cylinder that contains the core, any pair of perpendicular points on the two lines are points diametrically opposite each other on the fiber cross-section.

The ratio (1.33) of high to low refractive indices between core and cladding is the same as the ratio of refractive indices between water and air. This is a fortuitous coincidence for us because we can use the same table shown earlier (for water/air) to calculate angles of refraction in cladding from incidence angles in glass. Since a ray within the core that strikes the cladding surface will (exit the core and) penetrate the cladding if its angle of incidence is less than the critical angle, we see, from Figure E.3, that rays with *i* less than 48.8° escape to the cladding. All rays whose incidence angles are larger than 48.8° will reflect.

What this means is that when the light source is a *light emitting diode* its rays with *i* less than 48.8° at the outset are lost to the cladding. However, when the light source is a *laser* the light is essentially parallel to the longitudinal axis of the fiber and so few rays are lost.

Reflecting rays striking one surface will, a little later, reflect off the diametrically opposite surface since both surfaces of the cylinder are parallel. By geometry, the ray's next angle of incidence will be the same as the one that it had prior to its first reflection. Thus, once light is in the core, it does not escape. (It may lose intensity, though, due to absorption. Also, bends in the fiber as well as manufacturing tolerances may make the shape of the core not quite a perfect cylinder, thereby permitting some refraction.)

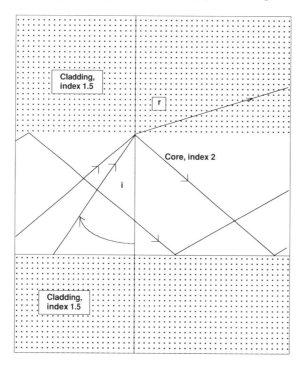

*Figure E.3. Longitudinal section of Fiber Optic core and cladding, showing that rays incident with angles "i" greater than 48.8° reflect at the core / cladding surface; others escape into the cladding.*

# Index